# The Media in
# Western Europe

# SAGE Communications in Society

**Dynamics of Media Politics**
Broadcast and Electronic Media
in Western Europe
*edited by Karen Siune and Wolfgang Truetzschler*
*for the Euromedia Research Group*

**New Communication Technologies**
**and the Public Interest**
*edited by Marjorie Ferguson*

**New Media Politics**
Comparative Perspectives
in Western Europe
*Euromedia Research Group*
*edited by Denis McQuail and Karen Siune*

**The Myth of the Information Revolution**
*edited by Michael Traber*

**Pressure Sensitive**
Popular Musicians under Stress
*Geoff Wills and Cary L. Cooper*

**Television and its Audience**
*Patrick Barwise and Andrew Ehrenberg*

# The Media in Western Europe

## The Euromedia Handbook

EUROMEDIA RESEARCH GROUP
Editor: Bernt Stubbe Østergaard

SAGE Publications
London · Newbury Park · New Delhi

© The Euromedia Research Group 1992

First published 1992

 SAGE Publications Ltd
6 Bonhill Street
London EC2A 4PU

SAGE Publications Inc
2455 Teller Road
Newbury Park, California 91320

SAGE Publications Pvt Ltd
32, M-Block Market
Greater Kailash – 1
New Delhi 110 048

**British Library Cataloguing in Publication data**

The media in Western Europe: The Euromedia
handbook. – (SAGE communications in society
series)
   I. Euromedia Research Group   II. Østergaard, Bernt S.
III. Series
302.23094

ISBN 0-8039-8575-4
ISBN 0-8039-8576-2 pbk

**Library of Congress catalog card number 91-50840**

Printed in Great Britain by Biddles Ltd, Guildford, Surrey

# Contents

# Notes on contributors

**Kees Brants**, lecturer at the Department of Communications at the University of Amsterdam, The Netherlands.

**Joan M. Corbella**, lecturer at the Faculty of Information Science, Universitat Autonoma, Barcelona, Spain.

**Els De Bens**, professor at the Department of Communications, University of Gent, Belgium.

**Panayote Dimitras**, assistant professor of political science at the Department of Economics, Athens University of Economics and Business (ASOEE), Greece.

**Joel Hasse Ferreira**, head of Urban Planning Office, Lisbon, Portugal.

**Karl Erik Gustafsson**, professor of mass media economics at the Gothenburg School of Economics, Sweden.

**Mario Hirsch**, journalist, teacher and researcher on economy and policy aspects of mass media, Luxembourg.

**Mary Kelly**, lecturer at the Department of Sociology, University College, Dublin, Ireland.

**Hans J. Kleinsteuber**, professor at the Institute of Political Science, University of Hamburg, Germany.

**Rosario de Mateo**, lecturer at the Faculty of Information Science, Universitat Autonoma, Barcelona, Spain.

**Gianpietro Mazzoleni**, professor of sociology of communications at the University of Salerno, Italy.

**Denis McQuail**, professor of mass communication at the University of Amsterdam, The Netherlands.

**Werner A. Meier**, media consultant and lecturer at the Department of Mass Communication at the University of Zurich, Switzerland.

**Helge Østbye**, senior lecturer, University of Bergen, Norway.

**Bernt Stubbe Østergaard**, director of Telsam Gruppen Ltd., Copenhagen, Denmark.

**Michael Palmer**, professor of communications at the Sorbonne University III in Paris, France.

**Vibeke Petersen**, head of section, General Directorate of P&T, Copenhagen, Denmark.

**Ulrich Saxer**, professor at the Department of Mass Communication at the University of Zurich, Switzerland.

**Karen Siune**, professor at the Institute of Political Science, University of Århus, Denmark.

**Claude Sorbets**, research director at the University of Bordeaux, France.

**Helena Tapper**, researcher and lecturer at the Department of Communications, University of Helsinki, Finland.

**Josef Trappel,** head of Audiovisual Eureka Secretariat, Federal Chancellery, Vienna, Austria.

**Wolfgang Truetzschler**, lecturer in communications at the Dublin Institute of Technology, Ireland.

**Jeremy Tunstall**, professor of sociology at the City University, London, United Kingdom.

**Peter Wilke**, researcher at the GEWOS-Institute in Hamburg, Germany.

# Introduction

This book gives a nation-by-nation introduction to historical media developments since 1945 and the present national media scene. The book is the result of a concerted effort by media researchers to give a coherent presentation of the many-faceted media scene. It is a reference guide to press, broadcasting and new electronic media in each of the 17 countries, and enables the reader to make cross-national and cross-media comparisons. Each chapter follows common guidelines, developed over several years of cooperation.

The book appears at a time when national media policies are characterized by fast change. A decade of de-regulation at the national level now faces a new decade of re-regulations on a European level, due to the increased interdependence in the European media environment.

It seems to be almost a law of nature that mass media expand to fill available space. Today that space is itself expanding. The "natural barriers" limiting the number of available frequencies for terrestrial television transmission, the prohibitive cost of setting up and running a television channel and the close cooperation between industry, public broadcasters and the national Telecommunications Authority (PTT) have all been broken down by technological developments and the entry of new actors on the media scene. This has led to shifts in the balance of power and to a certain extent also the rules of the game.

Traditional press and publishing companies have expanded their media activities and moved into television, and media tycoons with access to large scale international finance capital have launched multinational electronic media services. Their "logic" challenges the existing public broadcasters as well as the political media policy makers.

These changes have given the consumer access to new media services. However, many policy makers are worried by the lack of response from the media industry to the needs voiced by "concerned citizens", e.g. the democratization of media access.

Public regulatory measures designed to ensure diversity, fairness and minority interests were previously based on monopolies. These are now being circumvented in many different ways at once, forcing policy makers to constantly re-think the media landscapes. No Western European country has escaped baptism by fire in one form or another. In all countries the national broadcasting and telecommunications monopolies have been reduced and the electronic media market has been opened for commercial producers and financiers. Motivating forces have been:

— economic: strong media and advertising interests have put pressure on media policy makers to allow commercial exploitation of the electronic media, on the grounds of consumer unwillingness to accept increased licence fees;

— technical: the increase in the number of terrestrial television channels with national coverage (typically from 3 to 5), the easier access to neighbouring countries' television programmes via cable and the plethora of programmes distributed via television satellites have given television viewers many new programmes.

The consumer reaction has been unmistakable – across the board acceptance of advertising-financed programmes and programmes interrupted by commercials. In some respects the commercial invasion of television and radio has now surpassed even the US in ferocity. In some countries the old public service broadcasters (PSBs) with large staffs and the obligation to serve public interests defined by the politicians, who did not anticipate the popular demand for more programming and more entertainment, have crumbled in the face of the commercial onslaught. Some PSBs have panicked and now have programming schedules indistinguishable from their private competitors. Other PSBs have risen to this new challenge and kept their dominant position, but no PSB has remained unchanged and in most countries the new channels have quickly grabbed half the viewership.

Many European households now have access to 10–20 television channels either via cable or satellite broadcasts. Previously change came slowly and imperceptibly. Now it is fast and hard, and we can see it coming. This underscores the need for researchers and regulators to achieve a clearer recognition and understanding of the common traits in this transition across Europe.

## A coherent nation-by-nation presentation

This book offers the reader a coherent presentation of national press, broadcasting and electronic media. Authors of the individual chapters are noted national media experts, who over the last five years have met twice yearly in order to develop the framework for this book combining the diversity of media developments in all parts of Western Europe with an overall European perspective.

Each country chapter is introduced by a short summary of geographical and demographical features and the political situation in Government and Parliament. Then follow the developments in the printed press and electronic media since 1945, giving an overview of historical elements, the actors and the processes leading up to today's media situation in the country. The third section gives a more detailed description of the printed press, covering press legislation, the most important newspapers, ownership, financing, political affiliations and an analysis of important press issues such as cross-media ownership. This leads on to a section on the electronic media, beginning with national, regional and local radio and television. Here is information on the emergence of a large number of private radio and television channels in the wake of the monopoly breaking that has swept over Europe and the new media which have appeared – pay-television, even pay-per-view television and the telematic media, videotex and teletext. Each national author analyses these new channels, the new owners and their media strategies. In the chapter conclusions the authors sum up the important national trends in mass media developments. The salient issues and policy problems facing the important actors in the media field are analysed in their national contexts.

Each chapter has a statistics section giving vital facts about media use and access, numbers and types of channels, the main newspapers and media economics such as turnover, financing and ownership.

All manuscripts were written before May 1991 and changes after this date have not been incorporated, although several such developments are anticipated in the trends and issues discussions.

## The Euromedia Research Group

The Euromedia Research Group was established in 1982, and has since met regularly to address the central question of convergence in Western European media policy. The group now stands as one of the longest living independent media research groups in Europe, accepting gratefully the good-will and hospitality of the various universities with which the members are associated. The first research findings of the Group were published in 1986: a book on *European Media Policy* published by Campus Verlag and a comparative analysis, *New Media Politics*, published by Sage. Now five years later, the Group again publishes its findings in two parallel volumes – this book and a companion volume, *Dynamics of Media Politics*, presenting a comparative analysis of media developments and issues since 1985 in Western Europe, both volumes published by Sage.

Europe
September 1991
Bernt Stubbe Østergaard

# 1

# Austria

## Josef Trappel

### National profile

Geographically Austria is situated in the heart of Europe and is considered one of the "bridges" between East and West because of its status as permanently neutral since the Second World War. With its small home market of around 7.6 million inhabitants living in a surface area of 84 000 km², Austria is not one of the powerful economic forces in Europe. Nevertheless, Austria plays a crucial role in international diplomacy and has influenced the policy of various international bodies. Several departments of the United Nations have their headquarters in the Vienna International Centre.

Austria shares borders with Germany, Switzerland, Italy, Yugoslavia, Hungary, Czechoslovakia and Liechtenstein. Deriving from the time when Vienna was the capital of the Austro-Hungarian monarchy there are still some language minorities today living mainly in the southern and eastern parts of the country but the majority shares the German language with its large northern neighbour.

Austria is a parliamentary democracy with a federal constitution. The President is the head of state, but he does not play an active role in daily politics. In parliament there are four parties, of which the Socialist and the conservative People's Party are the largest. In the general election held in Autumn 1990 the Socialist Party (SPÖ) gained a relative majority of 43%, against the People's Party (ÖVP) with 32%, the National Liberal Party (FPÖ) with 17% and the Green Party with 5%. Since 1986 Austria has been governed by a coalition of the two largest parties, SPÖ and ÖVP, dominated by the Socialist Party, which has been in power since 1970.

Politics in Austria are marked by a strong tradition of democratic corporatism. The so-called "social partnership" between all groups in society has yielded a relatively stable social system but at the price of a lack of powerful control by a democratic opposition. All major decisions in Austria are taken only after reaching a certain consensus with the social partners.

Since the mid-1980s Austria has undergone a period of changing orientation in economic policy. The long tradition of state-owned industry has been challenged and a proportion of shares are now available to private investors. There are no major Austrian multinational companies. Because of the small domestic market and the hesitant policy towards foreign investment, Austria's enterprises suffer generally from under-capitalisation mainly because of the small domestic market and a hesitant policy towards foreign investment.

## Development of the press and broadcasting since 1945

At the end of World War II, Austria was divided into four sectors, each governed by one of the Allies.There were only four newspapers left in 1945. All over Austria the press media system was obliged to start again with almost nothing to build on (Paupié 1960). It was the availability of paper which enabled the publishers in the western and southern part of the country to start new newspapers earlier than in Vienna. Furthermore, a licence had to be obtained from the occupying forces and this was only given to politically "approved" persons. This might explain why the process of founding new newspapers was so slow. However, the Second Republic started with 35 newspapers and some regional editions. Since then developments have gone through 4 phases:

— From 1946 until 1957 there was a steady decline in the number of newspapers and of their overall circulation. In 1957 an all-time low was reached, with a mere 1.2 million copies printed in the whole of Austria.

— From 1958 until 1973 the first round of concentration took place. With the start of a new mass medium – television broadcasting – the number of newspapers declined further but at the same time circulation expanded. Within eleven years the number of copies doubled from 1.2 million in 1957 to 2.4 million in 1969. By then only 24 newspapers remained. In 1973 the figure dropped to 19 (Institut für Publizistik 1977).

— The period from 1973 until 1987 was marked by a stable supplier market on the one hand and a slow but steady increase of circulation figures on the other. Two newspapers dominated and still dominate the Austrian market. The popular tabloid *Kronenzeitung* circulates roughly one million copies every day and, together with the *Kurier* (440 000 copies), accounts for more than half of all newspaper-copies in Austria (1989). In this period papers of political parties lost market shares and were financially dependent on state subsidies and party funds.

— Since 1987 the balance has again been disturbed: the second wave of concentration hit Austria and foreign capital penetrated the market. During 1987 two party newspapers (one socialist, one conservative) shut down their presses. Another dramatic development has affected Austria's biggest papers. The two owners of the profitable *Kronenzeitung* decided to dissolve their agreement and one of them took over the shares of the other. He was not able to find sufficient financial backing in Austria and finally sold 45% of the company to the German *Westdeutsche Allgemeine Zeitung* (WAZ; 1.1.1988). Six months later, in June 1988, the WAZ landed its second coup. It bought 45% of the *Kurier*, which means that it is a shareholder in a company which in turn controls the leading opinion makers (weeklies: *Profil* and *Wochenpresse*) and some of the most successful general interest magazines (e.g. *Basta*).

After the war all Austria's broadcasting hardware was handed over to the occupying Allies. French, British, American and Soviet forces started their own services and hampered the installation of nation-wide broadcasting (Fabris et al. 1990). Only in 1954 was an agreement reached in which broadcasting was declared to be a national matter. Therefore the ORF (Österreichische Rundfunk – Austrian Broadcasting) was founded and in 1955, when Austria regained full sovereignty, the first television experiments started. In 1957 the Council of Ministers constituted the ORF as a public service company.

The first broadcasting legislation after the war came into force in 1967 and restructured the sector. Three radio channels and two television channels were defined as a minimum obligation for the ORF. Up to the time of writing the ORF is the only legal programme provider for radio and television within Austria which is licensed for terrestrial transmission.

## The press

### *Policy framework*

Apart from the European Convention of Human Rights (1950; Art. 10) and the Constitutional Law (Staatsgrundgesetz 1867, revised 1982; Art. 13), which ensures freedom of expression and prohibits any kind of censorship, press legislation is based on two pillars: the Press Act of 1922 and the Media Law of 1981 (Berka 1989). The Act of 1922 states that the freedom of the press is guaranteed. In the interest of national security, health and morality, and in the event of an infringement of territorial rights this otherwise absolute freedom may be reduced. There are certain obligations deriving from the Media Law of 1981: each periodical has to carry a clear indication of its owner, publisher and general political or ideological orientation. In addition, a certain number of copies must be delivered free of charge to the National Library and advertising must be clearly separated from the informational part of the paper. There is a right to reply, the protection of the private sphere and, of course, copyright legislation. Journalists enjoy "freedom of opinion", which includes their right to refuse collaboration on a piece of work which does not conform with the private opinion of the journalist. Also they can claim a "shift in the general orientation" of the paper and can then quit their job without losing the right to severance pay.

Newspapers and most of the periodicals enjoy three different kinds of state support. First, there is reduced VAT on printed products. Second, they can apply for postal distribution at a much lower rate than ordinary mail. Third, they can apply for state subsidies.

As indicated above, the Austrian newspaper industry has been characterized by a far-reaching concentration process. In 1975 a law concerning press subsidies was passed. Its effect was the stabilization of the industry for some years. The idea was to redistribute the Value-Added Tax back to the newspapers, but the total amount was reduced substantially in the following years. An amendment in 1984 directed the subsidy into two channels: the "ordinary" subsidy, which is now granted to every daily newspaper, distributes a certain amount of money every year to each newspaper, regardless of its financial situation and need. The "special subsidy for the maintenance of variety" is granted to papers which are in financial trouble. In 1990 the "ordinary" subsidy for each paper was 2.75 million AS (197 000 ECU), and the total subsidy 43 million AS (3.1 million ECU). Another 35 million AS were distributed as "special subsidy" to nine papers, ranging from 1.6 million to 7.9 million AS each. Apart from these regular subsidies the federal government often supports investment by the media. Most of the papers are planning to extend their services (technical equipment, data transmission, print shops etc.) and expect up to 30% of the total investment to be financed by the state. In 1990 an additional extraordinary grant of some 164 million AS (11.7 million ECU) was given to (the same) nine papers, ranging from 7.8 million to 36.9 million AS. Even though regular subsidies are reduced, extraordinary grants usually balance out the losses.

*Structure, ownership and finance*

At the end of 1990 there were 17 newspapers on the Austrian market. Six of them are published in Vienna and account for 68% of the nationwide circulation of 2.79 million copies. The two biggest newspapers are the independent *Kronenzeitung* (1.1 million) and *Kurier* (0.4 million). There are only three party papers left and none of them exceeds a circulation of 65 000. The press subsidies scheme has not succeeded in the long term. The concentration process continued. Between 1987 and 1991 seven newspapers were forced to close down or readjust their ownership structure. Three of them disappeared completely from the market.

Newspapers account for the largest market share of advertising revenue and that share is increasing. The 1989 market share reached 32% with an annual growth of 11% (Nielsen Media Research 1990). Advertising is the main source of income for Austrian newspapers. Forty-two percent of the budget comes from sales, 58% from advertising. This ratio has been fairly stable for ten years (Lankes 1990; Schrotta 1981).

In 1988 an Austrian businessman and journalist launched a new newspaper for the first time in 16 years. In the quality paper market *Der Standard* competes with the well-known *Presse and Salzburger Nachrichten* and has found wide acceptance among the Austrian readership. This new launch showed once again the vulnerability of the weak and undercapitalized Austrian structure. It was impossible to set up the newspaper with domestic financial resources and therefore the German media corporation Springer now holds some 50% of the shares. Only one year later Springer extended its market presence further and took over 45% of the independent Tyrolean paper *TirolerTageszeitung* (Lankes 1990).

The newspapers under Austrian ownership reacted sharply to the new challenge. In the face of the new competitor *Der Standard* the quality paper *Die Presse* increased its journalistic staff and its coverage of foreign affairs and economic matters considerably. The *SalzburgerNachrichten* in turn launched a national edition and both of them increased their market range. It seems that there is a potential market for serious information and news coverage which has not been served satisfactorily up to now. In order to compete with the newspapers financed by foreign concerns the larger of the Austrian-owned papers joined forces and have since Autumn 1989 published a television supplement together.

Outside Vienna there is no real choice of newspapers. Most of the Austrian *Länder* have one dominant newspaper with a more or less monopolistic position challenged only by *Kronenzeitung*. In Upper Austria, Styria and Vorarlberg there are two papers, but the second one has a marginal circulation compared to the market leader. In Autumn 1990 a former journalist founded a newspaper in Lower Austria, in an area where not a single paper existed before. After only four weeks the newspaper-project came to a sudden end, when the financial backing crashed, as market experts had predicted.

The turbulence in the market is not yet over. The ownership structure is currently changing. It started with the investment of the WAZ and Springer. The money paid for the shares of the *Kronenzeitung* has still not been invested yet. Experts expect a new low-price, low-standard tabloid for the end of 1991, which could substantially harm the market leader's present position. This project has been announced by the former part-owner of the *Kronenzeitung* and now editor of a sensationally successful yellow weekly. He is using the time until the launch for building up huge print shops near Vienna. Also parts of the remaining 55% of the *Kurier* were put on the market again. They were taken over by a consortium linked with one of the biggest private banking houses (Raiffeisen) in October 1990.

Even though their status is independent, most of the newspapers have a more or less declared political affiliation. Seven of the ten papers outside Vienna have links with the conservative ÖVP. However, with the decline of the party papers themselves (Socialists and Communists run one, Conservatives two starving papers) and the launch of the new competitor *Der Standard*, independent journalism – regardless of the ownership structure – is increasing. Even the traditional socialist *Arbeiterzeitung*, which was founded more than 100 years ago by one of the fathers of social democracy in Austria, is now independent (currently changing its ownership structure and busy designing survival strategies).

*Readership*

The Austrians are not a nation of avid readers. Nevertheless, Austria's newspapers compete with national television in their daily reach. For some years now newspapers have been read by a stable 72% of the population while all television channels together reach 71% (source: Optima 1989). But there exist strong disparities between the newspapers. The *Kronenzeitung*, with its circulation of more than a million copies, reaches 42%, the *Kurier* follows in second place with a mere 14%. With one exception (*Kleine Zeitung* 11%) no other paper reaches more than 5% of the population. This illustrates the concentration not only in ownership and circulation but also in the political influence and power of the popular press in Austria. The most successful quality paper reaches only 3.3% of the readers. It would seem that the Austrians love easy reading and watching television.

However, over the last few years there has been a slight but noticeable increase in the circulation of the quality papers. All quality papers with nationwide circulation have increased their readership. In 1978 the *Presse* and the *SalzburgerNachrichten* reached 2.6% and 2.7% of the population respectively. In 1990 they had increased their market share to 3.3% and 3.4% (source: Mediaanalyse 1978 and 1990), the newcomer *Der Standard* surpassed them, reaching 3.8% of the population (1990). Whatever hope this data may hold, the *Kronenzeitung* beats them all. It increased its market share in the same period by 5% and was read in 1990 by 42.6% of all Austrians. They remain a people of "easy readers".

## Electronic media

### Legal framework

Austria's broadcasting is basically governed by two laws: the "Federal Constitutional Law to Safeguard the Independence of Broadcasting" and the "Broadcasting Act concerning Tasks and Organization of Austrian Broadcasting", both of 1974. The Constitutional Law defines broadcasting as a "public service" to include both terrestrial and cable operations and prescribes the passing of legislation which will guarantee objectivity and impartiality of the coverage, the variety of views and the independence of the institutions and individuals concerned with broadcasting.

The Austrian broadcasting corporation, the ORF (Österrecihische Rundfunk) is the only institution licensed to transmit programmes on a terrestrial basis within Austria. This monopoly is not specified in the Constitutional Law but in the Broadcasting Act. The ORF must operate commercially but on a non-profit basis. Its organizational and control structure is designed to ensure that all significant views in society are fully and fairly represented in ORF operations. The supreme governing body, the Board of Trustees, is composed of 35 representatives: 9 members are appointed by the Federal Government, 6 according to the relative strength of the political parties in Parliament, one by each of the nine Austrian counties (*Länder*), 6 by the Council of Viewers and Listeners and 5 by the employees. Along with control duties and investment decisions the main task of the Board of Trustees is the election of the virtually "almighty" Director General (*Generalintendant*) every four years. During this election campaign it usually becomes clear that the "Board of Trustees" is composed entirely of party members or individuals with strong political party links. At least at the level of the Director General the ORF appears to be dependent on party bargaining.

Besides the already mentioned obligation to operate at least 3 radio channels and 2 television channels the ORF is responsible for technical transmission all over Austria and also runs the short-wave radio channel "Radio Austria International".

Without any executive power but with the purpose of integrating the audience, the Broadcasting Act constitutes the Council of Viewers and Listeners which has the right to propose programme adjustments and technical supply. The elected State President has to appoint a Commission with 17 members, which is convened by the Federal Chancellery and which oversees the ORF's operations in accordance with the law.

For several years now cable systems have carried foreign programmes to the connected households, although up to now there has been no cable legislation. Whether a programme is released for re-transmission (unchanged and unedited) or not is decided by the Federal Chancellery in consultation with the PTT. The legal basis for these decisions derives from a ruling of the Constitutional Court of Justice in 1983, which limits the free transmission and retransmission of programmes oriented towards the domestic public apart from the ORF. According to the Constitutional Law even foreign programmes have to fulfil the outlined content requirements. Almost all German and Swiss channels available on satellites are distributed by cable systems. Both radio and television reception as well as the operation of individual satellite receivers are subject to the granting of a licence and payment of a licence fee.

*Structure, organization, ownership and finance*

The ORF has its headquarters in Vienna and operates a radio and television studio in every *Land*. Since the broadcasting reforms in 1984 there has been more emphasis on regional programme production and in May 1988 all the regional studios of the ORF started producing local television news, a reaction to the international trend towards localization. Radio channels are directed at different target groups. The first, national channel broadcasts classical music and high quality information programmes. The second channel is mainly devoted to popular Austrian folk music transmitted by the regional studios. The third channel is nationwide and broadcasts light entertainment and pop music for the target group of younger people. All three radio channels and the two television channels are transmitted all over the country; language and ethnic minorities do not have their own electronic media service.

Because of the geographic location at the centre of Europe, in large parts of the country households are able to receive foreign television and radio channels over the air waves. This may be a reason for the relatively slow expansion of the cable network. Most communities have started their own cable systems; the majority are joint-ventures of public and private companies. By the end of 1990 about 21% of all households were cabled and more than 40% were able to receive foreign programmes either over-the-air, cable or satellite. However, the only rapidly expanding cable-network is in Vienna, where there is no terrestrial overspill allowing the reception of foreign programmes. In this area some 50% of all households who pay licence fees are connected. Around 15 channels are currently available via cable.

With the advent of political change in Austria's eastern neighbour countries, new programme suppliers have entered the market. Based in

Czechoslovakia and Hungary some private Austrian business people have started radio broadcasts from beyond the national borders following the lead of their colleagues from southern Austria. Since the early 1970s some pirate stations have begun to attract audiences and advertising in Carinthia, where they even manage to provide a television service transmitting from Italy.

These "old" pirate stations have not really damaged the politically well balanced system in Austria, because they have never reached the central area of Vienna over-the-air. Now there are some "new" radio stations entering this profitable area, but up to now their market success has remained limited. They reach less than 2% of the population of Vienna and only 5% in Carinthia and Tyrol. Even though detailed information on ownership is not yet available, some investments come from people closely linked to political parties, and in at least one case (Tyrol) the leading regional newspaper is a major shareholder in a private radio station.

Compared to the public service broadcasters in other small states in Europe the ORF is financially quite comfortable. With an annual turnover of some 8.25 billion AS (590 million ECU; financial year 1989) the ORF is far ahead of the Swiss or Belgian public broadcasters. Forty-three percent of the income derives from licence fees and 39% from advertising. The remaining 18% come from licence granting, subsidies and "other income".

With around 3 200 employees and several thousand freelance workers, the ORF is by far the largest media company in the country. The licence fee that consumers have to pay is the highest in absolute terms in all Europe (GEAR 1989).

Advertising revenue goes mainly to newspapers and magazines. Print media receive 52% of all media advertising expenditure, electronic media 40%. Again compared to other West European countries the overall advertising market is relatively small but moderately expanding. Between 1988 and 1989 the market growth in real terms was 6.6%, the highest increase being in the press sector. Radio and television advertising increased below average with 1% and 3% respectively. Within seven years advertising expenditure per capita has doubled from 654 AS in 1983 to 1 367 AS in 1989 (Nielsen Media Research 1990).

*Programme policy*

Austria's broadcasting company ORF has expanded its daily transmission substantially in recent years. In 1989, 10 355 hours of television broadcasting were transmitted, 30% more than four years ago. Taking co-productions into account, the ORF TV programme schedule contains 41% own productions, 33% are purchased and 25% are repeats. Approximately one third of broadcasting time is allocated to entertainment, 16% to news and culture. Comparing the statistics of this supply structure with how it is used by the audience, one finds a wide gap between the categories "entertainment" and "culture". People spent 51% of all viewing time watching entertainment programmes but only 8% on cultural or educational programmes.

As a result of its strategy to expand air-time the ORF has been forced to buy additional inexpensive programmes of the international series type, produced in the USA, Germany or the UK, leading to a slowly increasing "self-commercialization" of the public service (Fabris and Luger 1986).

This tendency has continued from 1986 to 1990 and even affects the presentation of world news. The prime time news at 19.30 is introduced by headlines with background music. News and weather forecast are separated by commercials.

In 1990 Austria's television viewers spent an average of 115 minutes a day in front of their TV-sets. They dedicated 94% of the time to one of the two domestic channels. In spite of the growing competition of new media these percentages have remained surprisingly stable over the past four years. In households equipped with cable television the ORF reaches only 64% daily.

For the majority of the population, TV is used mainly for entertainment. The most popular programmes with a share of often over 50% are Austrian folk music shows, international crime series and game shows, mainly produced in West Germany.

Radio programming is much more decentralized in Austria. Each of the nine county studios produces its own programming carrying regional and local content for the second channel . In 1990 there was a programme reform which changed the radio schedule radically. With the aim of meeting the needs and habits of the population better, more time is now dedicated to local affairs and in the popular third channel the structure is now more oriented towards the successful private commercial radio stations in Switzerland and Germany. Of course, late night sex-counselling via telephone must not be left out in the new structure.

*Local TV and radio*

As outlined above, the legal framework does not allow private competition in the Austrian market, either for radio or for television. The ORF re-adjusted the programme schedule last year to emphasize local coverage. Local radio programmes were introduced as early as 1981, local television operated by the ORF followed in May 1988. Daily at 18.30 there is a half-hour local television feature on the second channel which is produced by the county studios.

*Foreign media availability*

Austria's media market is traditionally penetrated by products from its "giant language partner": Germany. Particularly the magazine and book market in terms of market shares is under the firm control of German producers. Quite the opposite is true for television and radio. The audience prefer the domestic channels even when they can receive foreign channels by whatever means. It was mentioned above that roughly 40% of all households are able to receive at least one foreign television channel. Apart from the growing market for cable-TV in Vienna, a significant expansion of the availability of foreign programmes is not planned. Provincial cable operators are suffering from stagnation, and individual satellite dishes for a reasonable price came onto the consumer market only very recently. Around 15 foreign channels are currently (1990) available in the cable networks and more than half of them broadcast in German.

## Policies for the press and broadcasting

*Main actors and interests*

Efficient media policy is unknown in Austria and has been for more than a decade for two reasons: there is no central administration like a "Ministry of Communications", for example. Competence is spread over several ministries, including the Federal Chancellery. No standing committee or commission watches the media landscape, sectoral policy dominates and makes carefully balanced measures according to principles of common sense or agreement simply impossible.

Second, media policy in Austria must be seen as one of the areas where corporatist structures are much stronger than any market forces. The "iron triumvirate", consisting of the political parties, the ORF and the Publishers' Association, keeps all developments under its firm control. Neither the government nor parliament can be seen as independent agents – all decision-making is done by the "iron triumvirate". As early as 1964 – broadcasting was still in its infancy – the publishers declared their interest in the relatively new medium. They launched a referendum concerning the organization and programming structure of the ORF. All further developments in the electronic sector can be seen as the result of the search for compromise and agreement between the publishers and the ORF. In both of these organizations party interests are strongly represented. The last political debate on media policy took place in the mid-1970s, when the new media law was being drafted. Since that time and the passing of the law in 1981, media policy has been reduced to efforts aimed at maintaining the monopoly of public service broadcasting on the one hand and leaving the print media undisturbed on the other. In 1985 the

Publishers' Association and the ORF signed an agreement concerning the division of advertising revenue between the media. The ORF extended its weekly advertising time to include Sundays and public holidays, but agreed to leave regional advertising to the print media.

While all Austria's neighbours are replacing the monopoly of public broadcasting with more flexible systems, Austria's media policy has shown no sign of reacting to these developments. It was again the Publishers' Association and the ORF which took the initiative and agreed on limited franchises which would enable the newspapers to start regional commercial radio stations under the licence of the ORF (Radio Print). This agreement proposed the extension of the concentration process in Austria to an unprecedented degree: in the regions, the more or less unchallenged print market leaders would have had the monopoly on regional radio as well. It was not the strength of the opposition which prevented the agreement coming into force but the dramatic developments in the print market, commencing with the investments of the *Westdeutsche Allgemeine Zeitung* (WAZ) in Austria.

Facing the new monolithic block of the Mediaprint, a subsidiary of WAZ which organizes the distribution of *Kronenzeitung* and *Kurier,* the remaining newspapers started to rethink their radio ambitions. On the one hand, they were supporting a media concentration law to avoid further concentration and on the other they were well on the way to extending concentration to cross-media ownership. In the meantime the conservative party ÖVP presented a media concept, which dismissed Radio Print as a model. Social Democrats remain silent, unsure of how to further their political interests in the most efficient way.

*Main issues*

In the face of the second round of concentration, proposed anti-trust legislation including limitations on foreign media ownership in Austria is the central issue of the policy debate in the print media. Electronic media are concerned with the possible emergence of new competition, which seems to be at the top of any measures in public media policy. However, the ORF is trying to maximize its audience acceptance by adopting more and more of the strategies of its private competitors in Germany. These efforts are accompanied by the consciousness of the strengths of a public service. In his speech on the occasion of his re-election, the Director General of the ORF announced in late 1990 the expansion of news in general and the network of correspondents in particular. Austrian programme productions should be given preferential treatment.

## *Policy trends*

> In other words, the ORF seems ready to steer a cautious line between maintaining the public service ideal and self-commercialization. By developing this strategy, the ORF hopes to survive in new circumstances where it will no longer be in a position of controlling the market. (Signitzer and Luger 1988:23)

Part of this strategy is for the ORF to gain international experience in satellite-TV and in building alliances with other European public broadcasters. The ORF runs the non-commercial satellite-channel 3SAT in conjunction with German and Swiss partners. These and other international efforts are supported by the government, which has participated in several film and programme production funds and support schemes on a European level (e.g. sub-programmes of MEDIA 92; Eureka Audiovisual, Eurimage).

On the national level the issue of how to abolish the broadcasting monopoly is not yet ready for a decision. It is quite obvious that the megatrends of commercialization and internationalization in contemporary Europe have reached Austria now. In respect of Austrian ambitions to join the EEC, an adjustment of media policy is indeed required. Austria would enter the Common Media Market as a strong international competitor, with a broadcaster on a healthy financial base and technically well equipped. But this advantage might be lost if the now combined domestic forces are split by ruinous competition between various programme suppliers to the market of a small country with 2.96 million households and a relatively limited advertising market.

## Statistics

(1 ECU = 14 AS)
Number of inhabitants                                               7.6 m.

Broadcasting
Number of national TV-channels: (1985 and 1990)                       2
Number of national radio channels: (1985 and 1990)                   3

Advertising amount and division between media 1985 and 1989

|  | 1989 | | | 1985 | | |
|---|---|---|---|---|---|---|
|  | bn.AS | m.ECU | % | bn.AS | m.ECU | % |
| Newspapers | 3.37 | 241 | 32 | 2.58 | 184 | 37 |
| Regional newspapers/ | | | | | | |
| magazines | 2.16 | 155 | 22 | 1.16 | 83 | 17 |
| Press Total | 5.54 | 396 | 54 | 3.74 | 267 | 54 |
| Radio | 1.29 | 92 | 11 | 0.78 | 56 | 11 |
| Television | 2.89 | 206 | 28 | 1.91 | 136 | 28 |
| Elec. media Total | 4.18 | 298 | 39 | 2.69 | 192 | 39 |
| Outdoor | 0.68 | 49 | 7 | 0.50 | 36 | 7 |

(Source: Nielsen Media Research)

Household media equipment (1985 and 1989)

| | % of households | |
|---|---|---|
| | 1989 | 1985 |
| Households with TV-sets | 97.1 | 95.5 |
| More than one TV-set | 29.8 | 25.4 |
| Only b/w TV-set | 5.8 | 14.5 |
| VCR | 29.7 | 10.8 |
| Cable-households | 19.1 | 10.6 |
| Telephone | 85.5 | 82.2 |
| Car-radio | 56.9 | 48.2 |

(Source: Optima-Analyse 1985 and 1989.)

The press
Number of daily newspapers     17

Readership and circulation of the 10 biggest newspapers
(printed copies) 1990

| | Readership '000 | % | Copies '000 | Readership 1985 % |
|---|---|---|---|---|
| Neue Kronenzeitung | 2 681 | 42.6 | 1 075 | 40.7 |
| Kurier | 941 | 14.9 | 443 | 15.5 |
| Kleine Zeitung | 659 | 10.5 | 268 | 10.3 |
| Neue AZ | 235 | 3.7 | 138 | 2.2 |
| OÖ. Nachrichten | 307 | 4.9 | 115 | 4.6 |
| Tiroler Tageszeitung | 262 | 4.2 | 100 | 4.2 |
| Salzburger Nachrichten | 217 | 3.4 | 95 | 2.9 |
| Die Presse | 210 | 3.3 | 78 | 2.6 |
| Der Standard | 242 | 3.8 | 74 | n.a. |
| Neue Zeit | 123 | 2.0 | 73 | 1.7 |

(Source: Media-Analysen 1990; Pressehandbuch 1990; Medienbericht III 1986.)

## References

Berka, Walter (1989) "Das Recht der Massenmedien. Ein Lehr- und Handbuch für Studium und Praxis". Vienna, Cologne, Graz.

Fabris, Hans-Heinz (1989) "Kleinstaatliche Medienentwicklung im Europa der Großen'. Das Beispiel Österreich", Rundfunk und Fernsehen Vol. 2-3: 240–250.

Fabris, Hans-Heinz, Luger, Kurt and Signitzer, Benno (1990), "Das Rundfunksystem Österreichs", in Hans-Bredow-Institut (ed.), Internationales Handbuch für Rundfunk und Fernsehen. Baden-Baden: D 168—D 183.

Fabris, Hans-Heinz and Luger, Kurt (1986) "Austria" in Hans J. Kleinsteuber, Denis Mc-Quail, Karen Siune (eds.), Electronic Media and Politics in Western Europe: Euromedia Research Group Handbook of National Systems. Frankfurt, New York: 1–16.

GEAR (ed.) (1989) Euro-Factbook, Vienna.

Institut für Publizistik an der Universität Salzburg (ed.)(1977,1983,1986), Massenmedien in Österreich – Medienbericht I, II, III. Vienna.

Lankes, Gertraud (1990) "Österreichs Pressemarkt im Umbruch", in Verband österreichischer Zeitungsherausgeber und Zeitungsverleger (ed.), Pressehandbuch 1990. Vienna:11–13.

Luger, Kurt and Steinmaurer, Thomas (1990) "Die Medien-Metamorphose: Österreichs Medienlandschaft im Umbruch" in: Rundfunk und Fernsehen 2: 242–258.

Media-Analysen (Verein Arbeitsgemeinschaft) eds. (1990). Vienna.

Nielsen Media Research (1990) Entwicklung der Werbung 1989. Vienna.

Optima (1985 and 1989). Fessel + GfK, Vienna.

Paupié, Kurt (1960) Handbuch der Österreichischen Pressegeschichte 1948–1959. Vol I. Vienna.

Pürer, Heinz (1988) "Österreichs Mediensystem im Wandel. Ein aktueller Lagebericht", Media Perspektiven 11:673–682.

Schrotta, Werner (1981) "Die wirtschaftliche Entwicklung der österreichischen Tageszeitungen nach 1945" in: Amt der OÖ. Landesregierung (ed.), Das älteste Periodikum der Welt. Linz:57–60.

Signitzer, Benno and Luger, Kurt (1988) "Austria" in: Philip T. Rosen (ed.), International Handbook of Broadcasting Systems. New York, Westport, London: 15–24.

# 2

# Belgium

## Els De Bens

### National profile

Belgium is a small and densely populated country: 9 928 million people inhabit an area of 30 513 km$^2$, which amounts to 325 inhabitants per km$^2$. Almost 875 000 people are foreigners (9%). As Brussels is at the same time the EEC and NATO capital, more than half of the foreigners are European or American citizens; there is a large community of unskilled migrant workers from southern Europe, the Magreb and Turkey.

The largest part of the population lives in the Flemish region, 5 722 millions (i.e. 64%); 3 169 million (i.e. 36%) in the French-speaking part and 66 000 (0.7%) in the German-speaking region; almost one million people live in the bilingual area of Brussels.

The population is relatively old (46% older than 45 years); many families are childless and only 40% of the inhabitants belong to the active working population.

As a result of recent reforms of the state, Belgium has developed more and more towards a federalized country: 3 communities (Flemish, Walloon and German-speaking) with Brussels as a separate area (Gewest). This has caused a devolution of power from the central government to the regional governments. Belgium today has a very complicated state structure with a multitude of departments and services, so that bureaucracy is omnipresent.

Belgium has a multiparty system with a preponderance of christian democrats in Flanders and socialists in the Walloon part. No party has a clear majority, so that coalition governments prevail.

Belgium is a highly industrialized country, with a high standard of living, a decline of economic life in Wallonia and increasing industrial activities in Flanders. In Brussels more and more multinationals have established their administrative headquarters.

The gross national product in 1989 was 6 080 billion BF (41.6 billion ECU), which is 525 000 BF per capita. Belgium has a good social security system; 10% of the active population is unemployed, but for the last 2 years unemployment has been decreasing.

## Development of the press and broadcasting since 1945

### Print media

World War II caused many shifts in the Belgian press world. Newspapers that had appeared during the war were brought before special war courts in the postwar period of repression. Of the 65 pre-war newspapers only 39 continued to appear after the war. Even so, a number of new initiatives were taken to fill up the now empty spaces. Between 1944 and 1947, 20 newspapers were launched, but 17 of them had disappeared again by as early as 1947. The number of titles continued to decrease over the years: in 1990 only 28 papers are published!

Originally, the large newspaper groups were owned by individual families but gradually they became the property of financial holdings.

Belgium has always had a clearly distinguishable political opinion press. In Flanders it was the catholic press that always dominated. Between the world wars the socialist newspapers thrived to some extent in both communities, but after World War II the socialist press lost its hold.

The so-called neutral press was only successful in French-speaking Belgium.

Total circulation was subject to only minor fluctuations between 1955 and 1990, i.e. for a period of over 30 years. In 1955 the figure was 2 597 818 and in 1989 it was 2 130 846. There is a slight tendency for circulation figures to fall but the gently falling curve has occasionally been interrupted by new increases in circulation.

After World War II the Flemish press gradually caught up. From 1975 onwards it prevailed over the Walloon press (51% vs. 49%). The tendency became even more pronounced in the following years and the proportions are now 60% (Flemish) vs. 40% (Walloon). Because of the short distances in Belgium, all typically regional newspapers have gradually disappeared.

### The broadcasting system

After World War II the public broadcasting system in Belgium was given an absolute monopoly. Television broadcasting was introduced fairly late (1953) in Belgium, mainly due to the fact that Belgian television sets needed to be very complicated in order to receive both the French 819 line system and the European standard of 625 lines used elsewhere.

In May 1960 a new law was passed. It created two autonomous broadcasting institutions, one for Flanders (BRT) and one for French-speaking Wallonia (RTBF). Another new law in February 1977 created the Belgisches Fernsehen und Rundfunk (BFR) for the German-speaking part of Belgium.

As radio and television commercials remained illegal (until September 1987 in Wallonia and February 1989 in Flanders) licence fees constituted the sole source of revenue for the PSB. Over the years BRT and RTBF have received only a fraction (50 to 60% max) of the revenue from licence fees. Every year the budget of the PSB had to be accepted by the Flemish and Wallonian government.

An important factor that determined the audiovisual landscape of Belgium was the setting up of the cable networks in 1960. By the middle of the seventies half of the homes had been connected to a cable network. Today Belgium is the most densely cabled country of the world (91% of all TV households). In the beginning the cable companies only distributed the national programmes, but very soon the TV programmes of foreign TV-stations were distributed as well. Initially, only the foreign public service channels were given access to cable, but gradually some commercial stations were admitted as well.

As TV-commercials were forbidden, the law provided for the cable operators to cut out the commercials! In practice no such thing ever happened. As a matter of fact, cutting out commercials is contrary to the EEC stipulation of "the free exchange of services" (art. 59 and art. 60 of the EEC Treaty of Rome). And the European Court of Justice decided in its decree of 30 April 1974 that all television programmes – including commercials – are to be considered "services". Legal action taken in Belgium against the cable companies by consumers' organizations failed to change this situation.

The attitude displayed by the Belgian authorities in this affair was one of hypocrisy. The first commercial station to be allowed on cable was RTL. In 1983 the RTT (Regie van Telegrafie en Telefonie) even supplied an extra microwave link so that RTL could reach the Flemish TV-families more easily.

Whence this indulgence of the Belgian authorities towards RTL? The Group Brussel Lambert has a long-standing majority participation in RTL, through its holding company Audiofina. When the Belgian banker and media tycoon Albert Frère (Pargesa-Paribas) took over the Group Brussel Lambert in 1982, RTL became even more "Belgian" (Frère has control over 82% of CLT, including RTL). RTL became very successful and took away a large part of the audience, especially from RTBF.

The issue of TV advertising became a crucial one. The political parties were divided over it. BRT and RTBF joined the debate: they demanded at least a partial, but preferably the exclusive, right for radio and television advertising. It was not inconceivable that the decreasing audience ratings would be seized upon as a pretext to cut the allocated percentage of licence fees. Meanwhile, the ever increasing politicization of the PSB created a climate among public opinion in which the monopoly position of the PSB was resented to an ever increasing extent. Political pressure stifled the broadcast system. Promotions were not given because of qualifications but according to party loyalty.

The public broadcasting systems themselves deserved some of the blame: they readily joined the political game, and as a result of their many years of "inapproachability" in Belgium, both BRT and RTBF occasionally gave evidence of paternalistic and conceited traits. The permanently appointed employees, moreover, enjoyed the status of civil servants. Especially in the creative sectors, such a status of civil servant has proved too bureaucratic and too rigid, often nipping creativity in the bud.

All of these factors created a climate of public opinion in Belgium which grew more and more receptive to the idea of a breaching of the monopoly.

A number of private enterprises, and the world of finance at large, stimulated the introduction of radio and television advertising.

The PSB monopoly was first undermined by the illegal local radio stations. In September 1981 these radios were legalized in Wallonia and in May 1982 in Flanders. The monopoly of RTBF and BRT came to an end. Advertising remained illegal at first but under political and commercial pressures the ban on radio advertising was lifted in December 1985.

The television monopoly was legally broken in 1987. The legal framework and the development of the new commercial channels together with their impact on the public broadcasting system will be dealt with extensively in the section on the present situation of the electronic media.

**The press**

*Policy framework*

Belgium's constitution guarantees the complete freedom of the press. Articles 14 and 18 prohibit any form of preventive censorship, and repressive measures can be taken only if freedom of speech turns out to have been abused.

The law does provide for a number of restrictions on the freedom of the press. They are derived from fundamental rights, such as the individual's right to privacy and his protection against defamation. Further restrictions are based on the need to safeguard the public interest (national security, moral standards, the monarchy etc.).

When ownership concentration hit the Belgian press in the 1960s, no specific antitrust legislation was enacted in Belgium. The only measure taken to preserve the pluralistic character of the press was the establishment of a system of subsidies. In fact, the government had been helping the Belgian press indirectly since the end of the Second World War, for instance by means of reduced rates (mail, telephone, railway transport, paper and VAT).

In 1974 non-selective direct subsidies were introduced. They did not change the existing imbalance. Moreover, the sum to be distributed was small, about BF 200 million (1.4 million ECU), and inadequate to save newspapers in distress. Later a complex and partly selective system was adopted, giving small papers a trifle more than their larger and stronger colleagues. But in the meantime the overall subsidy itself had gradually become smaller, falling from BF 250 million in 1980 to 80 million in 1988.

## The major groups

Not only has the process of concentration resulted in a lower number of newspapers, it has also led to an even stronger decrease in the number of independent papers. Of today's 28 papers, a mere 9 are truly autonomous; the remaining 19 papers are parallel editions of the main papers, and differ only slightly from them.

In Flanders the market is controlled by 5 groups: VUM (*De Standaard, Het Nieuwsblad, De Gentenaar*), NV De Vlijt (*Gazet van Antwerpen, Gazet van Mechelen*), NV Concentra (*Het Belang van Limburg*), NV Het Volk (*Het Volk, De Nieuwe Gids*) and NV Hoste-Van Thillo (*Het Laatste Nieuws, De Nieuwe Gazet, De Morgen*). All the other papers have succumbed to the cut-throat competition.

The final battle was fought by *De Morgen/Vooruit*, the last remaining socialist-oriented  newspaper. In 1986 the socialist party decided not to continue its financial support to the paper. The reasons for the party's decision were twofold: on the one hand, the party was losing its hold on the editorial staff, which wanted to steer a more independent course; on the other, the paper's debts were becoming quite a burden. Once the decision was taken, the editors sounded the alarm and succeeded in setting up a heroic rescue operation, in which it was mainly the readers who raised money. The paper managed to hold out until the end of 1988, when the financial losses turned out to have become even larger, and eventually, in January 1989, the paper was bought by the centrist-liberal group NV Hoste-Van Thillo. A deal was struck with the new owner that the paper was to be allowed to maintain its free-thinking and progressive image, but it remains open to discussion whether this arrangement will stand the test of time.

Belgium's French-language press is dominated by only three large groups: NV Rossel (*Le Soir, La Meuse, La Lanterne, La Nouvelle Gazette*), SIPM (*La Libre Belgique, La Dernière Heure*) and Vers l'Avenir (*Vers l'Avenir, Le Courrier, Le Courrier de l'Escaut*). In 1986 and 1987 three smaller independent papers had to close down: the Brussels catholic paper *La Cité*, the catholic group around *Le Rappel* (based in Charleroi, along with *l'Echo du Centre* and the *Journal de Mons*) and a neutral independent paper in Verviers, *Le Jour*, which was bought by the group Vers l'Avenir. The sad story of these three French-language papers and of the Flemish *DeMorgen* shows clearly enough that increasing concentration pushes small papers off the market.

The remaining socialist newspapers (*Le Peuple, Journal et Indépendence* and *Journal de Charleroi* ) survive only because of financial support from the socialist party and the trade-unions.

Initially, all the groups mentioned above were family enterprises, but gradually they came to be controlled by financial holdings and banking institutions. Their ownership structure continues to be Belgian, with the exception of the Rossel group: in 1989 Hersant succeeded in acquiring a 41% stake in the group.

All these concerns have tended to become multimedia enterprises in the last few years. Quite a number of newspaper groups publish weeklies and freely distributed advertising papers.

Most Belgian newspapers participate in local radio via news and advertising networks. They also demanded participation when the introduction of new commercial television stations began to be considered, and their demands were met to a large extent: in Wallonia the press has a 31% stake in the new commercial station (31% being the legal minimum); in Flanders the press has 100% participation, the legal minimum being 51%.

*Financial aspects : circulation and advertising*

In 1989 the overall circulation of the Belgian press amounted to 2 028 231 copies, the Flemish press taking 1 204 431 or 59.38%, and the French-language press 810 300 or 39.95%. Over the past few years a decline in circulation figures has been noticeable mainly for the French-language press, whose share in the overall circulation figures stood at 46.50% in 1980.

The Flemish market leader is the VUM group, which publishes the so-called Standaard group (named after one of the papers *De Standaard*). The group's circulation was 382 424 in 1989.

With circulation figures of 291 092 NV Hoste-Van Thillo ranks second. NV Het Volk and NV De Vlijt (*Gazet van Antwerpen*) share the third place with about 190 000 each.

It is the group with the largest circulation, VUM with the Standaard papers, which is also the market leader with regard to revenues from advertising.

The Standaard papers and *Gazet van Antwerpen* derive some 55% of their income from advertising, and some 45% from sales. This is a very sound situation indeed, most other groups having about an equal share of revenue from sales and advertising.

Though *Het Belang van Limburg* (NV Concentra) has relatively small circulation figures, 103 812 in 1989, it boasts a steady growth, as in 1960 it sold only 50 000 copies. The paper enjoys a monopoly position in the province of Limburg, and its sales continued to increase even in the critical years 1975–1977, when all the other Belgian papers experienced a painful decline.

Among the French-language press the Rossel group continues to lead the market: the combined circulation of *Le Soir, La Meuse, La Lanterne and La Nouvelle Gazette* amounted to 444 309 in 1989. *Le Soir* alone accounted for 199 825 copies, which makes it the most widely read French-language paper in Belgium. However, in the past 20 years its circulation has dropped steadily; in 1970 the paper still sold nearly 300 000 copies! The same goes for the popular papers *La Meuse* and *La Lanterne*, whose circulation fell from 184 408 in 1970 to 130 361 in 1989. The Rossel group's only paper to sell more copies today than in the past is *La Nouvelle Gazette*: 70 300 copies in 1970, 111 123 in 1989. Oddly enough, *La Nouvelle Gazette* is the outsider in the neutral Rossel group since it has a marked liberal tendency. Perhaps the paper also owes its success to its typical local (Charleroi) flavour, which is that of a genuinely Walloon newspaper with a strong bias towards federalism.

The SIPM group ranks second as far as circulation goes. The group publishes *La Libre Belgique* and *La Dernière Heure*, which is actually a strange combination as *La Libre Belgique* is catholic and conservative, whereas *La Dernière Heure* is liberal. The latter newspaper was bought by *La Libre Belgique* in 1970, but a few years later M. Brébart of *La Dernière Heure* acquired a majority participation. Yet the two papers continued to have major problems, and they did not even have CIM verify their circulation; CIM is an officially recognized body which compiles reliable circulation figures. In 1985 the two papers were bought by SIPM. The new owners quote a circulation of 91 412 for *La Dernière Heure* and 86 105 for *La Libre Belgique* (1989).

The third major group of the French-language press is Vers l'Avenir, with 4 titles and 6 editions. Unlike *La Libre Belgique* and *La Dernière Heure*, *Vers l'Avenir* does have its circulation checked by CIM : 146 474 copies in 1989 as against 98 000 in 1970.

The remaining newspapers are marginal ones; they all belong to the socialist family and are kept alive by Wallonia's socialist party and socialist trade-unions.

As to the ratio of revenue from advertising on the one hand and from sales on the other, no recent figures are available. Thanks to their large share of the readership, the papers of the Rossel group are bound to take a large portion of the advertising cake.

Belgium spends little on advertising, at least when compared with other West European countries: a mere 0.7% of its GNP in 1989. Most of the advertising is done via the print media: 55.40% as against 27.14% via television, 1.68% via the radio, 14.31% via billboards and 1.41% via film theatres.

Needless to say, since the introduction of French-language and Dutch-language commercial television stations, the share taken by television in the advertising budget has increased. It is the weeklies in particular, rather than the dailies, which have felt the impact of this evolution. Indeed, the dailies, with the exception of the Standaard group, have taken a participation in commercial television.

### Quality and popular press

Belgium does not have any genuine popular papers or tabloids like the *Sun* in the UK, or quality papers like *Le Monde* in France. *De Standaard* and *La Libre Belgique* assume a somewhat more serious attitude; the others tend to present a more popular image.

### Political tendency

The Belgian press is strongly characterized by its political leanings. Only the papers of the Rossel group can be said to be "neutral" or "non-partisan", although *La Nouvelle Gazette* is a liberal newspaper.

In Flanders, 71.93% of the newspapers are catholic whereas 24.16% are liberal, and 3.89% socialist. The share taken by the catholic press has continued to increase in recent years.

In French-speaking Belgium 28.70% of the papers belong to the catholic press, 24.99% are liberal, 5.55% are socialist, and the majority, 40.74%, are neutral, i.e. do not follow any party line.

Clearly, there is a striking discrepancy between how Belgians vote and what newspapers they read: the share of the catholic newspapers in the overall circulation figures of the Flemish press is larger than the number of people who vote for the Flemish catholic party, and the socialist parties in Flanders as well as in Wallonia have more voters than there are readers of socialist papers.

*Het Volk* and *De Nieuwe Gids*, together with the French-language socialist newspapers, are the only papers which still have direct ties with a political party. Indeed, just as in other Western European countries, political-party newspapers are in decline in Belgium. Still, *Het Volk* and its parallel title are exceptions to the rule: they probably owe their 190 000 readers to their extensive sports pages and their *faits divers*; in addition, the group devotes much energy to its regional editions, and this may help to boost its popularity.

### Distribution and technology

The large newspaper enterprises rely partly on direct distribution. In addition to direct distribution they also use the services of a specialized distribution agency, Agence Messagère de Presse, which enjoys a near monopoly in Belgium. So far the Belgian newspapers do not co-operate as far as distribution is concerned.

In view of the recurrent train strikes and the less than perfect postal service, the large concerns are trying to build up distribution systems of their own. Hence, the distribution of the papers adds a substantial element to the cost-price of the newspapers. Actually, the increasing cost of distribution as well as the high price of paper are often cited by the publishers as arguments to raise the price of the newspapers.

Virtually all Belgian papers have changed over to on-line systems. The switch-over was carried out fairly smoothly in nearly all cases and certainly did not lead to serious social unrest as it did in Britain.

## Electronic media

### Legal framework

The legal framework of the public broadcasting system has already been discussed above in the historical overview. The different causes which led to the break up of the PSB monopoly have been explained as well.

Although Wallonia had established the legal framework for commercial television by means of the law of 28 January 1987, and Flanders with the law of 17 July 1987, a considerable time would elapse before the new commercial stations could actually start operations.

In order to make commercial television possible, a new law had to be passed allowing commercial advertising on television. Belgium has a very complex government structure and since at the time commercial advertising was still within national jurisdiction, it was the national government that first had to establish the legal framework. This was done by means of the law of 6 February 1987. However, the law was vague on many points. It was "forgotten" to stipulate how much, when and how television advertising had to be programmed. A supplementary Royal Decree (3 August 1987) detailed that commercial advertising had to be grouped in non-consecutive blocks of which the total duration should not surpass an annual average of 12 minutes per hour of broadcasting, while each individual block should last no longer than maximum 6 minutes.

As a consequence of the reform of the state, the authority over commercial advertising was transferred to the Communities from 1 January 1989 onwards. Both in Wallonia and Flanders a new law is being prepared to replace the old one, but in the meantime the new commercial stations VTM and RTL have had ample time to flout the legal regulations.

## Profile of the Walloon station, RTL-TVi

On the Walloon side of the country preparations for the establishment of a new commercial station had been going on long before the decree of 17 July 1987. RTL had been the unofficial Belgian commercial station for many years through its links with GBL and Paribas: in 1986 82.5 % of RTL was under Belgian control. Every year RTL obtained more than half of its advertising revenue from the Belgian advertising market. In order to give itself a more Belgian profile a Belgian subsidiary TV-Team was founded, which in 1985 concluded a deal with Audiopresse (the Belgian French-language press) to set up a commercial station.

In the meantime negotiations between RLT and the Executive Council of the French Community led to an agreement in the summer of 1986.

The draft decree to be passed by the French Community Council had in fact been finalized as early as 1986. Progress was however blocked by the fact that first the law on commercial advertising had to be changed on the national level.

After the passing of the law on commercial advertising (6 February 1987) and the decree of 17 July 1987, everything went very quickly. RTL-TVi received its licence as expected. RTL (TV-Team and CLT) have a participation of 66% and Audiopresse has an interest of 34%. The Walloon decree refers to "private television stations", in the plural, which contradicts the national law of 6 February 1987. For the time being, however, there is no danger to the monopoly of RTL-TVi. The licence has been granted for 9 years. In return for its advertising monopoly RTL-TVi has to invest in the Walloon audio-visual industry (through own production work, the purchase of programmes and co-productions).

RTL-TVi did however encounter unforeseen competition. The privatized channel TF1 attracted more and more Belgian viewers with its popular programming. In 1989 TF1 had an average viewer share of 20%, as against about 25% for both RTBF and RTL-TVi. Antenne 2 and FR3 had about 17% and the rest went to the other channels. TF1 opened up its advertising slots to Belgian advertising and the revenue for RTL-TVi kept diminishing. RTBF, which had always claimed the right to broadcast advertising and was losing viewers to TF1 in the same way as RTL-TVi, approached RTL-TVi. In June 1989 a decree granted RTBF permission to broadcast television advertising together with RTL-TVi from 1 September 1989 onwards. This "amalgamation" did not lead to the hoped for result because, instead of an increase in the advertising volume, part of RTL-TVi's advertising was simply transferred to RTBF. In a clever arrangement RTL-TVi had anticipated this possibility and made sure that part of the revenue went back to RTL-TVi, which left RTBF as "poor" as before: in 1990 the advertising revenues were distributed 24% to RTBF and 76% to RTL-TVi. In the meantime the struggle with the French stations continues.

*Profile of the Flemish channel,VTM*

After the publication of the cable decree of 17 January 1987, it took a considerable time before a national Flemish commercial station could start operations. The decree envisaged several types of non-public television stations, but on the national level the monopoly was given to one single channel, and for 18 years at that! (RTL-TVi received a licence for 9 years.) The lobby of the Flemish daily and weekly press was given satisfaction to a large degree: the law stipulates that 51% of the shares have to be owned by them. Later, it turned out that the VTM shares were owned almost 100% by the press: a detrimental form of multimedia concentration. In addition, there is the immediate concern for the safeguarding of independent television criticism.

VTM has undoubtedly become a success story in all respects, in contrast to RTL-TVi. Advertising revenues rose as high as 3 000 million BF. The financial success of VTM is obviously inextricably linked to its high viewing percentages. During the first launching month the target market share of 20% was surpassed: in February 1989 the viewing percentage rose to 27% and in December 1989 a percentage of 40% was reached. The trend continued in 1990. VTM's success is mainly due to a policy of very popular programming: much entertainment and lots of fiction, mainly American.

*The public broadcasting stations cornered*

Both BRT and RTBF have tried to counteract the success of their commercial competitors. It is obvious that no broadcasting system can remain indifferent to a sharp decline in viewers. In addition, both BRT and RTBF feared that the strong decrease in viewers might be used against the public broadcasting system. Reference has already been made to the difficult position of the public stations: too few resources (only about half of the licence fees) and the detrimental influence of a system of politicization that stifles creativity.

Even before VTM and RTL-TVi were set up, the public channels were faced with strong competition from foreign stations that reached the viewers via the cable networks (on average there are 16 foreign channels). However, neither public station had changed its proportion of "serious" programmes in the past: the proportion of "popular" versus "serious" programmes remained virtually unchanged during the period 1970–1987. What did change was the timing of the programmes: serious programmes were relegated more and more often to the early and late evening hours, while prime time was reserved for entertainment, mainly for fiction.

The advent of RTL-TVi and VTM, however, has led the public channels to choose a levelling down strategy, suffering as they were from a decline in viewers. "Serious" programmes are no longer scheduled at very disadvantageous hours, they have simply been discontinued. The amount of fiction and entertainment rose in the course of 1989 and 1990 especially on BRT1 and RTBF1. Both public stations are urgently in need of a new strategy in which a proper and new profile is presented. This search for a new identity of its own is made even more difficult in the case of RTBF because of its co-operation with RTL-TVi. In the past the public stations in Belgium were always financed exclusively with public means, i.e. without using revenue from advertising. This is in itself an excellent model if those resources are adequate.

This model was recently abandoned for RTBF and co-operation with the commercial channel was chosen instead. In Flanders, a first step towards commercialization of the PSB was made when advertising was allowed on BRT radio in 1990. When, at a later stage, the public stations in their turn are dependent on advertising in Belgium, the struggle with the commercial stations will become even more intense.

## Pay television: initiatives from abroad

As early as 1985 Filmnet was given permission to start a pay television service in Flanders. The legal framework for it was not created until the cable decree of January 1987!

Filmnet, which offers pay television in the Netherlands, Belgium and the Scandinavian countries, soon turned out to be no gold mine. In Flanders Filmnet has about 60 000 subscribers.

In Wallonia Canal Plus Belgique was started up in the autumn of 1989. In February 1989 an agreement was concluded between Canal Plus France and the French-speaking community. The shares were distributed as follows: 1/3 for RTBF, 1/3 for Canal Plus France and the rest for various Belgian enterprises, among which are Déficom and a Tractebel-dependent group.

On the Walloon side a lot of concessions were demanded: Canal Plus France had to agree that possible dividends would be reinvested in Wallonia and that it would participate in co-productions in Wallonia for a yearly amount that could not be lower than 80 000 million francs. In addition, Canal Plus has to give RTBF the opportunity to participate in every production planned in French-speaking Belgium.

Filmnet on the other hand did not have to fulfil so many requirements: for the first 4 years 5% of its productions have to consist of its own Flemish cultural productions. After 4 years this percentage is raised to 7.5%.

The break-even point of Canal Plus Belgique is estimated to be about 80 000. In 1992, it is hoped that the figure of 160 000 subscriptions will be reached. In July 1990 the number of subscribers was 13 200.

In Europe, Canal Plus France is the only successful pay film channel and probably this increases the chances of success for its Belgian subsidiary.

Yet the boom of new commercial channels will adversely affect the chances of survival of pay television networks in the near future. The competition of the videorecorder as home viewing cinema is growing as well: the penetration of VCRs is increasing rapidly in Belgium and the video film circuit is becoming ever more extensive.

*Local radio: a lost opportunity?*

The first illegal local radio stations started to appear in Belgium around 1980. They broadcast at irregular hours, operated illegally and carried on a campaign to break the BRT–RTBF monopoly. The idealists were, however, quickly joined by commercially inspired groups that turned the local radio stations into non-stop pop stations.

Legalization was bound to follow: technical norms were legally determined by the law of August 1981. The commercially oriented local radio stations continued to broadcast advertising illegally. Soon local radio networks developed in which the newspapers participated! For the small-scale local radio stations the future was bleak, but in January 1990 there was a turn for the better: a new law was passed prohibiting the formation of commercial local radio chains and once again promoting the old small-scale "pioneering model".

The big question is of course in what way the present chain forming will be counteracted by this law.

*The local television policy: a success in Wallonia but not in Flanders*

From the beginning the Walloon policy on local television was much more coherent than in Flanders. In Wallonia a certain model was taken as the starting point: local television had to be geared to one particular region with respect to content. This idea implied immediately that broadcasting time had to be limited. The Walloon government remained consistent in this and provided the resources in the launch phase. Later, a limited form of advertising was allowed which meant that local television stations had a mixed form of financing: public and private.

In Wallonia 11 stations were given a licence. In each region corresponding in size to approximately one voting district, only one channel could be operational. This limitation was very important, because it prevented proliferation and made government grants possible.

After a 14-year experience (the first experiments were set up in 1976) it has proved that most local television stations were able to build up a stable audience. Although the new Walloon audio-visual decree of 1987 provides for the setting up of purely commercial channels, the political will in Wallonia to limit themselves to the 11 existing channels remains intact. Until now, no new licences have been granted.

The Flemish cable decree and its implementing orders leave some crucial questions on local television unanswered: there are no clear views on the size of the region, the limitation of the broadcasting hours, the content, the way of financing. Applications for recognition keep flooding in by the dozen and if no clearer regulations are provided Flanders is heading directly for the Italian model: proliferation in which the stronger commercial stations push out all others and in doing so make chain formation inevitable. Four licences have been granted. One channel, AVS-Eeklo, started broadcasting in October 1988 for one hour a month. A new legal frame-work and policy are essential conditions in order to give local television in Flanders the same chance of survival as in Wallonia.

*Telematic media*

In Flanders teletext distribution has increased over the last few years (teletext decoders in 1990: approx. 17%). The teletext service is provided by the public broadcasting system. In comparison with, say, the Netherlands and the UK the number of pages is rather limited. An increase in the number of pages will probably lead to increased use. In Wallonia teletext was unable to gain a foothold because French-speaking Belgium chose the French Antiope system. Antiope is a very sophisticated form of teletext but the system is so expensive that no one has found a use for it. RTBF has in fact developed a teletext service of its own but it is broadcast over the open channel since the viewers have no decoders.

Videotex domestic use in Belgium is still in its infancy. Since 1988 the RTT has offered a videotex service but at the beginning of 1990 the number of subscribers was still only 7 000. By means of promotional campaigns the RTT is trying to sell videotex to a wide audience but the fact that the telephone links remain relatively expensive and that the content is not attractive enough keeps weighing heavily upon a further expansion.

## Policies for the press and broadcasting

Belgium has never been in the forefront as far as meaningful media policies are concerned. A lot of media laws have only confirmed situations that were already in existence. In short, Belgium has followed a media policy of *laissez faire*. Many media laws are ambiguous and can be interpreted in different ways. For the last few years media policies have been strongly oriented towards liberalism: new private initiatives have been supported such as commercial radio, pay television, new commercial television networks. Advertising regulations have been neglected, with no government interference, and the quotas on indigenous cultural productions have been sidestepped by games and quizzes. No measures have been taken against the increasing concentration of the media. On the contrary, in the new commercial stations there is an obligatory participation of the dailies and the weeklies.

Supportive measures for the press, such as direct government grants, have no effect whatsoever: the amounts are too small and the selection criteria too unselective. This has led to the situation that prosperous papers too receive a share of the very small overall amount available for subsidies.

The public stations' situation is becoming ever more difficult: there is a lack of funds, the stifling effect of political patronage and bureaucratic inertia, a loss of viewers and of their own identity. The commercial stations RTL-TVi and VTM turn out to have dragged along the public stations in a down-market process. The political will is lacking to look for a serious solution for the public broadcasting systems.

## Statistics

(1 ECU = 40 Belgian francs, Bfr)
Population 1989

| | | |
|---|---|---|
| Number of inhabitants: | | 9 928 million |
| Number of inhabitants per sq. km | | 325 |

Broadcasting
Public Service

| | | |
|---|---|---|
| Number of TV channels: | 4 | (BRT 1, BRT 2, RTBF 2, RTBF 1) |
| Number of radio channels: | 10 | (BRT: 5; RTBF: 5) |
| Commercial  (national) | | |
| Number of TV channels: | 2 | (VTM,  RTL-TVi) |

Commercial (local)

| | | |
|---|---|---|
| Number of TV channels: | 13 | (Flanders: 1; Wallonia: 12) |
| Number of local radio stations: | 510 | (Flanders: 402; Wallonia: 108) |
| Hours TV per week: | | 15559 |

Financing of the broadcast systems

| | | |
|---|---|---|
| PSB: Licence fees: | | 258 billion ECU |
| | Flanders: | 135 billion ECU |
| | Wallonia: | 123 billion ECU |
| Commercial TV: Advertising revenue: | | 147 billion ECU |
| | Flanders: | 90 billion ECU |
| | Wallonia: | 57 billion ECU |

Audience share

| | |
|---|---|
| PSB in Flanders: | 26% (BRT) |
| Commercial in Flanders: | 40% (VTM) |
| PSB in Wallonia: | 24% (RTBF) |
| Commercial in Wallonia: | 15% (RTL-TVi) |

Transmission

| | |
|---|---|
| Telephone: | 78% |
| Cable (ATV): | 91% |
| Satellite: | negligible |

AV -Equipment

| | |
|---|---|
| TV-sets colour: | 88% |
| VCR: | 30% |
| Teletext: | 17% |
| RTT-Videotex: | 7 000 subscribers |

Print media 1989

| | | |
|---|---|---|
| Total Flemish press | 1 204 431 | 59.38% |
| Total French-language press | 810 300 | 39.95% |

Political tendency of the Belgian newspapers

| Tendency | Flemish press | French-language press |
|---|---|---|
| Catholic | 71.93 % | 28.70 % |
| Liberal | 24.16 % | 24.99 % |
| Socialist | 3.89 % | 5.55 % |
| Neutral | - | 40.74 % |

Circulation according to groups

| Controlling group          Titles published | Ideology | Circulation |
|---|---|---|
| VUM – De Standaard,Het Nieuwsblad, De Gentenaar | catholic | 382424 |
| NV De Vlijt – Gazet van Antwerpen, Gazet van Mechelen | catholic | 90853 |
| NV Het Volk – Het Volk, De Nieuwe Gids | catholic | 189366 |
| NV Concentra – Het Belang van Limburg | catholic | 103812 |
| NV Hoste – Van Thillo: | | |
|   Het Laatste Nieuws, De Nieuwe Gazet | liberal | 291092 |
|   De Morgen/Vooruit | socialist | 46884 |
| NV Rossel – Le Soir, La Meuse, La Lanterne | neutral | 330186 |
|   La Nouvelle Gazette | liberal | 111123 |

## 32    Belgium

Circulation according to groups (continued)

| Controlling group | Titles published | Ideology | Circulation |
|---|---|---|---|
| SIPM: | | | |
| La Libre Belgique | | catholic | 86 105 |
| La Dernière Heure | | liberal | 91 412 |
| Vers l'Avenir: | | | |
| Le Jour | | neutral | na |
| Vers l'Avenir, Le Courrier de l'Escaut, Le Courrier | | catholic | 146 474 |
| Small independent newspapers | | neutral/socialist | 58 500 |
| TOTAL | | | 2 028 231 |

Advertising: division by media

| Media | 1988 | 1989 |
|---|---|---|
| Newspapers | 24.15% | 20.17% |
| Regional weeklies | 8.93% | 8.49% |
| Family magazines | 12.47% | 10.11% |
| Women's magazines | 14.26% | 9.28% |
| Other periodicals | 7.72% | 7.35% |
| Posters | 14.48% | 14.31% |
| TV | 14.33% | 21.14% |
| Cinema | 1.64% | 1.41% |
| Radio | 1.97% | 1.68% |

## References

Boone, L. (1978) Krantenpluralisme en informatiebeleid. Leuven.

Burgelman J. (1989) "Political Parties and their Impact on Public Service in Belgium. Elements from a political-sociological approach", Media Culture and Society, April (2), 167–193.

De Bens, E. (1986) "Cable Penetration and Competition among Belgian and Foreign Stations", European Journal of Communication, 1 (4) 477–492.

De Bens, E. (1988) "Der Einfluss eines grossen ausländischen Programmangebotes auf die Sehgewohnheiten: Belgische Erfahrungen mit einer dichten Verkabelung", Publizistik, Sonderheft: Sozialisation durch Massenmedien, 33 (2–3) 352–365.

De Bens, E. (1989)"Audiovisual media in Belgium. Political, social, cultural and economic developments", Soziale Konsequenzen einer europäischen Medienpolitik, Vol. 2, Studie für GDV der Europäischen Gemeinschaft, Hamburg, November: 1–34.

De Bens, E. (1990) "Het Recente beleid inzake de audiovisuele media in België", in Politiek Jaarboek 1989 Année Politique, Res Publica, Tijdschrift voor Politologie, Vol. XXXII (2–3). 299–311.

Gol, J. (1970) Le monde de la presse en Belgique. Brussels.

Heinsman, L. and Servaes, J. (1988) Hoe nieuw zijn de media: Een mediabeleid met een perspectief. Leuven.

Herroelen, P. (1982) 1,2, ... veel? Kroniek van 20 jaar Belgische radio en televisie. Leuven.

Lentzen, E. (1985) "La CLT",Courrier Hebdomadaire, CRLSP, 18 January:8–18.

Luykx, T. (1973) Evolutie van de communicatiemedia. Brussels.

Van Der Biesen, W. (1990) "Vlaanderen en zijn 5 dagbladen" and "Persconcentratie", Mediagids, Parts 13 and 15, Deurne.

Verstraeten, H. (1980) Pers en markt: Een dossier over de geschreven pers in België. Leuven.

Voorhoof, D. (1987) "De nieuwe mediawetgeving: krachtlijnen en knelpunten", Communicatie, 1:3–20.

# 3

# Denmark

*Vibeke G. Petersen and Karen Siune*

## National profile

Denmark has a population of 5.1 million spread over 43 069 km$^2$. The number of households is 2.4 million. Danish is the language spoken by everybody except a limited number of guest workers. Denmark is, compared to many other countries, a relatively homogenous society with respect to culture and values.

Denmark has been a member of the European Community (EC) since 1973, but there is an old tradition for cultural and political affiliation with the Nordic countries, and Scandinavia is often considered as one unit. This chapter will show many similarities with the other Scandinavian countries with respect to media structure and media politics.

The political system is a multiparty system with more than 10 political parties running at elections. No single party has a majority and the political system frequently has to make compromise decisions. The Social Democratic Party has for decades been the largest party with more than one third of the votes, and it has very often formed the government, mostly in coalition with smaller bourgeois parties. From 1982 Denmark has had bourgeois coalition governments under the leadership of the Conservative People's Party in strong cooperation with the Agrarian Liberals. In the coalitions a number of smaller parties have participated. Since the 1990 election the two major bourgeois parties alone have formed the government coalition.

Media policy is an issue for debate in Danish society, and all political parties have views on the media structure. Media politics has however never been the main election issue.

The Danish economy is basically capitalist and the state has a very limited involvement in industrial production. The standard of living is high as is the distribution of consumer goods. Denmark is one of the leading examples of a welfare society.

A relatively high level of unemployment, close to 10% of the labour force, and problems with the balance of trade and the balance of payments have been issues on the political agenda for many years. These issues have an impact on the debate on media policy as well as other policy areas related to economic growth and employment. New technology suitable for export and increased employment opportunities have been influential in relation to Danish media politics as described by Siune (1986).

## Development of the press and broadcasting since 1945

In Denmark telecommunications has been taken care of by the state or by concessionaries. The national Post and Telegraph Service has distributed ordinary mail ever since 1711, and besides P&T has been responsible for telegraphy, telex and national telephone services.

In 1926 a monopoly on broadcasting was given to Statsradiofonien. This institution changed its name in 1959 to Danmarks Radio but kept the monopoly on all radio broadcasting till the 1980s. In 1953 Danmarks Radio started broadcasting television. The organization of Danmarks Radio has always been regulated by law.

From the very beginning of Danish national broadcasting the condition was that it should be financed by licence fees. The costs for broadcasting should not burden the state budget as such. No commercials were allowed. Danmarks Radio got and DR still has, according to the text of the  law, the status of an independent public institution. The responsibility for broadcasting has been placed with a variety of ministries through the years. At present it belongs to the Ministry of Communications. Danmarks Radio's monopoly on national broadcasting was broken in the second half of the 1980s by the establishment of a second national television channel, TV2. Independent local television and local radio were allowed as experiments in 1983 and later made legal permanently (see below).

A second television channel had been debated for years when it was finally decided upon in 1987. The issue had been handled by the Government Commission for Mass Media, set up in 1980 to propose an overall media policy. A large majority of the Commission recommended in 1983 the establishment of a second national television channel independent of Danmarks Radio. TV2 was created as a reaction to the challenge from foreign channels broadcast to Denmark via satellites and transmitted to households via cable.

The law establishing TV2 in 1987 was passed in the Danish parliament, Folketinget, with a majority of just one vote. The opposition, the Social Democrats and the Socialists, were against the proposal because it introduced commercial financing of national television. The small centre party, the Radical Liberals — traditionally opposed to bourgeois cultural policy, supported the government's proposal in return for a decisive influence on the regional structure of TV2.

The ideas behind the new channel were several: to break the monopoly of Danmarks Radio was a prominent one, to introduce commercial television a second, presenting another Danish alternative to the foreign channels a third. Thus, the main arguments were based on a wish to protect Danish culture. The intention was also to give the Danish production companies a chance to produce for television.

In summary it can be said that broadcasting in Denmark has expanded a great deal in the period after the Second World War, but that the national expansion has always been heavily regulated. Local radio and television stations have emerged, now licensed locally and financed by advertising and private means. These stations are owned and operated by private broadcasting associations, companies and the like. They can also be owned by the press (more about local radio and television below). So private radio broadcasting has expanded during the 1980s, regulated, but with far fewer obligations than national broadcasting.

The vast increase in broadcasting outlets has taken place against the background of a drastic decrease in the number of daily newspapers since the Second World War. With the dwindling number came a restructuring of the press in provincial towns from competition to monopoly.

Since 1945 75 newspapers have died, leaving 48, of which 10 are national papers published in Copenhagen. Half of the 75 ceased to appear before 1960, and the latest large-scale close-down happened in the early 1970s when the Social Democrats decided to give up publishing independent dailies in all but two provincial areas (they still have close relations to one national daily). During the 1980s the concentration process has slowed down — a few new papers were launched and died within a year.

In the provinces where most of the closures took place, the post-war era meant the end of the traditional "four paper" system according to which each of the four major political parties (the Social Democratic Party, the Conservative People's Party, the Agrarian Liberals, and the Radical Liberals) ran their own newspaper. This situation of diversity and competition has given way to one of monopoly nearly everywhere — only three of these towns have more than one daily. Close behind came the "liberation" of most of the remaining papers from their party affiliation. It is commonly acknowledged, however, that about 90% of the Danish press is to be found at the centre/right of the political spectrum.

The relatively stable period of the last 15 years or so has mainly been characterized by a stagnation/decline in the circulation of provincial dailies, while the national papers, especially the two tabloids *Ekstrabladet* and *B.T.*, have increased theirs.

**The press**

*Legal framework*

Freedom of the press goes back almost 150 years to the Constitution of 1849. It gives everybody the right to impart information, and it prohibits censorship. Other laws specify and set the limitations of this freedom, notably the press law, the penal code and procedural law. The legal framework of the press does not encompass monopoly regulations, but it does provide for a (modest) state subsidy scheme.

The laws deal with editorial responsibility, the right of reply, the right to privacy, libel, defamation, incitement to crime, and the right of journalists to protect their sources, to mention the most important issues. In addition to the legal regulations there is a set of voluntary ethical rules about journalistic practice, administered by a Press Council. The rules were written and adopted by the publishers' association, but not formally recognized by the journalists' union. They are expected to be incorporated in a new law in 1991.

The main purpose of this law is to extend the press law's system of editorial responsibility to broadcasters and to expand the right of journalists to protect their sources.

Press legislation is the prerogative of the Prime Minister — who otherwise, in addition to heading the government, only looks after matters concerning Greenland and the Faroe Islands — and is thus marked as a field belonging under neither industry, trade, business nor communications.

*Structure and organization*

When the Prime Minister in 1980 set up the Media Commission to look into the development of the media and to recommend policy initiatives, one of the first tasks it took up was an analysis of the economic status of the press. It was recognized then — as it is now — that the press operates largely on the same conditions as private business (in contrast to the electronic media).

Unlike the other Nordic countries, Denmark does not have a tradition of active political intervention in the newspaper business, as for instance through direct subsidy. The existing subsidy — exemption from VAT and cheap postal rates — is difficult to evaluate precisely. It is generally set at about 500 million Dkr. annually (40 m. ECU). But although this form of subsidy helps the industry by enabling it to sell its product relatively cheaply, it does nothing to change structural problems.

As mentioned above, one such structural problem is the disappearance of competition at the local level. A number of idealistic attempts during the 1970s and 1980s to establish new papers or revive dead ones have shown that it is practically impossible to reverse the movement towards a monopoly structure.

Since 1970 a modest direct subsidy has been channelled to needy papers through the Finance Institute of the Press. On recommendation from the Media Commission a large majority in Parliament decided in 1984 to increase the annual state subsidy to the Institute from 4 to 14 million Dkr. (320 000 to 1.1 m. ECU). The money is used to give security for loans in connection with modernization of newspaper production, to plan the establishment of new papers, to carry out those plans, and to support financial reorganizations of existing papers.

The stated goal of such press policy initiatives as there are is, of course, to further the diversity and plurality of the media offer. The political rejection of more substantial direct intervention in the financial affairs of the press is mainly based on the fear of cementing the existing press pattern. By keeping alive papers that would die in the market place because of inefficient management, the state would only delay the necessary adaptation to modern society, the argument goes. Newspaper proprietors have consistently (if not always unanimously) added to this that direct subsidy would make the press dependent on the state in an unacceptable manner.

The Danish press is almost entirely privately owned, mostly in the form of limited liability companies, and often organized as foundations in order to prevent hostile take-overs. The companies typically have extra income through related activities such as publication of free sheets and other printing business. But the bulk of their finance comes from the sale of copies and of advertising space — in roughly equal proportions.

It is generally recognized that financing of the press increasingly will have to rely on a more efficient use of existing resources. Advertising volume is going down — between 1987 and 1989 by an average of 6.5% — and turnover is also decreasing, albeit not as drastically. The well-established connection between the state of the market and the advertising industry makes newspapers particularly vulnerable to overall economic trends in society. It is no consolation that readership patterns show that young people increasingly choose to do without a daily paper.

The fall in advertising volume in the press coincides with the introduction of broadcast advertising which came about during 1988. But so far no serious attempt has been made to establish a connection between the two or to draw policy conclusions, except at the local level. The press was allowed to own local broadcasting stations when commercial financing became possible. This, however, had more to do with giving the press an opportunity to participate in the electronic development of information exchange than with compensating them for lost advertising revenue.

*Circulation*

The total circulation of the 48 existing dailies has been fairly stable during the past 10–15 years at about 1.85 million. The 12 Sunday papers, which are Sunday editions of the daily papers, have a circulation of about 1.5 million. Also the division between different groups of papers has stayed much the same during the 1980s, with the 9 national papers taking about 55%, and the 39 local papers 45%. Within the group of national dailies, the two biggest newspapers, both tabloids, account for half the daily circulation (on Sundays they have a third of all sales in the country). Seen over a longer period, the success of the tabloids is notable: during the past 25 years they have risen from one sixth to one fourth of the total circulation of all newspapers — at the expense of the local papers.

It should be noted that this period witnessed the demise of the party-political press, the so-called four-paper system. This system, according to which each of the four most important political parties had their own local papers, has given way to a system of nominally independent papers with just a handful of politically tied titles left. It is a fact, however, that more than 90% of today's newspapers belong on the liberal-conservative side of the political spectrum, even if they do not function as party mouthpieces.

Nine out of 10 Danes read at least one daily newspaper. More than 8 of them buy it. But the numbers are slowly going down — 20 years ago, more than 100 copies were sold for every 100 households. So more people confine themselves to just one paper, and, what is more problematic for the industry, the rise in the number of households is not reflected in the total circulation of dailies. Perhaps most worrying is the fact that it is young people who are dropping out of the readership.

## Electronic media

Since 1988 Denmark has had a dual system of broadcasting: Danmarks Radio, the old monopoly, running one national television channel and three radio channels, and TV2 running one national television channel with 8 regional "windows". The whole of the population can receive the DR channel and 98% of the population can receive TV2.

All national broadcasting is regulated by law no. 421 of June 1973 with later amendments. In the same law community antenna network and other types of cable network are regulated, as well as local broadcasting.

*Organization of Danmarks Radio and TV2*

Danmarks Radio is organized as a central unit and located in the capital, Copenhagen. It has one provincial TV-production department. In contrast to this rather monolithic set-up there are 9 regional radio stations under Danmarks Radio. Due to political decisions TV2 has been placed outside Copenhagen. The purpose is to make it pay more attention to provincial life, and it has 8 regional television stations, each responsible for regional news and for providing the national channel with regional programmes.

According to the law a board of governors consisting of 11 members directs Danmarks Radio, and a board of governors consisting of 8 members directs TV2. These two boards are appointed by the Minister of Communication. The boards are not composed in the same way. The board of Danmarks Radio has 9 members selected by the Parliament, Folketinget, one representative from the employees, and a chairman appointed directly by the minister. The board of TV2 has five of its eight members appointed by the Minister and together they must represent knowledge about the media, business management and culture. Appointments last four years. The two boards are to be a-political, and active politicians defined as members of the Danish parliament are not allowed on the board. Besides the board of governors there are separate advisory programme committees for DR and TV2, also appointed for four years.

## The financing of DR and TV2

DR TV and DR radio channels are all financed via licence fees, while TV2 from the outset was financed by advertising (66%) and by licence fees (34%). This balance has since shifted somewhat, increasing the dependence on advertising. There are strict regulations of the amount and insertion of commercials and, although the regulations have become less restrictive, they have not disappeared.

Also regulated by law is the size of the licence fees, which are collected jointly for the two broadcasting organizations. The budgets for DR and TV2 are drawn up by the boards of governors, which also propose the size of the licence fees; however these must be approved by the Parliament, Folketinget. Until 1990 budgets were allocated annually, but a new law gives the broadcasting organizations three-year budgets. The new law came as a response to a plea from the broadcasting institutions which suffered from the annual problem of not knowing the size of the budget until very late. The licence fees were increased by 2% annually for the 3-year period. In 1990 sponsorship was allowed on both channels.

## Programme responsibility

Danmarks Radio is an independent public institution, committed to the responsibility of broadcasting radio and television programmes in the form of news, information, entertainment and art to the whole population. Quality, diversity and plurality are the main objectives. Fairness and impartiality are mentioned as objectives in relation to the transmission of information.

TV2 is labelled an independent institution, while the word public is absent. Programme responsibilities are not described in the same details as for DR, but also TV2 must emphasize quality, diversity and plurality. The purpose of TV2 is to produce news and current affairs, while all other programmes are to be bought from independent producers. Commercials are allowed. TV2 is obliged to broadcast 50% Danish/Nordic programmes.

Television is watched daily by 70% of the population and the total amount of time spent by the Danes watching Danish television is around 100 minutes. There has been an increase in the amount of daily viewing time, and a decrease in the amount of daily time spent reading newspapers. This is reflected in the issues of the public debate (see below).

## Local TV and radio

Local radio and TV started in Denmark in 1983 as a 3-year experiment. The Ministry of Culture gave licences and seed money to a limited number of stations — at the height of the experimental period, in 1985, 90 radio stations and 34 TV-stations were on the air. The radio stations were run on limited incomes, advertising was banned, and most of the money came from voluntary contributions, just as most of the broadcasters were unpaid amateurs.

At present there are about 350 local radio licensees. They broadcast on average 22 hours a week, and they do it on an income of only 200 000 Dkr. per year (average), according to official figures. One type of income which is not included here is (an unknown sum of) voluntary membership fees.

When the time came to replace the experiment with a permanent system two things were clear. There was a great deal of interest in local radio on the part of new broadcasters as well as listeners — therefore many new applications for licences were to be expected. And some form of secured financing would be required if the stations were to survive after the first bout of philanthropic support dwindled.

There was political agreement that the new system should be decentralized as far as possible, and that only frequency scarcity should limit the number of licensees. There was not, however, agreement on the issue of financing. The conservative government — which was and is a minority government — favoured advertising and no state support, whereas the liberal/social democratic/socialist opposition wanted partial public subsidy and no commercial income.

The resulting compromise law did not last very long. It did not allow advertising, it gave no state support, and it opened up for new entrants. The consequence was that large numbers of people applied for a licence, convinced that time would work for the commercial proponents. To nobody's surprise they were right, and in 1988 local radio was allowed to carry advertising within certain limitations: a maximum of 10% of daily broadcast time, and a maximum of 6 minutes per hour. As of mid-1990 they can also receive income from sponsorship.

The regulation of local radio is light, but whatever rules there are aim to keep it local and to make a sufficient number of licences available for everybody to join in. Frequencies are allocated by the Ministry of Communication, but all other licensing and supervision is done by local committees, who are obliged to hand out licences until there is no more broadcast time left (the licensees have to share frequencies, and they have to use the time allocated if they want to keep it). Only local associations with radio broadcasting as their only goal can obtain a licence. (A special provision is made for municipalities, which can run an information and/or open access channel.) It should be noted that the stations are allowed to be commercial, i.e. to earn money for their owners. Business interests may not have a dominant influence on a station (newspapers are excepted from this rule). Networking is forbidden except in very special cases.

The arrival of advertisements was accompanied by measures to counter some of the predictable effects of commercial financing, most notably that of killing off small or "narrow" radio stations. A "Robin Hood" fund was established to channel money from the rich to the poor stations by way of a levy of 10% on all income. Radio stations earning below a certain fixed amount of money per broadcast hour are entitled to subsidy from the fund for up to 28 hours of broadcasting a week. The actual amount is calculated on the basis of what is available in the fund — which does not have any state money coming in. From the start of the fund, August 1988, till the end of 1989 a total of about 16.5 million Dkr. was paid to eligible radio stations — about 150 in all.

As there is no regulation on programme content, such as local/home production, not much is known about this. During the experimental period — when the law required "a substantial" amount of programmes to be local — music accounted for about 50% of broadcast time, on average. The percentage is probably higher today. Whatever the content actually is, it seems to be in agreement with listeners' wishes. Almost the whole population has access to at least one local station, and on the average more than half listens weekly.

*Local TV*

The law on local broadcasting governs TV as well as radio, with a few special provisions concerning particularly advertising. Local TV was only allowed to carry advertising in 1989 — a year later than radio. As of October 1989, 84 local TV stations were "on the air" — of them 44 through cable. Over-the-air broadcasters share time on 30 transmitters. Altogether they are reported to broadcast about 1 500 hours per week — 18 hours per station on average.

As in the case of local radio there is little information available on programme content in local TV. No local quotas are imposed by the law, but the advertising rules stipulate that the amount of commercial broadcast time is to be calculated partly on the basis of the amount of local programming. Commercials must be broadcast in blocks of maximum five minutes. Each licensee is allowed only one block per day, and the block can only constitute 10% of the daily broadcast time devoted to local programming. There is no subsidy scheme for local TV.

*New electronic media*

Teletext, in Denmark called Tekst TV, was started in 1985 and is now to be found in 45% of all households. The service is organized by Danmarks Radio, and it consists of several hundred pages of information about news, sport, television and radio programmes, weather, traffic, business and leisure. This service can be used from 6 o'clock in the morning till midnight, and the content is updated continuously. TV2 also runs a teletext service, but so far with a very limited content. Experiments on regional television under TV2 offer job information on teletext. The service is free of charge for the consumers and considered a natural part of the public service. Teletext has never been an issue for discussion, and there is no special regulation of this service.

Government policy on videotext has been to let it develop according to market forces. It is now a liberalized telecommunication service, managed by the telephone companies, but with less than 5 000 subscribers.

The Danish industry does not participate directly in the development of the European Eureka HDTV project, but follows it closely. Danmarks Radio has planned experiments with HDTV programme production in 1992.

Since withdrawal from plans for a Nordic satellite in 1981 there has been no DBS policy or plan in Denmark.

*Foreign media availability*

Foreign channels reach Danish households via satellites and cable. As of January 1990, Danes had an average of 7 channels to choose from. Every second household can watch Swedish television, and German television can be watched by more than every third. The Danes watch Danish television more than foreign channels during the hours when it is available, but the use of foreign channels increases dramatically at the end of the day, when the Danish channels go off the air. TV3, the commercial Nordic channel broadcast to Scandinavia by satellite from London, is among the most popular foreign channels. According to surveys 67% of Danish television viewers watch TV3 sometime during a week, but according to analyses in 1990 TV3's share of viewing time was only 10% of households able to receive it. Other channels broadcast via satellite and reaching most of the Danish households via cable, like Eurosport and RTL, are viewed for approximately 10% of the total viewing time.

Antenna dishes are used for reception, but only in 3% of households according to estimates. The majority of households receive the foreign channels via cable, and the hybrid network transmits up to twenty channels to the households connected. Altogether, close to 70% of Danish households can receive foreign television channels either via the cable networks, via private antennas or over the air. There has been a progressive, demand-led extension of the cable hybrid network, showing a doubling from 1987 to 1990. At the beginning of 1991, approximately 40% of all households were connected to the hybrid network or to private networks. The broadband part of the system is expected to be in place in the early 1990s.

There is a local pay TV channel, Kanal 2, in Copenhagen. Danmarks Radio has considered a pay per view service, run in cooperation with the telephone companies' hybrid network. And in 1991 the telephone companies, in cooperation with the Swedish Esselte Entertainment, Nordisk Film and Sky News, plan to offer Danish households attached to the hybrid network a 24 hour service of American films and news.

## Policies for the press and broadcasting

During the 1980s the Danish media structure experienced a great many changes, in relation to newspapers as well as to broadcasting. More than anything it is the breaking of the TV monopoly that has changed the debate. Television is on the agenda more than any other medium, but in comparison with other issues, media are not very significant in the political debate. The public debate is very much focused on the two national television channels. How much are they viewed, and how do they compete? TV2 has been a great success. Within two years the new channel managed to get half the Danish population as daily viewers. At the beginning of 1991 daily reach was 64% for both channels. Ratings are an ongoing issue for debate, especially related to the issues of programme structure and the size of licence fees. Share of viewing time is almost equal for the two channels with approximately 50 minutes per day per channel. Danes are news freaks more than most; more than one third of the population watch the daily news on TV2 and half of them switch to the main news programme on DR TV immediately after. On top of this comes the amount of time spent on foreign channels.

The eventual establishment of a fourth national radio channel has been under discussion, the question being whether it will be allocated to Danmarks Radio, or to private investors, possibly to newspapers.

Sponsorship for programmes on national radio and television has been one of the issues on the agenda during the 1980s. After several bills had been put forward in Parliament it ended in 1990 with a law (no. 340 of May 1990) allowing sponsorship on all channels. The main actors in favour of sponsorship were the bourgeois government and the new television channels plus the local private broadcasters, while the opposition initially was very concerned about the possibility of damage to the public service orientation of national broadcasting. According to the law content and placement of a given programme must not be influenced by sponsors.

The issue related to content of broadcasting is very old in itself, but at the same time it is typical of a nation where commercial channels are relatively new. The discussion is closely related to the ideals of public service broadcasting organizations versus commercialized media, private or public.

Commercialization has been an issue for debate, and so has the threat to Danish culture from an increase in foreign programmes broadcast to all Danes. But Denmark was not in favour of the EC regulation requesting European programme quotas of 50%, the main reason being a negative attitude from political parties to EC regulations of national culture, an area that was considered to be outside the EC Treaty.

New technology was on the agenda in the beginning of the 1980s, and media policy at that time was closely related to issues like optical fibres, the broadband network and the hybrid, which combined coaxial cables and optical fibres. Expectations were great, but here at the beginning of the 1990s the Danish debate on media politics is very down to earth. Nevertheless, there have been several developments. A pilot ISDN project was started in 1989, and a commercial ISDN service will start in 1991–92. But the issue "Danish culture at stake" is no longer very prominent on the agenda for public or political debate.

The population and the different actors such as political parties and broadcasting institutions have all adjusted to the new media structure;

only changes in viewing patterns resulting from the new competition from more broadcasting outlets are debated. The Danish debate is still dominated by economic concerns, but new communication technology is no longer as prominent as it was during the 1980s, even if its importance continues to be recognized.

In summary it can be said that regulation and steering of the media structure in Denmark have not decreased. We cannot talk about deregulation, but there has been a series of re-regulations, some giving more freedom than before. Altogether the amount of regulation counted in number of pages of law is far greater today than it was 10 years ago (Minke 1990).

## Statistics

(1 ECU = 7.90 Dkr.)

| Population | |
|---|---|
| Inhabitants 1990 | 5 145 101 |
| Population density pr $km^2$ | 118 |
| No. of households | 2 400 000 |

| Broadcasting | |
|---|---|
| Number of television channels | 2 |
| Number of radio channels | 3 |
| Regional TV-stations (TV2) | 8 |
| Regional radio (DR) | 9 |

| | |
|---|---|
| Local TV | 80 (estimated) |
| Local radio licensees | 350 (estimated) |
| Video | 34% of all households |
| Satellite receivers | 3% of all households |
| Cable connections | 40% of all households |

| | |
|---|---|
| Licence fees, colour TV 1992 | 1 514 Dkr. |
| Licence fees, black & white TV 1992 | 974 Dkr. |
| Licence fees, radio 1992 | 222-Dkr app 20 ECU |

| Advertising | | |
|---|---|---|
| Total national media advertising spend (estimate 1989): | | 8 billion Dkr. |
| Print media: | | 87% |
| of this daily press: | 48% | |
| Audiovisual media: | | 13% |
| of this TV | 58% | |
| Radio | 9% | |

(Source: Hansen, F. (1990) Draft research paper "Reklameforbruget, dets sammensætning og nogle kritiske kommentarer", Handelshøjskolen, Copenhagen.)

## 46   Denmark

The press
No. of main independent national and regional newspapers:          48

Circulation of principal newspapers (1st half of 1990)
Ekstrabladet                                                              238000
B.T.                                                                     212000
Politiken                                                                 152000
Jyllands-Posten                                                          140000
Berlingske Tidende                                                       130000
Det Fri Aktuelt                                                           50000
(Source: Dansk Oplagskontrol, quoted in Politiken, 29 October 1990.)

## References

Mediekommissionen (1983) Mediekommissionens betænkning nr. 3, Betænkning om de trykte mediers økonomi og beskæftigelse. Betænkning nr. 972, Copenhagen.

Mediekommissionen (1985a) Mediekommissionens betænkning nr. 5, Betænkning om et øget dansk tv-udbud. Betænkning nr. 986, Copenhagen..

Mediekommissionen (1985b) Mediekommissionens betænkning nr. 6, Betænkning om dansk mediepolitik. Betænkning nr. 1029, Copenhagen..

Boesen, B. and Lund, E.B. (1989) Få styr på udviklingen, Aarhus: Danmarks Journalisthøjskole.

Frøbert, K.Aa. (1983) Massemediernes frihed og ansvar, Copenhagen. Akademisk Forlag.

Ministry of Communication, Committee on Local Radio and TV (1990) Status over ordningen for lokal radio og tv (Overview of local radio and TV), Copenhagen, June.

Minke, Kim (1990) "Media Structures in Denmark, Media Structures in a Changing Europe", in Innovation, Vienna 3 (2):253–267.

Notkin, A. (1990) Dansk Presse 1988/89, Pressens Årbog 1989. Odense.

Siune, Karen (1986) "Denmark" in H. Kleinsteuber, D. McQuail and K. Siune, Electronic Media and Politics in Western Europe. Euromedia Research Group Handbook of National Systems, Frankfurt: Campus.

# 4

# Finland

## Helena Tapper

### National profile

The total area of Finland is 338 145 km$^2$, with a population of 5 million. The Swedish minority comprises 6% of the population, but Swedish is recognized as an official language beside Finnish.

The country is divided into 12 provinces. Most of the population lives in Southern Finland with about 900 000 people living in Helsinki and the 3 neighbouring towns *(Statistical Year Book 1989*:40).

In March 1991 Finland held Parliamentary elections. The previous government was "red and blue" – a coalition between the Social Democrats and the conservative party ( the National Coalition Party) with the liberals (the Centre party) as the main opposition. The election gave a landslide victory to the Centre party, which is expected to head the new government. Other parliamentary parties are the left wing alliance, the Finnish Rural Party, the Swedish People's Party in Finland, the Christian League of Finland, the liberals and the Green Party.

Finland is a member of EFTA, the Nordic Council, and the Council of Europe. Negotiations are under way to find ways of joining the EEC and EFTA in a common European Economic Space. This idea has political and economic support in Finland, whereas politicians are still very divided on the question of direct membership of the EEC.

Finland has experienced a relatively stable period of economic growth since the mid 1980s but the beginning of the 1990s has seen the coming of a recession. The years of economic growth brought new media, local radio stations and plans for local TV. Advertising expenditure increased rapidly until the recession set in. New enterprises and media concentration have characterized the media field. Investors from outside the traditional media sector have invested heavily in the media, and become key shareholders in media enterprises. This has created confusion both in the traditional media market and among the policy-makers.

The average Finnish citizen reads 2.5 newspapers per day and spends 46 minutes reading them. It seems that Finnish people are still today a "reading nation", although electronic media consumption is increasing rapidly.

The service sector accounts for 58% of the GDP, secondary production 35% and primary production 7%. The service sector and the information sector are growing rapidly. The recent foreign developments have affected the Finnish economy badly, resulting in a fall in advertising expenditures and increasing difficulties for the smaller media enterprises. Concentration processes are strong in the media sector.

## Development of the press and broadcasting since 1945

The printed press has moved away from party-political alignment. In 1946 there were 104 newspapers. Thirty were non-political, 24 left-wing and the rest various shades of centre/right-wing. In 1989 the number of newspapers had fallen to 102. Sixty were neutral, non-political, and 14 were left-wing papers (Nordenstreng and Wiio 1990:52). From 1940–1980 35 newspapers died. Without a state subsidy many of the political second or third newspapers in one circulation area would have disappeared many years ago.

During the 1980s the newspaper publishers have moved into other media fields: local radio, telecommunications and cable-TV. They have also bought up small local papers. Especially the small area local papers, published once or twice a week, have been the survivors of the newspaper business.

The Finnish Broadcasting Company (YLE) was given a broadcasting monopoly in the Radio Act of 1927. The state owns 90% of YLE shares. The Parliament nominates the governing board for YLE. The Radio Act also regulates the role of YLE as a public broadcasting company.

In 1959 the principle of the broadcasting monopoly was relaxed, and other operators were in principle allowed to operate in the field.

TV broadcasting started in Finland in 1954 as a private experiment, TES TV. YLE started TV transmission in 1957, as did the commercial TV company MTV Finland. In 1964 the private TV company TES TV was bought by YLE and renamed TV 2.

The YLE de facto monopoly in broadcasting was breached in 1985 when the local radio stations came into existence.

# The press

## *Policy framework*

The main thrust of Finnish press media policy has been to ensure diversity of opinion. This was first formulated in the 1919 Constitution Act as an essential freedom of the press. To achieve this a strong public subsidy policy offers the press a wide range of subsidy forms.

The State Press Subsidy Board, a Parliamentary body, annually allocates the public subsidy. The main forms of subsidy are the distribution subsidy for the individual newspapers, for joint distribution systems organized by several newspapers and postal distribution of newspapers by the PTT. In 1990 the direct subsidy was 22.5 million ECU, out of which 13.5 million ECU were selective subsidies and 9 million ECU subsidies based on political party press needs.

Additionally there are tax rebates on subscription to newspapers and telecommunications subsidies for the news agencies and their customers.

The subsidy system reflects the political/parliamentary structure of the country aiming to retain the broadest possibilities for freedom of expression, and also a political party press. If the market forces regulated the newspaper market, Finland would today have less than half of its present press.

Since the mid-1980s there has been a strong concentration process in the press sector. The large publishers have bought local newspapers and taken a majority of shares in the regional papers. There is no legislation preventing press monopolies, however, the public policy measures are directed towards an anti-monopolistic media system.

In 1989 there were 102 newspapers in the country published 3–7 times a week (there are 66 papers according to the UNESCO 4–7 times a week classification). Since the population of the country is only 5 million the number of newspapers is relatively high.

## *Ownership and finance*

The majority of the newspapers are private companies, a limited number are associated with political parties. The 3 biggest newspaper publishers, *Sanoma* Ltd, the *Aamulehti* Corporation and *Turun Sanomat* Ltd, publish the 3 biggest newspapers in the country and they own other local and regional newspapers. Their circulation share of the 102 newspapers coming out 3–7 times a week was in 1990 3.3 million – which is 40%.

The biggest newspaper publisher is *Sanoma* Ltd: the *Helsingin Sanomat* newspaper has a circulation of 477 215 and the evening paper *Ilta-Sanomat*, 213 660. The *Aamulehti* Corporation publishes the second biggest newspaper, *Aamulehti,* with a circulation of 144 162, and *Turun Sanomat* Ltd the third biggest newspaper *Turun Sanomat* with a circulation of 136 517. The *Aamulehti* Corporation has in recent years purchased several regional and local newspapers.

However the rampant buying spree which previously characterized the biggest publishers has now declined as advertising revenues drop and recession grips the economy.

In 1989 the newspaper business accounted for 34.4% of the total mass media economy with advertising contributing about 75% of the total newspaper income. The rest came mainly from subscriptions.

Newspaper production expenditures are comprised of: editorial expenses 28%, administration and marketing 21%, distribution 17% and technical process 35% (Newspaper Publishers' Union).

## The structure of the newspaper market

Of the 102 newspapers, 27 are published daily. The biggest newspaper, *Helsingin Sanomat,* is the national newspaper. *Turun Sanomat* and *Aamulehti* cover large parts of southern Finland, the most populated areas of the country. There are 19 regional newspapers. They do not compete with bigger newspapers or the local newspapers. The local papers are a strong force in the newspaper market.

The trend in the newspaper market structure is towards bigger regional/national papers and very local papers. They are omnibus papers with no specific party political affiliations. In 1989 the conservative Coalition Party had 5 supporting newspapers (the biggest being *Aamulehti*), the liberal Centre Party had 13 supporting papers and the Social Democratic Party 8, the Democratic League 7 and the Swedish National Party 1.

## Electronic media

### Legal Framework

The Finnish broadcasting system consists of the Finnish Broadcasting Company (YLE), the MTV Finland Company, TV 3 and the local radio stations. Additionally there are cable-TV companies, the biggest is HTV covering Helsinki.

The broadcasting licence is granted by the government for a 10-year period. YLE had the only radio operating licence in the country till 1985 when the first local radio stations were given licences. The YLE licence fee is regulated by the state. The operating licence regulates the nature of programmes, and the role of the company as a national cultural institution. The latest operating licence was granted in 1989 (Nordenstreng and Wiio 1990:93)

The 1988 new Radio Act is technical in nature. It covers access to and use of the transmitters and the prevention of disturbances to broadcasting. It does not cover the role of broadcasting or YLE, and there is no legislation regulating the use of satellites.

The Cable-TV Act came into being in 1987. An operating licence can be granted to a Finnish citizen or association with sufficient economic resources and demonstrated capacity to operate in the cable-TV field. The operating licence is granted for 5 years by the government via the Ministry of Transport and Communications (Nordenstreng and Wiio, 1990:119).

The Cable-TV Act includes an obligation to reserve 1 channel or time in that channel for local programmes, additionally there is a "must carry" rule for YLE's programmes. The share of domestic programmes must be 15–50% of the total programme time for any 6-month period. The advertising time can be 10% of total programme time in a channel for any 6-month period.

There are principles for operating local radio but no legislation. These principles are: emphasize the local culture and information, do not transmit programmes on violence, immoral behaviour etc. and in general local radio must adhere to the principles of the broadcasting legislation.

*The structure of the media*

YLE has five separate operating units: the Radio Unit for Finnish programmes in the whole country; the Regional and News unit for the Finnish-speaking audience in the whole country and the foreign service; TV 1 national channel; TV 2 national channel and the Swedish Unit for radio and TV.

In June 1990 YLE reorganized its radio channels: Radio 1 is reserved for culture and arts (YLE's One), Radio 2 for pop music and news (Radio Mafia) and Radio 3 for regional programmes and news (Radio Finland). Radio 4 is for national programmes in Swedish, Radio 5 regional programmes in Swedish and Lapp. The new profiles for each channel are intended to clarify their role in the radio field, especially since the local radio stations have entered the radio arena in competition with YLE.

The YLE national TV channels are TV 1 and TV 2. Since 1957 there has been a commercial TV company, MTV Finland, operating via YLE's channels according to an agreement between the two companies. In the mid-1980s a third (commercial) TV channel, TV 3, began broadcasting in Finland. It is owned by YLE (20%) and MTV Finland (80%). Since 1990

TV 3 has been a subsidiary of MTV Finland. MTV is in turn owned by private enterprises.

The reorganization of TV channels will take place in 1993. The commercial programmes will be withdrawn from TV 1 and TV 2, and MTV Finland will operate only on TV 3. At the moment TV 3 reaches about 60% of the households, the whole country should be covered by 1993.

In 1989 28% of the households were connected to cable-TV, the estimated figure for the end of 1990s is 50% of the households. At the moment there are about 600 000 subscribers to cable-TV. The main owners of the cable-TV companies are local telephone/telecommunications companies and major newspaper publishers. Out of 198 cable-TV licences, 75 were granted to the PTT and the majority of the rest to private regional telephone companies (Nordenstreng and Wiio 1990:123).

The biggest cable-TV company is the Helsinki cable-TV company, HTV, with 162 000 cabled households. It also has pay-TV channels and recently started a subscription service: for 7.7 ECU per month subscribers receive BBC TV Europe, Discovery, Lifestyle, Screensport, CNN and Children's Channel (Österlund-Karinkanta 1990:9).

The cable-TV companies in Helsinki, Turku and Tampere established a new channel, PTV, in 1990 in order to increase advertising revenue. This channel has also been used by other cable-TV companies. They have a common schedule every evening from 7 p.m. to 10 p.m. Foreign satellite programmes dominate on most schedules, although there is also a small increase in domestic/local news programmes.

The programmes in Finnish cable-TV channels are:
—local, free channels,
—free satellite channels,
—pay-TV and
—the public broadcasting programmes.

The satellite channels are mainly TV 5, 3Sat, BBC TV Europe, Music-TV, Super Channel, Children's Channel, CNN, Discovery, Lifestyle, Screensport, Filmnet, Swedish TV, Estonian TV and Soviet TV.

*Local TV and radio*

In February 1991 the Ministry of Communications decided not to grant any operating licence for local TV. The applicants were supposed to get licences for a test period. The economic recession was cited as the main reason for the suspension of the licensing procedure.

The ministry did grant 3 new licences for local radio stations in early 1991 and 18 of the existing local radio stations were granted a larger operating area. In January 1991 there were 58 operating commercial local radio stations and 7 non-commercial ones.

Licences are granted for 5-year periods. The operating licence guidelines require a licensee to broadcast programmes 75% of the programme time. Commercials may not exceed 10% of programme time. However, the majority of the programme time on local radio is used to play foreign, popular music, making the contents of the programmes less than local.

## Telematic media

The videotex services have not demonstrated the wide customer appeal originally expected. According to a report published by France Telecom (*Eledis Journal* 1991:6) there are 20 000 users in Finland, of which 68% are professionals. Overall traffic reached 160 000 hours per month in 1989. The Helsinki Telephone Company runs one videotex service, Startel. Customers are mostly from the business world, or belong to special customer groups. The other, called Telesampo, is run by the PTT. Expanding fields in videotex are banking services and services for farmers.

Video conferences are rarely used. To some extent the conferences use satellites for foreign speakers. Electronic-mail is used in universities, government offices, research institutes etc. The Finnish PTT operates a public E-mail service called Mailnet based on the emerging international X.400 standard.

## Policies for the press and broadcasting

### Main actors and interests

The main actors in the media arena are the government bodies and the associations of the media. Additionally, there is a dependency between the media and the government bodies, e.g. the government grants the licences and formulates the principles for operating licences.

The Council of State grants, via the Ministry of Transport and Communications, operating licences for broadcasting. The Ministry not only grants licences but is also involved in policy formulation and legislation regarding broadcasting, cable transmission, press and telecommunications. It also regulates technical issues. The Ministry thus combines legislative and executive functions.

The Ministry of Education is more involved in the cultural aspects of media policy. The Ministry has assigned a high priority to audio-visual culture, its research and education. The Ministry is also active in the international media culture arena.

The PTT was recently divided into Post and Tele Units. The PTT is a central agency in the telecommunications field, competing in data/voice services with private telephone companies and other telecommunications operators. The PTT has moved away from the traditional state organization towards a commercial business organization.

In 1988 a special supervising agency, the Telecommunications Administration Centre, was set up to regulate TV licences and fees, radio frequency use and telecommunications equipment.

There is much lobbying done by the Local Radio Union, the Cable-TV Union and the Newspaper Publishers Union to influence government and ministry policies.

## Main issues

The main issues in the media field are deregulation in public broadcasting and telecommunications. The national public broadcasting company (YLE) is going through a period of changes, as a reaction to the many new television channels supplied via cable and satellite and the many new local radio stations.

Deregulation has led to increased competition, which again has strengthened the ongoing concentration. This is very clear in the newspaper sector as demonstrated by the *Sanoma Oy* company. As yet no cross-ownership legislation has been introduced.

The economic recession also poses a threat to the diversity of expression in the media. Advertising revenues are stagnating and there are more media wanting a share of them. The issue of press subsidy is now less debated, since it is seen as a necessity for the existing newspaper structure.

## Policy trends

The public media policy is directed towards international (European) media development and the division of the media arena between the large media companies, while at the same time attempting to ensure the survival of the small and medium-size companies.

The policy trend emphasizes visual communication, education and research, rather than purely cultural aspects. Central questions revolve around the issue of retaining strong national media, while ensuring freedom of speech via a diversified press. The local media arena, and the new media operating here, is also seen as important.

Media policy is an integrated part of the national cultural policy, while telecommunications is an industrial policy issue.

## Statistics

(1 ECU = 4.93 FMK)
Population                                                          5 m$_2$
Population density                                          14.8 pr km$^2$

Broadcasting
National radio channels                        3 Finnish + 1 Swedish
National TV channels                                        3 Finnish

Division of TV channel audiences – average % of daily audience
(Totals exceed 100% because viewers watch more than one channel)
National programmes

| TV1(YLE) | TV2(YLE) | YLE | MTV1 | MTV2 | MTV |
|----------|----------|-----|------|------|-----|
| 51% | 38% | 59% | 32% | 26% | 48% |

Other programmes

| TV3 | TV4 | SWED.* | Satellite | Cable | VCR |
|-----|-----|--------|-----------|-------|-----|
| 19% | 1% | 2% | 6% | 2% | 9% |

(Source: Kasari 1990:9)
* Swedish programmes retransmitted in Finnish television by YLE

Media economy
Total turnover 1989                      3 billion ECU (3,3% of GNP)
Newspapers                                                    34.4%
Magazines and journals                                        17.6%
Book publishing                                               12.7%
Broadcasting                                                  12.3%
Advertising (printed)                                         10.2%
Records and tapes                                              3.8%
Free sheets                                                    3.0%
Other media                                                    6.0%
(Source: The Newspaper Publishers' Union 1990:8)

The press
Circulation of newspapers

| Title | Circulation | Coverage | Party political relations |
|-------|-------------|----------|---------------------------|
| (7 days a week) | | | |
| Helsingin Sanomat | 477215 | national | indep. |
| Aamulehti | 144162 | regional | dep. |
| Turun Sanomat | 136517 | regional | indep. |
| Kaleva | 95461 | regional | indep. |
| Savon Sanomat | 90488 | regional | dep. |
| Uusi Suomi | 84762 | national | indep. |
| (6 days a week) | | | |
| Ilta-Sanomat | 213660 | national | indep. |
| Iltalehti | 1033808 | national | indep. |

(Source: The Newspaper Publishers' Union 1990:7)

## 56   Finland

| | |
|---|---|
| Advertising total in 1989 | 1.4 billion ECU |
| Newspapers | 60.3% |
| Free sheets | 4.5% |
| Magazines and journals | 9.4% |
| TV | 12.0% |
| Transport and outdoor advertising | 2.3% |
| Direct advertising | 7.9% |
| Radio | 3.3% |

(Source: The Newspaper Publishers' Union 1990:4)

## References

Eledis Journal (1991) Report on Electronic Data Interchange Systems. 6 Jan/Feb., ISSN: 0777-8589. XCOMS, Brussels.

Kasari, H. (1990) TV Audience 1989–90, YLE Reports, 5. Helsinki.

The Newspaper Publishers' Union (1990) Knowledge is Power. Helsinki.

Nordenstreng, K. and Wiio, O.A. (eds) (1990) Suomen viestintäjärjestelmä (The Finnish Communication System), Weilin & Göös. Helsinki.

Österlund-Karinkanta, M. (1990) Current Media Policy Issues in Finland, YLE. Helsinki.

Statistical Year Book of Finland (1989, 1990) Central Statistical Office of Finland. Helsinki.

# 5

# France

## Michael Palmer and Claude Sorbets

### National profile

Occupying a surface area of 549 000 km$^2$, metropolitan France has a relatively small population (about 56.6 m. inhabitants) and low population density (102 inhabitants per km$^2$). Eighteen percent of the population live in and around the capital. Traditionally, it has proved difficult to govern, because of its geographical diversity and of various socio-economic and cultural variations and disparities.

With the Parliamentary victory of the Right in 1986, the pendulum swung towards liberalism and privatization, after the socialist-led nationalization phase of the early 1980s. Between March 1986 and May 1988, a socialist President of the Republic "cohabited" in an uneasy peace with the new right-wing government of Jacques Chirac. In May 1988, François Mitterrand was re-elected President. In the new National Assembly, the socialists emerged with a relative – not an absolute – majority. This imposed constraints on the government headed by Michel Rocard, a (democratic) socialist: no more companies were to be nationalized or privatized; government posts were offered to leading figures – ostensibly without a political affiliation – of "civil" society; their reputation owed much to their media skills.

In 1991, the structure of the French economy remains marked by tensions and forces of the past. France has a mixed economy. Some observers claim indeed that the French economy has benefited both from the radical shot-in-the-arm applied by left-wing governments, and from the corrective measures subsequently taken by conservative governments. This continual process throughout the 1980s of "action" and "reaction" was particularly in evidence in the area of new communication technologies.

In 1981, the Left argued that the new technologies were a means of escaping from the economic crisis that was then common to many advanced industrial economies. The government launched a two-pronged action programme: the nationalization of key companies of the communications equipment sector (Matra, Thomson, C.G.E.), and a comprehensive industrial policy for the "electronics sector" or "filière" – a term used in the Farnoux report of March 1982. This policy straddled the entire Research and Development process – from the basic component or chip to a wide range of technologies, products and services (fibre optics, digitalization of telecommunications, etc). This policy was gradually abandoned. It failed to have the desired impact in combating unemployment; the attempt to encompass all the links in the electronics chain foundered; the contrasting positions of the various nationalized companies in their respective markets made the implementation of a coherent collective policy impossible. Furthermore, the government of the Left was forced to adapt its policy from 1982–1983 to the underlying trend towards the privatization of industrial production; the state adopted a lower profile in the management of the economy. Thus the policy of the Chirac government from 1986 merely accentuated a trend that had begun, albeit discreetly (around 1985) with the privatization of companies nationalized by the left in the early 1980s, and the privatization of other industrial groups. In the communications media sector, the privatization of France's leading (and oldest) public service TV channel, TF1, in 1986–1987, was strongly criticized; yet, in acting thus, the Chirac government was "building on" a policy that appeared during the socialist (Fabius) government of 1984–1986, with the emergence of private sector TV channels (La Cinq, and TV 6).

From the mid-1970s, beginning with the Giscard d'Estaing presidency successive governments sought to transform the French telecoms system from one of the most backward of advanced industrial societies to one of the most modern of the industrialized world. D.G.T-France Télécom also symbolized government determination to modernize French industry. French companies were obliged to be more attentive to the international environment and market possibilities, and were afforded assistance in facing the challenge of the emerging world leaders in communications technologies.

Within France, the decentralization policy of the Mauroy (1981–1984) government proved sufficiently far-reaching that no subsequent government dared call it into question (even on the Right). The transfer of various powers to the regions was seen as an integral part of the reshaping of the public sphere. In the communications sector, new media outlets and new operators emerged; it was realized both that the local context might be influenced by the national and international strategies of the actors or operators present at the local level, and that established actors might call on greater resources than newly emerging local actors.

## Development of the press and broadcasting since 1945

There are at least two possible interpretations of the development of the press and broadcasting (or, more generally, of print media and the audiovisual sector) during the past fifty years. Broadcasting and the press developed distinctly, and, insofar as there was contact, the new broadcasting media undermined the print media. According to this interpretation, the trend towards the concentration of ownership of newspaper publishing companies is endogenous, whereas the subsequent diversification of many media companies is due to the growing interdependence of the audiovisual and print media; this interdependence called into question the state control of broadcasting that dates from 1945.

The other interpretation involves a radically different approach. Communication technologies, rather than the media themselves, are the key factor. This approach highlights the perceived convergence between telecommunications and computing. Regulatory texts and policy have rarely, if at all, run counter to the main economic and technological trends of communications development. In recent years, laws, rules and regulations have attempted, rather, to provide a very loose framework for a sector that is in considerable flux. New actors have emerged and others disappeared; new media outlets have come on-stream, and long-established media have been revitalized.

### *The press*

The number of newspaper titles has declined since 1945: there were 11 general interest (i.e. non-specialist) Parisian dailies and 65 provincial dailies in 1988. Many partisan and committed, politically or otherwise, daily "viewspapers" folded whereas ostensibly middle-of-the-road or a-political titles fared better. The regional daily newspaper (as opposed to the "departmental" or "county" title) has expanded over the past two to three decades, often at the expense of the provincial markets of Parisian dailies.

The 1944 ordinance aimed to protect the press from capitalist forces and from foreign influences: the full financial details of newspaper publishing company accounts were to be published; the same entity (an individual or a company) was not to control or manage more than one daily newspaper. This rule was repeatedly violated. On the one hand, the state did little to offset the market trend towards the concentration of ownership; on the other, it subsidized the newspaper industry. A complex system of direct and, above all, indirect subsidies helped newspaper publishers modernize their plant and presses and thus indirectly helped them acquire other newspaper titles. In 1983–1984, the left-wing government headed by Pierre Mauroy attempted to update this text and the

Léotard law of 1986 modified the context in which newspaper publishing groups sought to expand their multimedia interests. From the vantage-point of 1990, it appears that it is indeed print-based multimedia groups that have emerged triumphant from the trend towards the concentration of ownership and towards diversification. These groups were precisely those that proved the most skilful in playing a system of fiscal aids and political connections: companies such as Hachette and Hersant thus emerged in the 1980s as leading actors in the new version of "the French media landscape".

## Concentration of press ownership

In France, the concentration of the ownership of print media occurred in two ways: expansion from a given title's original catchment area; and chain ownership of newspapers established across the country. Regional news-paper publishing groups (such as Ouest-France) belong to the first cate-gory; the Hersant and Hachette groups to the second. In both cases, a merger or the acquisition of majority control came about as a result of a process in which the company that was ultimately taken over was initially the aggressor. In both cases, likewise, a merger leads the successful com-pany to threaten yet another group. "Frontier disputes" between rival groups led them to agreements intended to avoid "newspaper wars", with compromises over who should distribute which title where.

The (shared) control of the advertising revenue of newspaper titles which pool their advertising space effectively dissuades any potential new market entrants. But such pooling of advertising revenue strengthens the hand of the advertising middleman; he has more say over the news/ editorial content because he "controls" the advertising columns. There are 17 such pooled advertising newspaper groups. Nearly every individual newspaper title has "surrendered" (at least in part) the control of its ad-vertising columns to bulk ad space vendors: the latter are sometimes sub-sidiaries of advertising groups like Publicis or Havas; others are an integral part of a press group, such as Hersant's Publiprint.

## Broadcasting

The Ordinance of 23 March 1945 formalized the state monopoly of broad-casting: this was assigned to Radiodiffusion de France (which later be-came Radiodiffusion-Télévision de France (RTF)). Television, like radio before it, developed very slowly at first. The earliest experimental broad-casts dated from the late 1930s; the three state channels only enjoyed full nationwide coverage by the early 1970s. Successive broadcasting reforms often complicated the resolution of technical problems.

Initially established as a public company accountable to the Ministry of Information, RTF, in June 1964, became an "Office" (ORTF), closely supervised by the government. In 1969, prime minister Jacques Chaban-Delmas, seeking to liberalize the medium in the aftermath of the "events" of May 1968, abolished the ministry of information. Three years later, the Act of 3 July 1972 confirmed the basic principles of the public service broadcasting monopoly.

When Valéry Giscard d'Estaing became President of the Republic in 1974, a purge occurred at the Maison Ronde (Broadcasting House) and a new Act (July 1974) substantially changed the situation. The "Office" was split up into seven public companies (*établissements* and *sociétés*) that together formed public service broadcasting: TF1, Antenne 2, FR3, Radio France, TDF, SFP, INA. Only in 1982 did the Act – of 29 July – at last end the state monopoly of TV programme channels. The 1982 law encouraged a diversity of channels. But in the new context PSB no longer had a clearly defined place, and the transition from a state to a public service broadcasting ethos proved an on-going process lasting a decade or more.

Technological progress, on the one hand, fostered the free radio movement – *les radios libres* – and, on the other, encouraged those in charge of the broadcasting and telecommunications transmission monopolies to profit from the new opportunities. The DGT, for instance, became involved in the provision of value added services and encountered the competition of private sector actors in satellites and telematics.

One of the overall aims of the 1982 Audiovisual Communications Act was to open up the media field to new actors and to allow traditional actors new opportunities. The provisions of the law were so couched as to allow subsequent decrees (*décrets d'application*) to fill in specific points. The process of deregulation proved even more extensive than that originally envisaged by the proponents of the law.

The law allowed for the development of a private audiovisual sector. Independent or "free" radio stations as well as videotex fell within its remit. The law distinguished between the media and their content. It recognized that it would be increasingly difficult to maintain the existing separation between "private correspondence" (the telephone network) and public broadcasting (TDF transmission equipment). The Act distinguished between media that were "rare" or "abundant". For instance, the state might concede a "public service" to a private concern, in the case of a severe scarcity of transmission facilities (terrestrial television channels, satellite transponders).

The Act established an independent broadcasting regulatory body, the Haute Autorité de la Communication Audiovisuelle (HA). The HA was to ensure the independence of public service broadcasting (PSB). The HA appointed the chief executives (PDG) of the national and regional public broadcasting companies and issued operating licences to local radio stations and cable TV operators. Members of the HA were appointed for nine years, according to a procedure similar to that used to appoint members of the Constitutional Council. The HA was to act as a buffer between public service broadcasting bodies and the government. Tension later arose between an Haute Autorité trying to assert its powers and a government seeking to preserve its ability to influence developments (and appointments) in the broadcasting sector.

While providing a formal structure for PSB, the 1982 law said little or nothing about how this was to be funded: the government, for example, continued to determine the fee charged for a TV licence; licence fee revenue was a, if not the, major component in the funding of PSB companies. The government and the regulatory body alike had to respond to the demands and pressures of often contradictory forces. Paradoxically, a government committed to a system that gave pride of place to PSB, experienced growing pressures to develop private sector broadcasting.

In 1986, the new right-wing Parliamentary majority voted in the communications law piloted through Parliament by the communication minister, François Léotard. This both signalled the end of the Fillioud law of 1982 and opened the path to deregulation, overseen by a new regulatory body that replaced the HA – the Commission Nationale de la Communication et des Libertés (CNCL). In May 1988, the new left of centre government of Michel Rocard secured Parliamentary support for the establishment of yet another regulatory body, the Conseil Supérieur de l'Audiovisuel, in place of the discredited (argued President Mitterrand and the Left) CNCL. Between 1982 and 1989, the issue of the broadcasting regulatory body replaced that of the status of broadcasting programme channels as the most contentious issue for communication policymakers.

**The press**

The 1980s saw several pieces of legislation intended *inter alia* to preserve the pluralism of newspaper titles, the diversity of press ownership, and to ensure the transparency of the accounts of newspaper publishing companies. The law of 23 October 1984 set up a "press transparency and pluralism commission": newspaper publishers such as Robert Hersant ignored the commission and a subsequent law, promulgated in August 1986, abolished it. The 1984 law was enacted under the socialists (the Mauroy–Fabius administrations of 1981–1986); the 1986 law under the conservative-liberal Chirac administration. Press policy in the 1980s, like broadcasting policy, was a political ping-pong game. With the advent of the democratic socialist left-of-centre Rocard administration (May 1988) the reform of the press no longer figured on the political agenda.

France is the EEC country which, with Italy, has the most complete and varied system of direct and indirect press subsidies: the figure involved represents some 12–15% of the total turnover of the French press. The principle of such aid dates from the Liberation (even if the press enjoyed certain advantages, such as preferential postal tariffs, long before); every year, Parliament examines these "aids" when it debates the government's budget proposals. A state fund operates to favour financially weak political daily newspapers: in 1988, beneficiaries included the Catholic *La Croix-L'Evénement*, the Communist party's *L'Humanité*, the right-wing *Présent*, and the left-of-centre *Libération*.

The trend towards the concentration of ownership is less advanced in France than in other EEC countries. In 1986, the ten leading newspaper and magazine publishing groups accounted for half of the total turn-over of the press, and the top thirty for three-quarters. (In the UK, four companies accounted for 80% of the turnover of the companies publishing national dailies.) Yet the issue of mergers and takeovers involving newspaper titles is politically acutely sensitive.

Occupying the first or second rank in classifications of French press publishing companies, the Hersant "group" was the bane of the French socialists, especially in the early and mid-1980s. Hersant epitomized the failure of such anti-concentration measures as existed in France. The 1944 ordinance stipulated that no one *personne* (an individual, or a company) should publish, directly or through an intermediary, more than one daily: in 1976 dailies published by the Hersant group included the regional daily *Paris-Normandie* and three Parisian dailies with national pretensions – the conservative *LeFigaro*, the popular (in style and content) *France-Soir*, and (the moribund) *l'Aurore*. Tainted with a collaborationist past (in Pétain's France, 1940–1944), and known for his outspoken anti-communism and contempt for (some of) the journalists who worked for him, Hersant was the *bête noire* of socialists and journalist trade unions. The 1983 press bill was largely seen as directed specifically against him. Yet, heavily amended, the 1984 press law fixed limits on the concentration of ownership that, in effect, did not force the Hersant – or any other – group to divest itself of any of its titles: no group was to control titles whose combined circulation exceeded 15% that of national dailies, or 15% that of regional dailies, or 10% of the total circulation of both.

The 1984 law was not retroactive. And Hersant rode roughshod over it. In January 1986, he acquired the company publishing *LeProgrès*, the major regional daily published in Lyon, France's second biggest city, and various satellite titles – irrespective of protests of government ministers and of the press transparency and pluralism commission. Hersant stated:"I am merely anticipating the next law." So it proved: after the Parliamentary elections of March 1986, and the appointment of the Chirac government, a new press law was promulgated in August and completed following the "observations" of the Constitutional Council on 27 November; it abolished the commission and reduced the requirements intended to ensure the transparency of the accounts of communications companies. Above all, the 1986 communications legislation imposed limits on the concentration of ownership by companies with multimedia interests – in the press, radio, and in terrestrial, cable and satellite television. These limits were, however, relatively generous. For example, a group may control up to 30% of the circulation of the daily press, provided that it does not control other media; if it has substantial interests in the broadcasting media, it may control up to 10% of the circulation of the daily press. The law did not take into account the ownership of weekly or other non-daily titles. The Hersant group, once again, did not have to divest itself of any titles; and, in February 1987, the CNCL, the regulatory body set up by the 1986 law, awarded the franchise to operate the fifth terrestrial TV channel in France to a consortium in which a Hersant company, TVES, was the lead operator, with a 25% stake.

*Ownership and finance*

The horizontal and vertical integration of leading communications groups increased during the 1980s: print media groups diversified into other media; companies or conglomerates diversified into the hardware or software of the communications sector from which they had previously been absent; leading French print media groups pursued their expansion in Europe and abroad, and foreign groups acquired or launched titles in the French daily newspaper and magazine press. French press groups were not authorized to diversify into radio and television until the mid-1980s; previously, their expansion was mainly confined to publishing and advertising. During the 1980s, the structure of the French media market has become more similar to that of other European countries; the struggle for the control of French press groups, often considered previously primarily in terms of political influence, is increasingly decided by strictly financial considerations.

Nonetheless, when considered in a European context, the French press continues to present three major weaknesses: the readership of daily newspapers is ageing and declining; advertising revenue is relatively limited (both in absolute terms, and in terms of the decline of the press's share of total advertising expenditure); French press companies are under-capitalized and profit margins are low.

These factors accentuated during the 1980s the trend towards the concentration of ownership discernible since the early 1950s, especially in the daily newspaper market. The increase in the sale-price of a daily has been substantially greater than the rise of the cost of living: expressed in constant francs, a paper that sold for 4 fr. 50 in 1988 cost the reader 1 fr. 10 in 1947. Titles disappeared or else merged and shared advertising revenue: from the mid-1960s, the modernization of printing technologies and plant, and the advent of commercial television (advertising was authorized on PSB TV channels from 1968) led to a perceived shortfall in press revenues that accentuated the trend to the concentration of ownership. These factors were again significant in the 1980s, with the advent of electronic publishing, offset printing and photocomposition, on the one hand, and, on the other, the passage between 1983 and 1986 from three public service TV channels (whose advertising was limited to 25% of total revenue) to six channels that all carry advertising and where, in the main, the "commercial logic" prevails.

According to France's leading economic news magazine, *L'Expansion* – itself the flagship of France's twelfth biggest press group – fourteen groups had a turnover exceeding 1 billion francs in 1988. The 5 leading groups were Hachette-Presse, Hersant Group, Editions Mondiales, Ouest-France and CEP Communications.

Hachette-Presse exemplifies the difficulty of analysing the ownership structure and conglomerate interests of French communications groups. Hachette-Presse is a division of Hachette: with a total group turnover in 1988 of 24.4 billion francs (29.05 bn in 1989), the latter was the 28th biggest French industrial company. Its president, Jean-Luc Lagardère, also heads the electronics (civilian and military communications) group Matra, ranked number 35 among French industrial companies; Lagardère's right-hand man, and indeed his associate in the acquisition of Hachette in 1981, is Daniel Filipacchi of Publications Filipacchi – the publisher of titles such as *Paris-Match* – ranked number 8 in the print media groups.

During the past decade, the Hachette group, like that of Robert Hersant, tested the provisions of French common law and communications law concerning "the dominant position" acquired in certain market sectors by the emerging multimedia conglomerates. In late 1990 (September–October) Hachette obtained the authorization of the broadcasting regulatory authority, the CSA, to replace the Hersant group as the lead operator in the consortium holding the franchise for La Cinq.

The attempt in 1990 by France's leading multimedia group to acquire control of France's second main private sector TV channel (estimated share of the TV viewing public: 12%) posed a series of issues relating to pluralism and the concentration of ownership. These specifically concerned: the treatment of La Cinq by *Télé 7 Jours* (Hachette-owned), France's leading TV programme listings magazine; the control of the advertising budgets and airtime of La Cinq; the possibility of vertical integration with production companies that were already, in effect, Hachette subsidiaries; and, in sound radio, the links between Europe 1, Europe 2 (a purveyor of programmes, not a radio network) and Skyrock (an FM radio network of the Filipacchi group, whose advertising revenues and airtime are run by Europe 1).

*Structure and organization*

French newspapers are generally divided into Paris-based titles (with "national" pretensions) and provincial (regional and "departmental" or county) daily newspapers. Some titles published in Paris are genuinely national: they are to be found on sale in many of the 50 000 newspaper sales-points across France (*Le Monde, Le Figaro*, for instance). But other Parisian titles, such as *le Quotidien de Paris*, while they may count politically as part of the "national" press, have low circulations (well under 50 000 copies, for example); they are on sale primarily in Paris and other major cities, and through subscription (*La Croix-L'Evénement* is primarily distributed via subscription).

In 1988, there were 11 general interest (i.e. non-specialist) French daily newspapers published in Paris. There were 65 provincial dailies. The provincial titles accounted for 70.8% of the total circulation of the French daily newspaper press. In many regions of France, there is one dominant title, published in the major city of the region. From the 1950s to the 1980s, there long existed tacit agreements between the leading titles of neighbouring regions not to engage in a "newspaper war" and compete for sales and – even more important – advertising revenue in "border" areas.

Between 1952 and 1988, the total circulation of the French daily press rose from 9.6 m. to 13.05 m. copies: but given the growth of the French population, newspaper readership overall is declining.

The relatively poor performance of French daily newspapers (compared to their British and German counterparts) is partly offset by the strength of the magazine and "periodical" press.

Three groups dominate the "periodical" press sector: Hachette (publisher of *Télé 7 Jours*), Editions mondiales (with *Télé Poche* and *Modes et Travaux*) and Prisma Presse (with *Femme Actuelle, Prima*, and *Téléloisirs*).

**Electronic media**

The situation in 1990 had largely been shaped by the Léotard communications law of September 1986, which the Lang–Tasca law of 1989 partly modified. The left-of-centre government in office from May 1988 decided not to repeat "the errors" of previous governments, which had repealed the audiovisual legislation of their predecessors. A central issue of the period between 1982 and 1989 was the status, functions and powers of an independent regulatory body for the audiovisual sector. The controversy surrounding the creation of the three successive bodies – Haute Autorité, Commission Nationale de la Communication et des Libertés, Conseil Supérieur de l'Audiovisuel – highlighted the issue of their membership and mode of appointment: on each occasion, the opposition suspected that the body would be indirectly controlled by the government; they saw each major decision of the regulatory body as proof of this self-fulfilling prophecy.

By 1990, it appeared that the heated and impassioned climate surrounding previous broadcasting reforms was a thing of the past. The CSA was entrusted with the preservation of pluralism of the means of expression (and their ownership); the issues of advertising and sponsorship in broadcasting fell within its remit; it appointed the chief executives of public service broadcasting organizations; it issued licences to run radio stations and to operate private television channels (either terrestrial or relayed by satellite) and the licences to operate cable networks.

## *Television*

Meanwhile, the television industry gained in complexity throughout the 1980s. This was due largely to the increase in the number of channels and their different legal status and funding. By 1990, there were channels with local, national and European programmes, audiences and ambitions. Some TV channels were terrestrial; others were relayed by cable and/or satellite; some satellite TV channels were relayed direct to home (DTH) like TDF1; others used telecommunications satellites like Télécom 1-2. Given this complexity, we shall first briefly describe the situation in 1990.

## *Public service television*

The Tasca law of 1990 created a "super-president" or overlord for the two public service channels, Antenne 2 (A2) and France Régions 3 (FR3), launched respectively in 1964 and 1972. Their 1990 budget was respectively 3.3 bn francs and 3.4 bn francs. Their revenue breakdown was as follows:

| Channel | Advertising | Licence-fees | Sponsorship | Other |
|---------|-------------|--------------|-------------|-------|
| A2 | 54.5% | 40% | 1.2% | 4.3% |
| FR3 | | 20% | 80% | |

The super-president was to marshall the joint resources of these PBS channels and ensure that they complemented one another in the competition against private sector channels and secured 40% of the total audience. FR3 chafed against the obligation – in principle, temporary – to surrender transmission time and broadcast (on Saturdays) programmes of the new public service channel beamed via TDF1 (from April 1989). Because it could otherwise only be received by satellite (and because households with satellite reception equipment numbered under 100 000), this channel, the SEPT (Société d'Éditions de Programmes de Télévision), appeared in dire need of the publicity or "window of opportunity" conferred by the use of FR3 transmission time.

Defined "as a cultural channel with a European vocation", the SEPT is owned by various public service broadcasting organizations: FR3 has 45%, l'Institut National de l'Audiovisuel has 15%, Radio France has 15%, and the State has 25%.

The public service television channels are: A2 (national channel), FR3 (national and regional channel – it has 12 regional stations), SEPT (European channel), TV 5-Europe (European channel launched in November 1983, transmits programmes broadcast by various French-speaking countries, by satellite), R.F.O. (transmits radio and TV programmes to French overseas territories and possessions).

*Private TV channels*

Canal Plus was the first private sector channel to be launched (November 1984); this subscriber channel is owned by a company holding a public service operating licence (issued in December 1983); the company's shareholders include Havas, CGE, CDC, Société générale, CCF, the l'Oréal group; company personnel and the general public own some 25% of the stock. After severe initial difficulties (the number of subscribers failed to meet anticipated target figures), Canal Plus has created, during the past few years, a host of subsidiary companies, and acquired minority interests in others, notably in the fields of audiovisual production, tele-matics and home shopping (by TV): it has also sired subscription TV companies in Belgium, Spain and elsewhere, and has interests in newspaper publishing, satellite and TV reception equipment companies. Canal Plus has more than 2.8 m. subscribers and has substantial profits. It was France's 29th service company in 1988, with a turnover of 4.3 bn francs (TF1, France's premier TV channel, ranked 33rd, with a turnover of 3.4 bn). It expects a steady growth in the number of subscribers in France and abroad, and is well placed to profit from the development of cable and satellite television.

TF1 (Télévision Française 1) was the first channel to be launched in France (8 December 1935); it was the first to carry commercial advertising (1968); from 1975, it broadcast in colour; and it was the first and only public service channel to be privatized (in 1987). The general public holds 33.8% of the stock and company employees 10%; 56.2% of shares are owned by a group of shareholders, the most important of which is the Bouygues construction company, in effect the "owner-operator" of TF1, with 25% of the stock; the other major shareholders of this group include Pergamon, Maxwell, Maxwell media S.A., Editions mondiales, Bernard Tapie, Société générale, and three other banks. Since 1989 Berlusconi has acquired stock and Maxwell announced he wishes to sell out.

In February 1987, the CNCL awarded the licence to operate the fifth channel, La Cinq, to the Hersant and Berlusconi groups (which each had 25% of the stock of the operating company) for ten years. This licence superseded that awarded in 1985 (under the socialists) to a consortium of the Berlusconi, Seydoux and Riboud groups, which the Chirac government rescinded. M 6 (Métropole télévision) is in a similar position: the Chirac government rescinded the operating licence issued under the socialists in 1985–1986 for a TV music channel, TV 6 (promoted by a consortium of advertising, cinema and radio companies – Publicis, Gaumont and NRJ); the CNCL, in March 1987, awarded a licence to operate a new general interest channel, M 6, owned by a consortium led by the CLT and the Lyonnaise des Eaux group.

The central issue in 1990 was no longer that of government interference but the ability of the advertising market to finance five general interest channels. Total advertising spend in 1989 was in the order of 11.5 bn francs. The growth in the size of the overall advertising "cake" slowed down from 15.5% in 1988 and 12.9% in 1989 to an anticipated 9% in 1990 (Source: IREP – l'Institut de recherche et d'études publicitaires). While the size of the TV "share" of the cake had increased substantially in the 1980s, there were growing fears both that companies were preferring to advertise via non-media outlets (direct marketing, sales promotions, etc.) rather than the media, and that the TV advertising market did not generate revenue sufficient to fund five general interest channels. The junior communications minister, Catherine Tasca, stated that there was one general interest channel too many. La Cinq had an audience share of 12% and a deficit of 2.5 bn francs; M 6 had an audience share of 8% and losses of 1.2 bn. TF1 emerged triumphant during the 1986–1990 period in the competition for TV advertising revenues, a competition waged against both private sector and public service channels. In 1989, A2 failed to attract its target advertising revenues and had losses of 321 m. fr.; it responded by preparing a 1991 budget in which anticipated revenue from licence fees exceeded that from advertising. To help offset their continued losses La Cinq and M 6 battled to acquire full nationwide reception and, following the success of Hachette in replacing Hersant as the lead operator of La Cinq, there was (again) talk of some form of alliance between La Cinq and M 6, aimed primarily against TF1.

TF1 and Canal Plus are profit-making: in 1989, their net profits were 220 and 740 m. francs respectively. But TF1 represented a very heavy initial investment (6 bn francs in 1987 to acquire the licence to operate the channel for ten years); its profits, on a turnover of 5.3 bn, were relatively modest. La Cinq and M 6, in their programme schedules (which contained many low-quality American programmes), contributed to the inflation in the cost of acquiring programme transmission rights, while failing to contribute to the production of French quality programmes; they occupied TV broadcasting frequencies that others dearly sought. In short, the increase in the number of channels did not lead to a corresponding increase in the quality of programmes on offer, and programme schedules, indeed, tended to a certain uniformity.

*Local television*

As with "national" TV channels, it is necessary to distinguish between terrestrial and cable TV  channels. In 1990, there were three local terrestrial TV channels: Télé-Toulouse, 8 Mont-Blanc and Télé 30 Lyon Métropole. They all carry local programmes and relay Euromusique or CNN programmes, and they are all loss-making.

Fifteen cable network TV channels form the other category of local TV channels. They are located in towns which have a cable network and which assigned one channel to a local TV company. In the Cable Plan of 1982 (see below), local cable TV networks were assigned a major and vital role; by 1990, this was no longer the case.

*Cable*

In November 1982, the Mauroy government announced the cable plan, advocating the large-scale systematic cabling of the country. The minister presented cable as "a massive, consistent and orderly solution to satisfy multiple communication needs". But it was not before May 1984 that the government announced how the plan was to be implemented. The two-year interval was taken up with the discussion by all the parties concerned as to how to achieve the initial objective, namely connecting 1.5 m. homes in 3 years and the bulk of the population within about 15 years. In 1984, some 2% of households were cabled. The decision taken in the spring of 1984 represented a compromise between several sets of projects and strategies and an attempt to fulfil the main industrial objective, viz. developing optical fibre technology. The cable plan rapidly encountered opposition from several parties. Local authorities had recently gained in power as a result of decentralization legislation; for electoral (and other) reasons, they were little attracted by the massive investment cable required. The decision to assign to a state organization (the DGT) the overall control of the implementation of the new technology antagonized the manufacturers of cable equipment who proved unable to produce what was required within the agreed price and time.

Following the Léotard communications law of 1986, the government officially abandoned the cable plan. The DGT was no longer in sole control of the implementation of the plan; likewise, the decision to use only optical fibre (and therefore maximize the interactivity potential of videocommunications) was abandoned. The result was that France would be cabled in a piecemeal fashion. Fifty-four local authorities had signed agreements with the DGT prior to the abandonment of the cable plan; another 49 undertook to be cabled, but on an ad hoc basis.

In 1990, some 2.4 m. cable connections had been laid down; there were about 386 000 individual or collective subscribers. The penetration rate was about 16%. It was anticipated that by the end of 1990, there would be 500 000 subscribers for 3.3 m. connections, and, by 1992, 1.3 m. subscribers for 6 m. connections.

The cabling of France therefore, entered by the late 1980s a more realistic phase. The industrial dimension remains present; but this is no longer piloted by public operators, the DGT and TDF, but by private operators. The latter build the networks and have gone into audiovisual production; they promise to be the carrier for technical and commercial integration at the local, national and transnational levels and in multimedia activities.

## Satellite

The decision to build a joint Franco-German satellite – taken by Valéry Giscard d'Estaing and Helmut Schmidt in 1979 – was never rescinded. But, with the passage of time, it appeared that the technology initially chosen was obsolete and unreliable. Successive governments were tempted to abandon a costly project (4 bn francs); but they yielded to the arguments of the industrial groups manufacturing the satellites and TV reception equipment. At stake was the future of the European TV industry (and what was left of the European electronic industry). The goal was High Definition Television and the imposition of the European standard, the D2 Mac Packet. In October 1990, it seemed that the TDF1-2 satellites, launched during the previous year, were unable to provide more than a minimal service: they could transmit the signals of only three channels. Both before and after their launch and entry into service, however, these satellites (or rather access to one of their transponders) were considered by various multimedia groups vital to their development.

Between 1988 and 1990, the CSA awarded the operating licence for use of the five channels that could be beamed via the TDF transponder to one German-language channel and three (and a half) subscriber TV channels. The companies applying for a place on the French "hot bird" planned to dovetail satellite with their cable or terrestrial transmissions. Commercial considerations were, at most, a secondary concern for the various satellite operators, especially the SEPT. The aim, rather, was to have access to the maximum possible means of transmitting programmes and thereby facilitate expansion: thus, a general interest terrestrial channel like TF1 wanted to gain access to scrambled or encoded transmission (as is the case with some cable and satellite technologies); the CSA, however, rejected its application. The same general aim lies behind Canal Plus' strategy in its dealings with cable operators and behind the latter's strategy in diversifying into a range of media.

## Telematics

TDF's teletext system, Antiope, has been in decline whereas Minitel gained an increasing number of subscribers (especially for professional, as opposed to domestic, usage). Seven years after it was launched as a commercial proposition, the minitel videotex service could be accessed from 4.7 m. terminals, most of them distributed free by the PTT-France Télécom. The videotex industry employed 10 000 people, and had a turnover of 2 bn francs.

## Radio

In this sphere also, the political and professional agenda altered rapidly. The issue of pirate radio stations has been one of the key factors in bringing about the changes in the regulation of the audiovisual sector in the early 1980s. In the late 1970s, the threat to the state broadcasting monopoly posed by pirate radio stations led to their repression; but the socialist candidate François Mitterrand in the Presidential election of 1981 came out in their support.

Private radio stations gradually gained in legality. "Associations" were allowed to operate radio stations in a 1981 law; from 1984, private stations were authorized to carry advertising; in 1986, they were allowed to progress from a purely local dimension and form networks operating on a national scale. This seemingly haphazard process had many consequences: FM radio was the scene of considerable inventiveness with the trying out of new programme formats and content; but it also saw the death of attempts at convivial (and amateur) sound broadcasting; newspaper publishing groups diversified into radio, and some municipal authorities tried to create their own (propaganda) stations. The main victors to emerge from this turbulent scene were new professional broadcasters (such as NRJ), who dominated the growing number of networks (and their affiliates).

Radio "turbulence" has now ended. The actors who traditionally do-minated sound broadcasting in France have emerged triumphant and reinvigorated from the severe (FM) competition. The long-established "peripheral" radio stations (RTL, RMC, Europe 1) are now established on the FM wavelength (in addition to their traditional medium wave fre-quencies). The public service national radio station, Radio France, diver-sified into local broadcasting; in 1990 Radio France boasted a wider range of stations – France Inter, France Musique, France Culture, but also (the distinct and autonomous) Radio France Internationale and several suc-cessful innovations of the 1980s, the "round the clock" news service, France Infos, and 47 local radio stations – at the level of the town, district or coun-ty.

## Policies for the press and broadcasting

It has been said that France is a country of great geographical and cultural diversity, counterbalanced by a heavy-handed central government. The resultant underlying tension periodically explodes, in the form of political crises and national traumas, with Frenchmen divided into radically oppos-ing camps. The present mood of relative calm, and of quiescence between the Left and the Right, may well be due less to the development of con-sensus politics than to the inability of political ideologies to apprehend and analyse the forces making for social change.

Broadcasting has long been highly politicized in France. Criticisms levelled at "audiovisual" policymakers and managers include "government interference", excessive bureaucracy and the promotion of a "homogenous culture". As a symbol of Parisian centralism, state broadcasting was a tar-get for various regional movements (Basque, Breton, Alsatian, Corsican, and Occitan) that strive for recognition of their cultural identity and press for local self-government. The broadcasting reforms of the past decade, therefore, have to be seen in this general context. The reforms (of many sectors of public life) implemented after 1981 by the first non-conserva-tive government for 23 years – the "government of the left" appointed by François Mitterrand after his (first) election as President – reversed, or tried to break, century-old trends. Undertaken at a time of economic crisis, they disturbed established social and political attitudes and forces. Media policy issues in the 1990s may prove less contentious.

## Statistics

(1 ECU = fr. 2.33)
Population
Number of inhabitants (m.)                                          56.6
Population density per km²                                           102


Broadcasting
National TV channels – Audience and budget in 1989

| Channel | Audience share | Budget |
|---|---|---|
| TF1 | 40.9% | 5 307.0 m. fr. |
| Antenne 2 | 22.8% | 3 306.1 m. fr. |
| La 5 | 12.6% | No figures published |
| FR3 | 10.4% | 3 344.6 m. fr. |
| M 6 | 6.9% | 421.0 m. fr. |
| Canal + | 4.5% | 5 399.0 m. fr. |
| Other channels | 1.9% | NA |
| Total | 100% | |

Number of national radio channels                                     7

Number of videotex subscribers                                     4.7 m.
Number of cabled households                                        2.4 m.

The press
Independent national dailies                           Circulation in 1989
Le Parisien                                                       395 593
Le Figaro                                                        394 248
Le Monde                                                         316 220
L'équipe                                                         253 669
France Soir (1987 figure)                                        284 752
Libération                                                       166 628
Paris Turf                                                       112 500
La Croix-Evénement                                                96 720
L'Humanité (1988 figure)                                          91 104

Number of independent regional dailies                               45

# 6

# Germany

## Hans J. Kleinsteuber and Peter Wilke

### National profile

Describing the national characteristics of Germany at this time is far from easy. The country was divided as a result of World War II and two separate political entities existed for 45 years. For the first four years after the war these were occupation zones, but in 1949 two states were established. In the field of mass media, two totally different systems emerged that very much resembled the models of their respective political "camps", led by the United States and the Soviet Union.

As a consequence of the fast developing unification process since October 1989 almost all indicators have changed or are changing, or more precisely, the system of the West has been adopted by the East with some modifications. Because of this situation, the overview presented here concentrates on West Germany. But we also briefly describe the "socialist" system of the former German Democratic Republic (GDR) and analyse the emerging framework for a common media system in a unified Germany. The term Federal Republic of Germany (FRG) means the Western part of the divided Germany, but since 3 October 1990 it refers to the unified German state.

The (former) FRG made up the greater part of Germany, its territory – including West Berlin – covered 248 621 km$^2$, with a population of 62.7 million (1989). The density of population (ca. 250 inhabitants per km$^2$) is among the highest in the world. It was concentrated in heavily industrialized regions of the country like the Ruhr and Rhine Valley, West Berlin, Munich, Stuttgart and Hamburg. High incomes and economic wealth ensure high expenditures for advertising and media consumption. The figure for total advertising expenditure was in 1989 22.6 bn DM and showed rates of growth (from 1988: + 9.2%) which were clearly above GNP-growth rates.

The territory of the former GDR covered 108 333 km$^2$. The population was around 16.4 million, mostly clustered in East Berlin and the south of the country (Leipzig, Dresden). As the political system was shaped according to that of the Soviet Union, decision-making, including the media, was under control of the ruling communist party, the SED. After the fall of the wall that had divided both countries until November 1989, the East German system virtually collapsed. In March 1990 a freely elected and non-communist government took over and later the East German parliament decided to join the Federal Republic. Since 3 October 1990 both Germanies have been united, consisting now of 16 federal states (*Länder*) in the Federal Republic.

## Development of the press and broadcasting since 1945

### *The creation of the present system*

After the unconditional surrender in 1945 the Allies introduced a completely new media system in East and West Germany. As a result, the mass media are almost solely the product of the post-war years. The press was to be reintroduced under a system of licences and all old newspaper owners (until 1945) had to be excluded from press activities.

In the Soviet part, the occupying power immediately started to favour the Communist Party and its "transmission" organizations and made survival increasingly difficult for publications of other parties. After the formation of the SED (Socialist Unity Party of Germany) in 1946, the media system was brought in line with official SED policy. *Neues Deutschland* – the central party paper resembling the Soviet *Pravda* – became the leading newspaper. Radio and later television were also closely controlled by the SED.

### *Newspapers in the FRG*

The Western Allies clearly decided in favour of a gradual rebuilding of a private and commercial press. The new owners had to be individuals with an anti-Fascist and pro-democratic background. Even so, quite a few former Nazis made their way into the post-war media. From July to September 1945, in total 169 papers were licensed: 71 in the British Sector, 58 in the American, 20 in the French and 20 jointly in West Berlin. In the course of this licensing process nearly all the old publishers were excluded.

With the founding of the Federal Republic in 1949 and the enaction of the Basic Law as its constitution, the practice of compulsory licensing ended. Responsibility for press policy was handed over to German authorities and the market opened for all kinds of interest. Immediately the old publishers tried to get into business again and a wave of new papers entered the market. Within six months the number of publications rose by around 400 to a total of 568.

But the following years proved that the "licensed press" had established itself firmly; since 1945 in fact, nearly all of today's internationally known German publications like *Der Spiegel, Die Zeit, Der Stern* or *Die Welt* were licensed in the post-war years. Only a few old newspaper publishers were able to survive, mainly on the local level or with specialist magazines. In the 1950s the distinction between licensed press and old publishers became more and more meaningless. In 1954 the publishers founded their umbrella organization, Bundesverband Deutscher Zeitungsverleger (BDZV). In 1956 publishers and journalists founded a body for self-regulation, the Press Council (Deutscher Presserat). It is modelled on the British Press Council, comprising publishers and journalists.

The years after 1950 brought the conflicts typical of such a press system, namely conflicts of competition between broadcasting and press, the relationship of press and political power, press concentration and introduction of new technologies. One of the continuities is that the print publishers have attempted since the 1950s to gain access to broadcasting. Therefore, one of the first conflicts was advertising in public service broadcasting, which was attacked by the publishers as they feared heavy competition for advertising revenue. However reports of independent commissions (like the Michel-Report of 1967) as well as court rulings established the right of public service broadcasters to advertise, as long as it did not endanger the financial health (i.e. the diversity) of the press.

Another controversy influencing the German press system was linked to discussions on state security in the 1960s. The leading news magazine *Der Spiegel* was accused of having published defence secrets, its publisher and the journalist responsible were jailed, the premises searched. This "Spiegel Affair" (1962) ended with a clear victory for press freedom: the publisher was acquitted and the instigator of the action, Minister of Defence F. J. Strauss, was forced to resign. As part of the Cold War, amendments to the Basic Law were discussed for the case of a national emergency and some media control was proposed. But when the articles were passed in 1968, the freedom of the press, as laid down in Article 5 of the Basic Law, remained unchanged. Both the Spiegel Affair and the discussions on state security consolidated and strengthened the freedom of the press in Germany.

As in other Western countries, the main internal danger for the press is its high degree of concentration. Although the German press is at first sight diverse with an exceptionally high share of local and regional papers, the figures show a clear process of concentration since the 1950s, accompanied by an increase in cross-ownership. The number of "independent editorial units" (i. e. units that produce a complete newspaper with all its sections) has fallen constantly, mainly for economic reasons. The greatest steps in the concentration process followed the general recessions in 1966–67 and 1973–74.

*Historical development of broadcasting*

In 1945, the occupation forces also insisted on the broadcasting media starting from scratch. The British established one unified radio organization located in Hamburg, covering almost the entire North and West of Germany (except the US-occupied port of Bremen, which still has its own small broadcasting corporation). The radio station in Hamburg (NWDR) was set up on the lines of the centralized BBC structure, and its first director, Sir Hugh Greene, later became Director General of the BBC. In later years, the NWDR was split into NDR Hamburg, WDR Cologne and SFB Berlin.

The Americans left a more regionalized broadcasting structure in their occupation zone, based on *Länder* borders, and therefore similar to their own, rather decentralized system. The Americans planned to establish a commercial system (like they did in occupied Japan) but were forced to drop these plans on account of British resistance.

The French occupation zone covered two independent territories along the French border, i. e. two German *Länder* of that time. Their radio organization is still in existence today (SWF Baden Baden) and serves two regions with – by today's standards – rather artificial borders.

During the late 1940s broadcasting was handed back to German management. The structure created by the Allies was firmly established and widely accepted at that time and changed amazingly little in the following years. It was mainly adapted to the needs of the German federal system.

*Historical development of the media system in the former GDR*

Until the end of 1989 the media system of the GDR was under the tight control of the SED. With the help of the Soviets, the SED had established a centralized information system between 1945 and 1959, in which the mass media were supposed to function as "instruments of the worker and peasant power". They were instructed to serve as "propagandist, agitator and organizer" of the masses.

The structure of the national and regional daily press did not change much after 1952. Thirty-nine daily newspapers were published of which the SED directly edited 16. The others were owned by the parties of the so-called Democratic Block (CDU, LDPN, NDPD, DBP) or mass organizations like the unions and Socialist Youth. The SED press dominated with a circulation of 6.6 million.

The SED had founded four main institutions to control the media: the Press Office of the Ministerial President, the Department for Agitation and Propaganda under the Central Committee of the SED, the state-owned news agency Allgemeine Deutsche Nachrichtenagentur (ADN) and the Office for Paper Distribution. Formal political censorship was not practised, but the SED gave out detailed guidelines on how to report the news. The education of journalists was monopolized under party super-vision (in Leipzig) and journalists who did not conform were threatened with expulsion. The result of this "guided" system of news management was a highly homogenous and dull press; access to foreign, especially West German, publications was barred.

The radio and television system was also directly influenced and or-ganized by the political leaders and the SED. Radio started as early as 1945 under Soviet control and reached full supply of the population in the mid-1950s. The first television programme was transmitted in December 1952, actually on Stalin's birthday. Due to problems in the industrial production of TV-sets, television supply reached its peak only very late in the 1960s.

Much of the population of East Germany could always receive Western television, exceptions being the Southeast around Dresden (therefore called valley of the unsuspecting) and the Northeast around Greifswald. Western radio was freely available everywhere. Until the 1970s the SED-leadership tried to ban Western reception, but afterwards it was tolerated. Even cable systems carried Western channels and TV-sets were provided with the Western colour specification (West Germany transmits in PAL, the East in SECAM). West German television had ratings up to 40 and 60% during prime time; Eastern news programmes in particular were rarely watched and often only reacted and responded to the Western mes-sage (for instance the notorious "Black Channel" presented by Karl Eduard von Schnitzler). Most recently entertainment shows and Western films were on the increase, in order to draw viewers away from watching Western programmes.

**The press**

*Policy framework*

The present media system is based on a short Article of the Basic Law. It says:

> Everybody has the right to free expression and publication of his opinion in word, writ-ing and picture and the right to obtain information without hindrance from sources generally accessible. The freedom of the press and of reporting by broadcasting and film is guaranteed. There must be no censorship. Art. 5 (1)

Apart from these general guidelines, which are part of the human rights section of the constitution, the Basic Law offers little further reference to the media framework of the country. The reason is simple: after World War II and Germany's unconditional surrender the system of the press and broadcasting was only gradually handed over to German management. Those who had been working on the constitution had only a limited mandate to decide upon the future structure of the German media.

Traditionally press laws were put out by the federal government (the first press law stems from 1874). The Basic Law stipulates (in Art. 70) that lawmaking for the press rests now with the individual *Länder*, but the federal government may put out a common frame of regulations (Art. 75). All "old" *Länder* have issued press laws that define what "press" actually means and regulate its obligations and privileges (the "new" *Länder* will follow). The *Länder* Press Laws, although varying in detail and formulation, follow the normative content of the Basic Law and ensure a democratic press. They establish key principles such as the freedom from dependency on registration or licensing. And they describe central functions of the press like the dissemination of information, participation in opinion-forming etc. The laws contain an obligation of accuracy for the press and the right of reply.

In the 1970s the social–liberal government tried to introduce the Federal Press Law (as demanded in Art. 75) as a general framework for the more specific regulations of the *Länder*. It included paragraphs on editorial statutes (meaning journalist co-determination) and freedom of opinion for journalists, as was demanded by journalist unions. The publishers' organizations fought fiercely against this bill and won: still there is no Federal Press Law.

The press regulations mentioned impose only a few material restrictions on the press, in fact, the freedom of the press turns out to be very much the freedom of the proprietors of newspapers and magazines. This fact is especially reflected in the legally protected right of the publisher to define the general political line of the publication (*Tendenzschutz*); therefore the extensive German co-determination (*Mitbestimmung*) law is much restricted for publishing companies.

A special regulation for the press was included in the Federal Cartel Law in 1976. The critical definition of market dominance was stricter for the press than for other products. The level for notification to the Cartel Office was lowered to 25 million DM in the case of mergers between press companies. Since 1976 the Federal Cartel Office has intervened several times against attempts to merge press companies, e.g. it stopped Burda from buying into the Springer company in 1981. But its policy approach is generally not hard-line.

*Structure and organization*

The structure of the West German press is characterized by:

— a high number of titles,

— many strong local newspapers,

— only a few national papers,

— a great number of magazines,

— the weak position of the party press,

— a dependency on advertising income,

— a high degree of economic concentration.

At the end of 1989 the number of "independent editorial units" (meaning full publishing entities that produce all parts of a paper) for daily newspapers was 119 and the total number of titles 1344. This reflects a situation where the press appears to be highly diversified and local, but in fact much is contributed by central offices. The circulation figures show that the local and regional press is very important in West Germany: 90% of the subscription press claims to be local. Traditionally, the share of subscription newspapers is high in West Germany. In 1989 they had a circulation of 13.8 m. Only 5.6 m. were sold in the street. But – as already mentioned – the *Heimatpresse* (home press) is in many cases only legally independent. For financial reasons these papers closely work together with larger newspapers or other local and regional papers.

Compared to the time before World War II only a few national papers exist. The national papers cover mainly a liberal and conservative spectrum. Apart from the *Tageszeitung* (Taz), which started in 1979 as an 'alternative' paper but is quite established now, there is no left-wing daily. All major newspapers claim to be independent or non-party-political, but in fact a large number are highly sympathetic to the conservative Christian Democratic Party (CDU, in Bavaria CSU).

The phenomenon *BILD Zeitung* deserves a special mention in describing the West German press. This daily newspaper with its extraordinarily high circulation (4.3 m.) uses the tabloid format and questionable reporting standards and shows traditionally a strong right wing orientation.

All in all, 484 general magazines (with 105.1 m. copies) and 850 specialized periodicals (with 15.1 m.) are published. A new type of newspaper, which became much stronger after 1945, is the weekly. It presents less actual news and more analysis and background information. Very successful and important is *Die Zeit* (circulation ca. 500 000), a liberal and independent paper. The protestant church publishes the *Deutsche*

*Allgemeine Sonntagsblatt* (ca. 100 000) and the catholic church the *Rhein-ischerMerkur* (ca. 100 000). A news magazine, modelled on the American *Time* magazine and with a virtual monopoly in its market is *Der Spiegel* (circulation ca. 1 m.). With its investigative style of journalism, it has made quite a number of scandals public and is counted as the most influential political publication in the FRG. The market for general interest maga-zines is still quite lively, *Stern* by Gruner und Jahr (controlled by Ber-telsmann) being the most successful and the best known, with a liberal and investigative format.

### Ownership and finance

The West German market for daily newspapers is dominated by a few groups of publishers. The largest market share is controlled by the Axel Springer Group with ca. 27% in 1989 *(BILD, Welt, Hamburger Abendblatt, BerlinerMorgenpost* etc.) Second position is taken by the WAZ-Group with 6% *(Westdeutsche Allgemeine Zeitung* etc.), which is more a regional publisher. Other regional groups (some with national papers) follow with 1 to 4% of the market.

The largest 10 publishing groups represent 53% of the total circulation. This ranking has remained unchanged in recent years. Advertising con-tributes 60–70% of all revenue in newspaper business. Newspapers take a share of about 45% of all advertising expenditure (all print media: near-ly 70%) in 1989, but commercial broadcasting is cutting down this share.

The Springer-group as a whole (which controls more than 70% of all dailies in the two largest cities, West Berlin and Hamburg), is well known for its conservative attitude, reflecting the views of Axel Springer himself. He was influenced by experiences of the Cold War, considered himself a militant anti-communist and used his papers to propagate his views. Before he died, he changed his press empire to a joint stock company, with especially selected conservative shareholders (among them his widow and Leo Kirch).

Although the Axel Springer Verlag ranks as the largest newspaper publishing group in Europe, it is only the second largest media group in Germany. The multi-media conglomerate Bertelsmann, which is active on all major German markets as well as world-wide, produced a turnover in 1989 that was three times higher.

### Press in the GDR until November 1989

A unique feature of the GDR was the high per capita consumption of newspapers. With a total circulation of 9.7 m., 583 copies of newspapers were sold per 1000 inhabitants. But the reason for this impressive figure was mainly political: low prices and a general tendency to subscribe to *Neues Deutschland* besides the local paper. The SED party press played a dominant role and directly controlled two thirds of the daily circulation. On the other hand, magazines (for instance TV guides) were produced in limited numbers only and were therefore scarce. New subscriptions were only accepted if old ones were cancelled.

Although paper scarcity prevented any innovations in the press system after the late 1970s, the supply was still diversified (if measured only by the number of titles):

— 1 812 titles existed,

— 39 daily newspapers with a circulation of 9.7 million in total,

— 30 weekly and monthly papers (9.5 million circulation)

— 667 papers published for businesses by the SED (2 million)

— 508 magazines of general and special interest

— additionally a great number of regional and local information papers.

## *The press after unification*

With the political liberalization of the GDR, control over the press collapsed and the journalists gained a very high degree of independence. But immediately after the opening of the border, Western publications flooded into East Germany and competed with the old publications. Especially magazines and the yellow press gained large market shares (papers like *BILD* started to produce regional editions for East Germany). Many of the old publications died. In the early days of the "non-violent revolution" quite a number of new publications, often with an "alternative" concept, appeared, but hardly any survived.

The only type of publication that seems to be little harmed by the change are local dailies, based on subscription (regardless of whether they had a communist past). Practically all of them have developed relationships with Western publishers and adapted rather well to the new situation. The largest publisher of the country, the SED-owned Berliner Verlag, was purchased in 1990 by a consortium consisting of Bertelsmann and Maxwell. Smaller papers have been sold to Western companies in 1991.

**Electronic media**

*Legal framework*

As was described above, the Basic Law stipulates that the sole responsibility for broadcasting rests with the states (*Länder*) of the Federal Republic as part of their "cultural sovereignty". Exceptions are only those radio corporations whose main function it is to provide foreign countries with information and which therefore are based on federal legislation: Deutschlandfunk (DLF) and Deutsche Welle (DW). The organizational and legal structure of all other broadcasting corporations is defined in *Länder* laws and, if more than one state is involved, in agreements between several *Länder* (e.g. ZDF). The result is a uniquely decentralized broadcasting system, with production centres in every region of the country. Central political influence is exercised on *Länder*-level; the Bonn government mainly uses the PTT as a political tool.

Another crucial legal actor in broadcasting policy was and still is the Federal Constitutional Court, stating its opinion in leading decisions, namely in 1961, 1971, 1981 and 1986. Whereas the Court defended the public service system in earlier decisions (especially in 1961 when it banned a commercial TV venture by the federal government), its ruling in 1986 argued that commercial broadcasting is protected by the constitution, provided that some basic principles are guarded, like secured financing and public service being able to take care of what they called a basic supply of programmes.

With the advent of new electronic technologies (cable and satellite) all *Länder* drafted media laws in the 1980s, that specifically regulate the electronic media outside the conventional public corporations, mainly by handing out commercial radio and TV licences and deciding what programmes may be fed into cable systems. For this purpose new supervisory bodies (*Landesmedienanstalten*) were created, each with a council, that resembles those of the public broadcasters. A national framework of regulations is laid down in agreement between all *Länder* (*Medienstaatsvertrag*). In 1990 this federal structure was also introduced in the newly established *Länder* of the East, thereby marking the end of the old GDR's centralized TV broadcaster DFF. The final structure has to be established by the end of 1991.

The German PTT is a purely federal institution, based on federal law and administered by a formally independent Telecom, supervised by the Postal Ministry in Bonn. The Telecom enjoys a relative strong position in conventional broadcasting (including ownership of most of the transmitters) as well as in cable and satellite technology (managing most cable systems and a number of satellites like TV-Sat and Kopernikus).

*Structure and organization*

The traditional public service broadcaster is an independent and non-commercial organization, financed primarily by fees, which resembles to a certain extent the British BBC and will be referred to as an *Anstalt*. The typical *Anstalt* provides public service radio and TV channels to a region, which in many cases means a *Land* (like WDR in North Rhine-Westphalia or BR in Bavaria). But NDR is the joint corporation for the Northern *Länder* (Schleswig Holstein, Hamburg, Lower Saxony). All the regional corporations together founded the ARD (Arbeitsgemeinschaft der Rundfunkanstalten Deutschlands) and contribute according to their size to the first TV channel. In addition they independently organize a regional Third Programme for TV (again sometimes in cooperation with other corporations).

Under ARD coordination, about 40% of all programmes are fed in centrally, such as national news, weather, sports and movies. Programming on the first (ARD) channel is nation-wide, except on weekdays from 6.00 to 8.00 p.m., when a regional (in the city-*Länder* like Berlin and Hamburg local) programme is offered.

The Second German Television, ZDF (Zweites Deutsches Fernsehen), is based on an agreement of all (old) *Länder* and located in Mainz. The five new *Länder* of the former GDR and East Berlin (that has merged with West Berlin) will each establish their own *Anstalt*. Alternatively some may act together or join an existing *Anstalt* in the West. Since December 1990 ZDF and ARD have been transmitted in the Eastern part of the country.

All *Länder*-broadcasters offer between three and five radio channels in their respective region, some of them regionalized or localized. Usually one channel offers the popular music format with advertisements, while other channels specialize in more conservative music, classical music or talk programmes. Former national radio channels from East and West that served primarily propaganda purposes have been converted to a cultural and a news channel, but final decisions on their future have not been taken.

All broadcasting corporations are governed by an independent broadcasting council (Rundfunkrat), whose representatives are supposed – according to the Federal Constitutional Court's ruling – to reflect the "socially relevant groups" of society. These delegates are either elected in parliament or they are selected and sent from groups like parties, business and labour organizations, churches, farmers, sports, women, culture etc. Even though in theory only a few or none have been sent directly from the major political parties, the councils are heavily influenced by party interests. The reason is that German parties are relatively strong in all areas of the political and social system and penetrate practically all of the "socially relevant groups".

The head of the *Anstalt* is an elected Director General (*Intendant*), usually a rather powerful position. He as well as his representative and all heads of departments (and often the journalists as well) are selected along party lines; proportional representation by the major parties CDU and SPD is the rule.

The public broadcasters also offer two minor cable channels, called EinsPlus (ARD) and 3Sat (ZDF, together with the ORF and SRG), mainly with cultural programming.

In the mid-1980s commercial competition started to challenge the public system. In 1991 two major channels are offered by RTLPlus and Sat1; in some parts of the country they transmit terrestrially or else they are on cable and satellite. Two minor channels are Tele5 and Pro7 on cable and satellite (rarely terrestrial). All commercial broadcasters offer the familiar mix of mass entertainment together with some short news and very little cultural programming.

## Programme policies

The two public national channels ARD and ZDF and also the Third regional channels are required by law to offer a comprehensive and integrated programme that is politically balanced. There is direct competition between ARD and ZDF, but also limited coordination, especially at events like sports or politics that require a joint effort. The Federal Constitutional Court demanded that the public broadcasters provide the country with a "basic supply" of programmes, whereas the commercial competitors are much freer to adapt to audience choice.

Based on these incongruences the commercial broadcasters have started a battle for ever larger market shares that is reflected in rating figures. In 1989 the average German watched television 135 minutes a day. The national market shares were as follows: ARD 43 minutes, ZDF 40 minutes, Third Programmes 15 minutes, RTL Plus 15 minutes, Sat1 13 minutes. Only 9 minutes are spent on minor public or commercial channels and foreign channels. It has to be taken into consideration that commercial TV is offered on a terrestrial basis only in parts of the country. The figures are quite different for cabled households, where viewers watch a total of 148 minutes; 63 minutes are spent on the three public (ARD, ZDF, Thirds) and 55 minutes on the two major commercial broadcasters (RTL Plus and Sat1). The remaining minutes are spent watching minor channels.

*Ownership and financing*

As public service broadcasters, the *Anstalten* are mainly financed by a monthly licence fee (combined fee for radio and television: DM 19 per month). In addition, considerable revenue is derived from 20 min. of advertising each weekday (about 20% of all ARD revenues, 40% for ZDF). Whenever the question of a licence fee increase comes up, the public broadcasters prove to be extremely vulnerable to political pressure. This is even more of a problem, as all *Länder*-parliaments have to agree on a common fee. A system of financial support from the large broadcasters (like WDR) to the very small ones (like RB) takes care of some financial balancing; a similar system of support for East Germany is planned. The commercial broadcasters earn all their money from advertising of course.

The commercial TV broadcasters in Germany are mainly owned by the leading national media companies, but some non-media and foreign ownership may be found. The main owners of Sat1 are Springer and the leading film distributor Leo Kirch, who for years fought a heavy battle for control but finally compromised. Other shareholders are the publisher Holtzbrinc k and smaller newspaper firms. RTL Plus is controlled by the Luxembourg CLT (46.1%) and UFA/Bertelsmann (38.9%); other participants are the WAZ company and other publishers. The leading influences in Tele 5 are CLT, Berlusconi and the Springer company. Pro7's dominant owner is Leo Kirch's son Thomas (49%) and it should be counted as part of Kirch's media empire.

The main pay-TV company Premiere took over the activities of the older Teleclub channel (owned by Kirch) and started in March 1991. It has the following shareholders: UFA/Bertelsmann (50%), Canal Plus (25%), Teleclub (25%).

*Foreign media availability*

West Germany, being a medium-sized country in the heart of Europe with many neighbouring countries, traditionally receives a large number of channels from the outside: RTL Radio was quite influential already in the 1950s. Spillover was especially strong from German-speaking neighbouring countries (GDR, Austria, Switzerland). On cable systems today up to about half of the channels come from other countries. But at least nine German-produced TV-channels are available on cable, so interest in non-German programmes (mainly in English, also French and Turkish) is low (ratings no higher than 1%).

The former GDR situation is outlined in the section on the historical development of the media system in the former GDR.

*Local TV and radio*

In the decentralized system of the FRG, regional (mostly *Länder*-wide) broadcasting is offered on the ARD channels, rarely on commercial TV. Local public TV is offered in some large cities, where city-*Anstalten* are located, especially in Berlin, Hamburg and Bremen. In a few places commercial channels are required to offer some local TV as a prerequisite of their licence.

Public radio is rarely national, mostly regional and again sometimes local. Commercial radio is local in the large cities and in Bavaria, Baden-Württemberg and North Rhine-Westphalia; in other places it is organized as a *Land*-wide network.

*New electronic mass media*

Among the countries of Europe with large populations, Germany has the highest percentage of cabled households; it has also more households cabled than any other European state, about a quarter of them. In the 1970s cabling was heavily disputed between the major parties and especially the SPD was accused of holding back this new technology to protect the public broadcasting system. After the Bonn government changed to the CDU in 1982, the Telecom (PTT) started to invest tremendous funds in the cable infrastructure; nearly all cabling is done by Telecom. The main interest behind this policy was to support commercial competition and to weaken the public system. Furthermore, the Telecom administration was ordered to search for additional terrestrial frequencies. As a result, RTLPlus and Sat1 found the opportunity in quite a number of larger cities for conventional transmission.

The Federal Republic, being a highly industrialized country, started to invest in national direct broadcasting satellite (DBS) in the 1970s (TV-Sat 1 and 2), but the first of the satellites launched never worked while the second one met little interest among broadcasters. Seeing the success of Astra, that also carries a number of German channels, the Telecom developed and launched a specification for smaller satellites (DFS/Kopernikus 1 and 2) with hybrid qualities. They proved to be much closer to the broadcasters' requirements, but when the second satellite was up, it was mainly applied to connect telecom lines between the two parts of the newly unified Germany.

In the early 1980s new telematic technologies were introduced, very much like those in other parts of Europe. Teletext (the German specification is called Videotext) reached (in 1989) about 5 m. households. About 44% of all households used a VCR in 1989.

The general technological backwardness of East Germany is also reflected in a low penetration of cable (though cable systems always carried

Western programmes), in late introduction of teletext (tests started in 1989) and the virtual non-availability of VCRs until 1989.

## Unification in broadcasting

As a result of the unification process the East German broadcasting system as an institution disappeared. Starting in December 1990 the former first DFF-channel took the ARD-programming and in return some East German programme material is fed in. In the same month ZDF was introduced on a formerly unused network of transmitters. The old second DFF-channel became the new Third Programme (DFF-Länderkette) of East Germany, the only channel that keeps some of the old GDR tradition. By the end of 1991 the old broadcasting system, still centralized in Berlin, will be abolished and *Länder-Anstalten* will be founded to step into its place. Public radio is already offered in each *Land*.

Western influences and Western interests are strong in the integration process. The appointed politician mainly responsible for this procedure was transferred from Bavaria. As soon as the public sector is transformed into the new order, the remaining frequencies will be occupied by Western commercial broadcasters, for whom this territorial extension comes as a welcome addition to their markets.

## Policies for the press and broadcasting

### Main actors and interests

The central actors in German media policy are the political parties, especially the *Länder*-organizations of the two large parties, CDU and SPD, that control much of the public broadcasting sector. During the 1980s they initiated new broadcasting laws for the commercial sector and assigned themselves central positions in the newly founded supervising bodies. The federal government generally exerts little influence, its main tool being the Post/Telecom. But during the peak months of unification it used the unclear situation to determine much of the process of broadcast integration.

The most influential business actors are the large media companies (like Bertelsmann, Springer) that had dominated publishing for a long time and successfully started to demand licensing of commercial broadcasting. They now occupy leading positions in radio and television in addition to the print media, thereby causing new problems of media concentration. Most of them (Springer, Bauer, Burda) tend towards the CDU and find in this party a ready ally for more commercialization. The Bertelsmann company behaves in a more independent manner and is sometimes seen as closer to the SPD. Foreign actors do exist, but their in-fluence is limited (RTL, Berlusconi).

### Main issues

Until the beginning of the unification process in late 1989, the central theme of the 1980s had been the introduction of commercial broadcast-ing. The CDU favoured this policy direction and started to license such broadcasters in *Länder* where it had a majority. The SPD tried to oppose this policy but found that it could not stop it and finally jumped on the bandwagon. After years of strong polarization, media policy is now again based on a broad consensus between the *Länder*. In 1986 the Federal Con-stitutional Court sanctioned the commercialization process, but cautioned against double monopolies (including press and broadcasting) and de-manded the protection of the bases of the public system.

### Policy trends

The 1980s, especially the second half, brought tremendous change for the German media system, especially in broadcasting. The most important event was, of course, the fall of the East German regime and its disap-pearance in just one year (1989/90). This process was accompanied by the virtual disappearance of the Communist-inspired media system of the GDR and the nearly total takeover of the Western press system and the adoption of Western public service broadcasting. Introduction of com-mercial programmes in the East came a little later.

The second important change was the introduction of commercial broadcasting on a large scale. In 1980 there was a public service monopo-ly, whereas in 1990 audiences that had a choice (because they were cabled) spent nearly half of their total TV time on commercial programming.

The third change is that the old polarization between the major parties (CDU vs. SPD) and to a lesser extent important social groups (business vs. labour) over media policy and the introduction of commercial TV and radio has very much disappeared. All *Länder* began to allow commercial broadcasting and established respective licensing and supervising bodies. In public statements CDU- and SPD-*Länder* might still differ somewhat, but in practice they cooperate, as has been the rule in this largely consen-sual political system.

The fourth result is that the future of the public broadcasting system looks rather gloomy. East German broadcasting had to be transformed into a public system, but is plagued by high overstaffing, backward tech-nology and extreme centralization. It is not yet clear who will pay for reform and decentralization. Also licence fee increases will be very difficult to arrange, as all 16 *Länder* parliaments (increase from 11 after unification) have to agree and act jointly.

Finally, regulation of commercial broadcasting proved to be mostly unsuccessful as the authority of the *Länder* regulatory bodies remained weak. Commercial broadcasters threaten to move to another *Land*, if they do not get what they expect.

*Degree of policy integration*

As was described before, Germany is a rather decentralized country in terms of political decision-making. PTT policy rests with the Bonn government, newspaper regulation with both federal and *Länder* governments, broadcasting mostly with the *Länder*. Conflicts might arise, but are usually solved as a compromise between all actors involved (but unsolved conflicts remain, e.g. over the federal government's approval of the EEC television directive that the *Länder* claim as their exclusive domain). This decentralized structure makes the integration of the new East German *Länder* into the Federal Republic relatively easy. But this integration, in fact, means the introduction of the Western system in the East. This process of "colonization" is highlighted by the fact that nearly all press and broadcasting production centres will remain in the West, the East being just a welcome market extension.

As was described above, a federal press policy does not exist at present, since the SPD's attempt at one in the 1970s failed miserably. The large publishing companies expanded into electronic media in the 1980s and a system of broadcast regulation was established. But the rather large and highly politicized regulatory bureaucracy is proving rather ineffective. It rarely limits commercial behaviour, and has been unable to cope with cross-ownership problems, but so far it has made the introduction of non-commercial local radio, based on community initiatives, nearly impossible.

Since the end of 1989 the large print and broadcasting companies have extended their influence into East Germany. A policy concept to cope with these market expansions and to check the power of the large media companies is not in sight.

## Statistics

(1 ECU = 2.05 DM)
Population: FRG and GDR together                                79.1 m.
Population density per km$^2$                                       221

THE FOLLOWING STATISTICS ARE FOR WEST GERMANY (FRG) ONLY

Broadcasting
Number of radio licences (Dec. 1989)                         24.14 m.
Number of TV licences (1989)                                 27.42 m.
Cost of monthly licence fee (starting Jan. 1990)
Radio                                                        DM  6.00
Radio and television                                         DM 19.00

Public television
3 terrestrial networks:                  ARD, ZDF, (regional) Third Programmes
2 programmes on satellite and cable:                    3Sat, EinsPlus
Private TV channels (all nationwide)
Major commercial channels (terrestrial and on cable)      RTL Plus, Sat1
Other commercial channels (on cable, rarely terrestrial)    Tele 5, Pro 7
Foreign channels on cable:
                 Super Channel, Eurosport, Screensport, TV 5, TRT et al.

| Television channels | Number of minutes per year |
|---|---|
| ARD | 230 474 |
| ZDF | 272 841 |
| ARD – regional channels | 321 043 |
| ARD + ZDF, morning TV | 61 632 |
| Third Programmes, total | 1 236 849 |
| 3 Sat | 175 898 |
| EinsPlus | 168 191 |

ARD – Contributing broadcasting corporations and respective Länder and their share in national programming in 1990
Bayerischer Rundfunk BR (Bayern)                                      17%
Hessischer Rundfunk HR (Hessen)                                        8%
Norddeutscher Rundfunk (Schleswig-Holstein,Hamburg, Niedersachsen)    19%
Radio Bremen RB (Bremen)                                               3%
Saarländischer Rundfunk SR (Saarland)                                  3%
Sender Freies Berlin SFB (Berlin)                                      8%
Süddeutscher Rundfunk SR (Northern part of Baden-Württemberg)          8%
Südwestfunk SWF (Rheinland-Pfalz, Southern part of Baden-Württemberg)  9%
Westdeutscher Rundfunk WDR (Nordrhein-Westfalen)                      25%

New electronic media
Video cassette recorders, penetration 1989                          44%
Teletext (Videotext) 1989, % of all sets                          18.3%
Videotex (Bildschirmtext) 1989, number of users                  179 831
Households passed by cable in 1989                        18 356 000 = 58%
actually cabled households of those passed            7 691 000 = 42%
Households cabled (Sept. 1989)                                     22.8%

Division of advertising revenues between media (1989)

| | |
|---|---|
| Newspapers | 44.2% |
| Magazines | 33.5% |
| Television | 13.4% |
| Radio | 4.6% |
| Billboards etc | 3.3% |
| Cinemas | 1.0% |

Newspapers in West Germany (1989)

| | |
|---|---|
| Number of newspapers, total | 1344 |
| Independent editorial units | 119 |
| Number of daily newspapers | 358 |
| local and regional | 345 |
| national | 6 |
| Sunday papers | 5 |
| Weekly papers | 42 |

Circulation
400 per 1000 inhabitants (data for 1990)

| | |
|---|---|
| Total circulation | 26.5 million |
| Daily newspapers | 20.8 million |
| Subscription, local and regional | 13.8 million |
| Subscription, national | 1.3 million |
| Street sales | 5.7 million |
| Sunday papers | 3.9 million |
| Weekly papers | 1.8 million |

| National newspapers | Circulation | Political profile |
|---|---|---|
| BILD | 4 300 000 | very conservative |
| Süddeutsche Zeitung | 380 000 | liberal |
| FAZ | 360 000 | conservative |
| Welt | 220 000 | very conservative |
| Frankfurter Rundschau | 195 000 | soc.dem/liberal |
| Tageszeitung | 70 000 | green/left |

Market share and concentration in newspapers (1989)

| Group | Circulation | Market share in% |
|---|---|---|
| 1. Axel Springer Verlag, Hamburg | 5 423 897 | 26.68 |
| 2. Zeitungsgruppe WAZ, Essen | 1 219 039 | 6.02 |
| 3. Süddeutscher Verlag, München | 721 954 | 3.56 |
| 4. DuMont Schauberg, Köln | 658 165 | 3.25 |
| 5. Stuttgarter Zeitung | 638 259 | 3.15 |
| 6. Münchner Zeitungsverlag/D.Ippen | 601 717 | 2.97 |
| 7. Frankfurter Allgemeine (FAZ) | 495 779 | 2.44 |
| 8. Rheinisch Bergische Druckerei | 414 760 | 2.05 |
| 9. Verlagsgruppe Madsack | 393 316 | 1.94 |
| 10. Ruhrnachrichten | 285 316 | 1.41 |

Media companies: ranking and turnover in 1989

| | |
|---|---|
| Bertelsmann AG | 13.00 bn DM |
| Springer AG | 3.00 bn DM |
| Heinrich Bauer | 2.00 bn DM |
| WAZ Gruppe | 1.65 bn DM |
| Holtzbrinck | 1.53 bn DM |
| Burda | 1.17 bn DM |
| Leo Kirch Gruppe | 0.90 bn DM |
| Rheinpfalz Gruppe | 0.75 bn DM |
| Süddeutscher Verlag | 0.69 bn DM |
| Sebaldus | 0.66 bn DM |

## References

ARD-Jahrbuch (ARD-Yearbook) (since 1969). Cologne.

Bausch, H. (ed.) (1980). Rundfunk in Deutschland. Munich: Deutscher Taschenbuch Verlag (5 Vols).

BDZV (published annually). Zeitungen. Bonn (Yearbook of the Publisher's Organization).

Braunschweig, S., Kleinsteuber, H. J., Wiesner, V. and Wilke, P. (1990) Radio und Fernsehen in der Bundesrepublik. Cologne: Bund.

DLM-Jahrbuch (Yearbook of the 'Landesmedienanstalten', published biennially since 1988) Munich.

Geserick, R. (1989) 40 Jahre Presse, Rundfunk und Kommunikationspolitik in der DDR. Munich: Minerva.

Holzweissig, G. (1989) Massenmedien in der DDR. Berlin: Holzapfel.

Humphreys, P. J. (1990) Media and Media Policy in West Germany. The Press and Broadcasting since 1945. London: Berg Publishers.

Kleinsteuber, H. J. (1982). Rundfunkpolitik. Der Kampf um die Macht über Hörfunk und Fernsehen. Opladen: Leske.

Media Perspektiven (published annually). Daten zur Mediensituation in der Bundesrepublik. Frankfurt.

Meyn, H. (1990). Massenmedien in der Bundesrepublik Deutschland. Berlin: Colloquium.

WIlliams, A. (1976). Broadcasting and Democracy in West Germany. Bradford University Press and London: Crosby Lockwood Staples.

ZDF-Jahrbuch (ZDF-Yearbook – since 1962) Mainz.

Periodicals: Media Perspektiven, Rundfunk und Fernsehen, Publizistik, Medium.

# 7

# Greece

## *Panayote Dimitras*

### National profile

Greece is one of the smallest European countries, located on the southern part of the Balkan peninsula, in the south-eastern end of the continent. Its $132\,000\,km^2$ are inhabited by some ten million people. This relatively small density ($76\ inh/km^2$) is due to the landscape of the country (a large part of continental Greece is mountainous) and to the consecutive waves of emigration (an estimated two million Greeks emigrated during the last one hundred years, of which less than 500 000 eventually returned to Greece). The low density figure, though, hides a significant discrepancy: one third of the total population (some 3.5 million) live in the $427\ km^2$ metropolitan area of the country's capital, Athens (a density of some 8 200 $inh/km^2$ as opposed to 55 $inh/km^2$ in the rest of continental Greece).

Greece has a homogeneous population: some 98% of its citizens primarily speak the same, Greek, language, and, at least nominally, identify with the same, Orthodox Christian, religion.

Except for the communist left (running as the Progressive Left Coalition in the end of the 1980s), the country's two-and-a-half party system is notorious for the absence of organized, principled parties. Instead they depend on the personality of their leader; both major political parties that have ruled Greece since the restoration of democracy in 1974, the conservative New Democracy (1974–81 and from 1990) and the Pan-Hellenic Socialist Movement (PASOK, 1981–89) share this characteristic. The average citizen feels a profound mistrust towards the state: this civic behaviour was inherited from the period of the four-centuries-long Ottoman occupation and was perpetuated by the dysfunctioning of the centralized, Napoleonic, administration imposed upon Greeks after independence: the predominantly traditionalist politicians have consciously opted for the dysfunctioning of a state whose imported structure they never liked.

## Development of the press and broadcasting since 1945

A country with a dysfunctioning administrative and economic system could only have dysfunctioning media. The first Greek government after World War II forbade the publication of the wartime newspapers; but, after the December 1944 communist uprising, the ban was lifted. The ensuing civil war, that lasted until 1949, prevented any effort to cleanse Greece from the collaborationist elements, generally as well as in the press. In the first twenty-year post-war period, the circulation of these dailies more than doubled, from an average of 320 000 in the early and mid-1950s to over 700 000 in the mid-1960s: at the same time, the internal synthesis of the circulation changed, as the morning papers' lead over the afternoon ones in the early 1950s gave way to an uncontested lead of the latter ever since. On the other hand, some two thirds of the circulation was concentrated in Greater Athens, which had at the time about one quarter of the total population.

Immediately after the military coup in 1967, 6 newspapers chose or were forced to close down: during the seven-year dictatorship, only 9 newspapers circulated, heavily censored in the beginning, less so towards the end; their circulation oscillated around 600 000. The restoration of democracy in 1974 led to an understandable blossoming of the press: with 3 of the 6 newspapers shut down in 1967, and the official communist one outlawed in 1946, reappearing to bring the number of newspapers to 13. Circulation rose by 50% to exceed 900 000 copies in 1974–75. As the right settled in (through 1981), circulation fell to as low as 750 000 by the end of the decade. Again, political change (a socialist government between 1981 and 1989) led to more newspapers being published, an average of 16, and to a substantial boost in circulation which reached an average of nearly one million copies between 1984 and 1989. This increase came almost exclusively from the copies sold outside Greater Athens, which accounted thenceforth for nearly half the total circulation; in the same period, the morning papers' circulation fell to less than 10% of the total. Moreover, the 1980s saw the entry into the print media business of outside businessmen who, in 1990, controlled 7 of the 16 dailies.

A constitutional act in 1945 gave birth to the National Radio Foundation (EIR). However, mainly because of the civil war, it took 8 years for the government to give EIR a legal framework. With Law 2312/1953, EIR became a Legal Entity of Public Law and acquired the monopoly over all electronic media. Radio broadcasting in Greece was regulated by that 1953 Law until 1975, with only minor alterations.

Television first appeared in 1960 at Salonica's International Fair (an annual September affair), in order to advertise the Fair's exhibited products. This private, limited, television station operated legally until 1968, and illegally until 1969. The first effort to broadcast a regular television channel was not made until 1966. When that channel proceeded from the experimental stage, a new law (745/1970) was introduced: it changed the title of the state broadcasting authority to National Radio and Television Foundation (EIRT) and provided the framework for the operation of the first television station. In 1975, finally, EIRT was changed into a state-controlled joint stock company, ERT (Greek Radio & Television).

The state monopoly, however, was, from the beginning, violated by the armed forces. Indeed, as early as 1951, a bill allowed them "to install radio or television stations ... for the information, the education, the entertainment and the general improvement of the cultural level of the Armed Forces; furthermore, in times of war, to strengthen the spirit of the fighting Nation". The armed forces' dominant role in the post-civil war, strongly anti-communist Greek state, led to an unchecked expansion of that radio network into a fully equipped service, antagonistic to EIR (and later EIRT). The 1970 legislation recognized that reality and provided a legal framework to the Armed Forces' Information Service (YENED), which had also installed an initially primitive television station in 1965. This unique situation of a nationwide armed forces network ended in 1982, when YENED was transformed into a civilian, state-owned broadcasting service, ERT-2 (Greek Radio and Television-2). ERT and ERT 2 merged into one company (ERT) in 1987.

Until the 1980s, the Greek media scene was a "paradise", in the initial, Persian meaning of a walled garden. The printed media were in the hands of traditional publishers, while the state monopoly controlled broadcast media. The 1990s brought the "fall from paradise", as the calm "walled gardens" were substituted by fierce competition: in the print media, between traditional publishers and wealthy businessmen who have also acquired or published newspapers; in broadcasting, between state and private media.

## The press

Article 14 of the constitution guarantees the freedom of speech and of the press, forbidding "censorship and any other preventive measure". Seizure of newspapers or of any other print medium is forbidden except with court order in the cases of: an offence against Christianity and any other "known religion", or against the president of the republic; the publication of information on sensitive defence matters or which could threaten the territorial integrity of the country; and the publication of obscene material. Three convictions after such seizures led to temporary or permanent closing down of the newspapers. The constitution also calls for laws to define the right to reply, as well as the conditions and qualifications for the profession of journalist, and it allows for a law to mandate that the financing of the newspapers and magazines be made publicly known. Finally, it specifies that press-related crimes be tried promptly.

The press law dates from 1938, though it was amended many times since. It provides for the right to reply and for criminal and civil suits for libel; criminal suits, though, have an 18-month prescription period which practically guarantees impunity in the slow Greek judicial system, despite the swift procedure mandated by the constitution. A minimum sale price for the daily and weekly newspapers is set by the government. From 1988, the owners must be publicly known, which means that even press-related joint-stock companies ought to have personalized stocks for their shareholders.

By the end of 1990, 16 national dailies were published in Athens (for circulation figures of the 10 largest, see the statistical appendix): the morning *Avgi* ("Dawn" in English, communist), *Kathimerini* ("Daily", centre-right), *Logos* ("Speech", centre-left), *Rizospastis* ("Radical", communist); the afternoon *Apogevmatini* ("Afternoon", centre-right), *Avriani* ("Tomorrow", centre-left), *Eleftheri Ora* ("Free Time", extreme right), *Eleftheros* ("Free", centre-right), *EleftherosTypos("FreePress",centre-right),Elef-the-rotypia("FreedomofthePress",centre-left),Epikairotita* ("Current Events", centre-left), *Estia* ("Focus", extreme right), *Ethnos* ("Nation", centre-left), *Mesimvrini* ("Noon", centre-right), *Nea* ("News", centre-left), *Nike* ("Victory", centre-left). Besides, two dailies in Salonica, the morning *Makedonia* ("Macedonia", centre-right) and the afternoon *Thesaloniki* ("Salonica", centre-left) had a regional circulation in Northern Greece, while there existed scores of local dailies, most with no more than four pages. Besides, there were four national financial and four national sports newspapers.

Newspaper ownership brings the publishers considerable influence (many dramatic events — revolutions, government changes etc. – were initiated or heavily influenced by the most powerful publishers), name recognition and respect across the political spectrum. A number of businessmen from the shipping industry and other sectors which frequently deal with the government (public contractors, arms dealers, etc.) entered the field and slowly displaced the traditional publishers. In 1990, only one of the pre-1974 publishers was still in business: Lambrakis, the heir to the most powerful press group from the inter-war period (with the daily *Nea*, 4 weeklies, 1 fortnightly, 2 monthlies, 1 yearly, one radio station and a 20% share in the most successful private television station Mega), still the country's biggest both in terms of turnover and in terms of profit. Besides him, three national dailies (*Avriani, Logos, Niki*) along with one sports daily, one radio station and one television station belonged to the recently successful, but traditional publishers, the Kouris brothers; the daily

*Eleftherotypia* and a 20% share in Mega to another traditional publisher, Tegopoulos; the other traditionally owned papers were the extreme right and the communist ones (the latter belonging to political parties), with low circulation except for *Rizospastis*. On the other hand, the new businessmen owned seven national dailies with more than half the total circulation: four bought traditional titles (*Apogevmatini, Ethnos, Kathimerini, Mesimvrini*) while three published new papers (*Eleftheros, Eleftheros Typos, Epikairotita*).

In the early 1980s, newspapers were running large deficits and were therefore very dependent on the state banks' "soft" loans, and hence on the government. In the late 1980s, however, almost all major press groups were making profits due to increases in newspaper sale prices which exceeded average consumer price rises. Also advertising revenues in newspapers rose by 50% and advertising in magazines increased almost 300%. Circulation kept going up from 1981 to 1989: but, in 1990, there was a downward trend which brought the corresponding figure to the low levels of the period 1976–81. Possible explanations for this trend were: the beginning of private television which offered satisfactory news coverage (already, in Greater Athens, circulation had fallen with the advent of non-state-owned radio); the events of 1989 (collapse of communist regimes and formation of a short-lived ecumenical government) which led to major readership losses in the communist and pro-PASOK populist press; and the comeback of the right in power (if we recall that circulation was always higher under centrist or socialist than under right-wing governments).

Traditionally, each newspaper has passionately supported one political party: in the 1980s, the centre-right ones favoured New Democracy, the centre-left ones PASOK, and *Avgi* the Eurocommunists and *Rizospastis* the communists until the two coalesced into the Progressive Left Coalition supported by both newspapers. As a result, more than three quarters of the readers of each newspaper were voters of the corresponding party. This trend survived into the 1990s, although, after the Koskotas scandal, some centre-left papers had become rather to very critical of the PASOK leadership; more recently, some centre-right papers had also become more critical of ND than everbefore. Overall, the circulation of the centre-left newspapers was nearly 60% of the total, both in 1981 (when PASOK came to power) and in 1990 (when PASOK lost power and fell in crisis).

According to their content, Greek dailies range from extremely populist newspapers, that are not only passionately partisan but also violently slanderous, to serious newspapers trying to emulate the authoritative European press (*The Times, Le Monde*, etc.). Among populist papers are *Avriani*, which 'pioneered' the style, and *Eleftheros Typos*: both have accumulated scores of criminal and civil convictions for libel, while the latter was the leader in circulation in 1988–1990. Among the serious papers is *Kathimerini*, the only morning newspaper with growing circulation in the recent years, and the only paper with growing circulation in 1990, the year of the crisis. More generally, most governments have at some point accused the press of 'yellow journalism', a view which many Greeks share. All governments have also attempted to influence the majority of journalists and newspapers, using some 40 million ECUs per annum in subsidies and "secret funds" (*Kathimerini*, 8 December 1990) and by keeping some 70% of the important journalists on the state payroll, sometimes with "phony jobs".

**Electronic media**

The constitution excludes broadcast media (along with the cinema and the record industry) from the legal protection offered to the print media. This exception is formulated in article 15, which also provides for direct state control of radio and television, whose responsibilities should include "the objective and fair broadcasting of information and news, as well as of products of literature and arts", and "securing the programming quality required by their social mission and the cultural development of the country". For a long time, "direct state control" was interpreted by conservative and socialist governments as tantamount to exclusive state ownership of electronic media.

The extreme pro-government bias of state-owned and government controlled radio and television led to social pressure for deregulation, led by a group of intellectuals called Channel 15 after the constitutional article. Public opinion's favourable reaction to that pressure made some opposition party mayors decide to start radio stations in 1987; in turn, this forced the socialist government to accept the principle of non-state-owned local radio stations in the 1987 law and implement it with a 1988 presidential decree. Furthermore, the success of those "free" radio stations paved the way for private and municipally owned television stations: in late 1988, the socialist government decided that the state-owned company, ERT, should start over-the-air free retransmission of foreign satellite television programmes (having previously threatened to "shoot down satellites which overfly Greek air space"); and the opposition mayors of Salonica and Piraeus started local television stations. Finally the conservative–communist coalition government in 1989 gave in to the intense lobbying of the newspaper publishers and radio station owners and allowed private and municipal local television, including cable, pay-TV and satellite re-transmission stations. They also limited ERT's monopoly to national broadcasting and transferred state control of the electronic media to a National Radio and Television Council.

Today, therefore, broadcast media in Greece officially function within the framework of the laws 1730/1987 (on ERT) and 1866/1989 (on the National Radio and Television Council), the presidential decree 25/1988 (on local radio stations), and the ministerial decision 22255/2/1990 of the Minister to the Prime Minister (on the National Radio and Television Council). The state's constitutionally mandated control of the media is in the hands of the National Radio and Television Council (ESR). ESR's responsibilities are: to recommend three candidates "of high reputation and professional competence" to each government-appointed position on the ERT board, from which the government will select one; to recommend to the government the dismissal of members of the ERT board; to advise the government on granting licences to private and municipally owned radio and television stations; to issue codes of ethics for journalists, programmes, and advertisements in broadcast media; to oversee the coverage of the activities of parliament and of electoral campaigns by ERT; and to rule on violations of these codes or of other laws by the stations.

The state-owned company ERT (Greek Radio and Television) holds monopoly rights to national radio and television broadcasting, but the government can give operating licences to local private and municipally owned radio or television stations. ERT is a public company organized as a joint stock company; its only stockholder is the Greek state.

ERT has two national television channels based in Athens (ET-1 and ET-2), and a third one based in Salonica (ET3) with limited broadcasting range (Athens, Salonica and a few other cities); 4 national radio stations (ERA-1, ERA-2, ERA-3, ERA-4); 21 regional stations, whose programming partly coincides with that of the national stations; one local radio station in Salonica; and a short-wave Voice of Greece servicing most parts of the globe.

In 1988, 40% of ERT's income came from a special mandatory fee that every customer of the state-owned Public Power Corporation (DEI) pays, regardless of whether the customer owns a radio or a television set. From December 1984, this fee has ranged from 1.8 ECU to 15 ECU annually, according to the value (not the quantity) of the consumption of electricity. Forty-two percent of ERT's income came from advertising and 18% from the state budget.

Local, private and municipal radio stations were allowed in 1988 and television stations in 1989, with licences granted to them by the government on the advice of the ESR. However, until late 1990, the ESR, because of its dysfunctioning, had failed to draft any such recommendations: as a result, some 600 local radio stations and a score of, mostly local, television stations including a pay TV channel in Greater Athens, were operating illegally, while awaiting the processing of their applications; some television stations had, in the meantime, extended beyond their Greater Athens "local" base to cover more than 70% of the country.

A non-transferable, two-year licence to operate a local FM radio station can be granted by the government, upon the recommendation of the ESR, to a local authority, a company controlled and managed by Greeks, or to a Greek citizen. Networking is forbidden; local radio stations can broadcast cultural or entertainment programmes of other stations up to 10% of their daily programming time. Retransmitters cannot be used, unless they are necessary in order to cover the whole region (locality is defined in terms of prefecture). The emphasis of the programme should be local.

A non-transferable, seven-year licence to operate a local television station can be granted by the government, upon the recommendation of the ESR, to a local authority or to a company, in which case, no individual can directly or through his/her relatives own more than 25% of the personalized shares, and foreign capital cannot control more than 25% of the total capital. The companies must be reliable, and their members should not have been convicted for press-related crimes. Being a local authority or having media-related experience among the shareholders is considered an advantage when applying for a licence. No shareholder can have shares in more than one station. At least 50% of the schedule, excluding news and current affairs, must be European productions, while the licence contract should specify "a satisfactory quota of national productions per programme type". Presidential decrees should specify the procedure by which 1.5% of the annual gross income (minus taxes and contributions to state agencies) of the state or non-state television companies is invested in Greek feature films also to be shown in cinemas; and 0.3% of the annual gross income is donated to two national organizations for the blind.

Advertisements on radio and television must not exceed 10 minutes per hour, or 8% of the total daily broadcasting time. Advertising spots interrupting television programmes are forbidden.

In 1990, according to Focus data, 99% of the three million Greek households had a television set, 83% a colour set, and 47% a video recorder. Audience surveys provided evidence of strong ratings for the, usually private, local stations, well ahead of the national or regional state stations. In December 1990, the private channels Mega and Antenna led the ratings with shares of 32% and 24% respectively, with ET-1 far behind in third place with 16%, ET-2 with a mere 7%, followed by the private New Channel (4%) and Channel 29 (3%); other channels had a total 7% – of which less than 1% was for ET-3, satellite channels 3% and videos 4%.

The main private television stations, with a coverage of more than three quarters of the country despite the "locality" constraint, belong to shareholders owning other media as well: Mega, on the air since November 1989, is owned by the Lambrakis group (the leading private media conglomerate), the Bobolas group (second), the Tegopoulos group (fourth), the Alafouzos group, and the Vardinoyannis group. Antenna, on the air since January 1990, belongs to the Kyriakou group which owns the radio stations with the same name.Their advertising-financed 8am–2am programming is based on the kind of programmes that attract sizeable audiences: series, movies, games, children's shows, music, sports, and news. Educational television and documentaries have no place here. Their news coverage is of better quality than the state stations and, especially for Mega, more objective. On the other hand, they too had the bad (state broadcasting) habit of starting many programmes later or earlier than announced, or making unannounced last-minute changes. Nevertheless, their efforts were successful, as, less than one year after their beginning, Mega and Antenna had larger audiences and drew more advertising than the state channels. Overall, only one third of their programme was Greek, as compared with more than half for the state channels. Naturally, the private channels' revenue was almost exclusively drawn from advertising.

From autumn 1988, satellite television channels have been available in most parts of the country, through over-the-air retransmission by, in most cases, ERT: at the end of 1990, for example, Athenians could watch Super Channel, Eurosport, MTV, CNN, RAI Uno, RAI Due, TVE-International, Horizon, TV 5, RIK (Greek Cypriot), besides the three state channels and the fourteen private channels with limited or round-the-clock programmes. Except for a few neighbourhoods in Athens and in Thrace, Greece was not cabled; moreover, the new telematic media had not been introduced by late 1990.

## Policies for the press and broadcasting

The media have for a long time been at the centre of the political debate in Greece. At the beginning of the 1990s, three issues were being discussed:

— inadequacy of the legal framework for both the print and the electronic media,

— cross-ownership and media concentration,

— objectivity of news and current affairs programmes in the state-owned broadcast media.

The existing legal framework was inadequate and outdated. From the provisions listed above, many were never applied or have repeatedly been violated. ERT did not have the national broadcasting monopoly as many radio and television stations covered most areas of the country. The dismissal of ERT's board in late 1990 was not based on the recommendation of the National Radio and Television Council (ESR), and the latter's recommendation for a new board was legally inappropriate, as it included 27 names for 9 positions rather than 3 names for each of the 9 members. Moreover, all private and municipal radio and television stations operated without licences as the ESR had failed to act upon their applications for new licences or for renewals. More than a year after its creation, the ESR had not drafted a code of ethics. The rules issued by the ESR for the 1990 election campaign were overruled by the State Court. Most private television stations were known to practically belong to one owner each, through ways which circumvented the 25% upper limit per individual; among the owners of the two stations which were given three-month trial licences in 1989 and the ones which operated stations in 1990 were the two press groups with an accumulation of so many convictions for press crimes. The 50% European production quota was not observed. The television stations did not invest in Greek movies nor did the private ones contribute to the national organizations for the blind. Advertisements often ran for more than ten minutes per hour in prime time programmes, and many interrupted them. Sometimes, products were advertised for more than the upper limit allowed in radio stations.

The reason for the inadequacy of the legal framework for the print media was that it was introduced a long time ago; publishers and journalists have resisted the introduction of any new comprehensive law in recent years. On the other hand, the laws on broadcasting were introduced under pressure for deregulation: so inadequately prepared, the legislators felt ideologically compelled to limit private and municipal broadcasting, but no subsequent government was willing to enforce this legislation in order to avoid conflict with the powerful media. By the end of 1990, it was reported that the New Democracy government was thinking of adapting the framework to reality at least by legalizing national private broadcasting.

Other countries have made legislation to discourage or forbid the concentration of media. In Greece the laws gave preference to the media companies in granting the licences for private radio and television stations. The result was the creation of a powerful oligopoly around the five shareholders of the most successful private television channel, Mega. The traditional publishers Lambrakis and Tegopoulos, and the new publishers Alafouzos, Bobolas, and Vardinoyannis, own five national dailies with nearly half the total circulation; their media groups gross nearly half the total turnover of the non-state media and make more than half of their total profits; in fact, Lambrakis is the country's largest private group, Bobolas is second and Tegopoulos fourth. Finally, it has been documented that they agreed to use the other media they owned to promote their television channel. Only marginal political parties and some intellectuals have criticized this arrangement as a threat to real freedom of the press; in vain, since the three main political parties appeared satisfied with it.

The main problem of the state electronic media has been the lack of impartiality in the news and other political broadcasts. Both radio and television "grew up" in non-democratic periods of Greek history: radio in the Metaxas dictatorship and the German occupation, and television in the Papadopoulos/Ioannidis dictatorship. Hence, these mass media became a propaganda tool of the government, as has been the case in all dictatorships. The democratic governments which succeeded the dictatorships fell to the temptation of using the same tactics.

Therefore, news coverage was often reminiscent of Third World or non-democratic countries.

A decisive effort to separate the state media from direct government control was made between the summer of 1989 and the spring of 1990. Then, and for the first time since 1952, Greece was governed by coalition governments. The latter created the ESR, with eleven members selected in such a way as to exclude a one-party majority. However, instead of using the opportunity to appoint an independent ERT management, the three parties agreed to share the positions on ERT's board and its various managerial positions among themselves, so as to ensure loyalty. Still, the end result was the most balanced newscasts state television and radio had ever produced. When a one-party (conservative) government came to power in mid-1990, it quickly did away with the short-lived ERT spring. Using ministerial decisions, whose doubtful legality was challenged in the courts, ESR and ERT boards were broadened to 19 and 11 members in such a way as to give the government control over the two bodies; consequently, in all ERT managerial positions the loyal New Democracy journalists replaced the ones chosen by the ecumenical government, including those who were favourable to the conservative party. Nevertheless, Greek public opinion was less concerned with ERT's partiality at the close of 1990 than ten years before, because the private channels filled the gap. In fact, it was noticeable that the state media made no effort to respond to the competition of the private radio stations and television channels, thus quickly losing their predominant position and, consequently, their advertising share. So, by the end of 1990, ERT, still with its 7 000 odd personnel (including hundreds of journalists who did not work but just received a paycheck so as to be under government control), was running huge deficits which the state's budget had to cover. This situation led to government plans for merging some radio stations and privatizing ET-2, something that had not been implemented by early 1991.


## Statistics

(1 ECU = 200 drs.)

| | |
|---|---|
| Population | 10 m. |
| Number of households | 3 m. |

| | |
|---|---|
| Number of national radio channels | 4 |
| Number of national television channels | 2–5 |
| Number of local television channels | ca. 20 |
| Number of local radio stations | ca. 600 |
| Number of national political daily newspapers | 16 |
| Number of regional political daily newspapers | 2 |
| Television penetration | 99% |
| Video penetration | 47% |

| | |
|---|---|
| Advertising (1990, ECU) | 269 m. |
| Television | 115 m. |
| Magazines | 81 m. |
| Newspapers | 51 m. |
| Radio | 22 m. |

Greater Athens and Salonica TV audience (AGB, December 1990)

| | |
|---|---|
| Mega | 32% |
| Antenna | 24% |
| ET-1 | 16% |
| ET-2 | 7% |
| Other Greek channels | 14% |
| Satellite channels | 3% |
| Video | 4% |

Average daily circulation of the 10 largest national political dailies (October 1990)

| All dailies | | 838 890 |
|---|---|---|

| Title | Political profile | Circulation |
|---|---|---|
| Morning dailies | | 72 282 |
| Kathimerini | centre-right | 36 043 |
| Rizospastis | KKE organ | 25 673 |
| Others | | 10 566 |
| Evening dailies | | 766 608 |
| Eleftheros Typos | centre-right | 170 050 |
| Nea | centre-left | 143 603 |
| Eleftherotypia | centre-left | 114 145 |
| Ethnos | centre-left | 94 660 |
| Apogevmatini | centre-right | 75 571 |
| Avriani | centre-left | 47 314 |
| Epikairotita | centre-left | 42 208 |
| Niki | centre-left | 39 786 |

# References

Dimitras, Panayote Elias (1988a, 1990) 'Griechenland: Radio und Fernsehen in Griechenland' in Hans Bredow Institut, (ed.) Internationales Handbuch für Rundfunk und Fernsehen. Hamburg: Nomos Verlag.

Dimitras, Panayote Elias (1988b) "Grèce", Cinemaction/Télérama Les Télévisions du Monde. Paris: Cerf-Corlet.

Dimitras, Panayote Elias and Doulkeri, Tessa (1986) "Greece" in Hans Kleinsteuber, Dennis McQuail, and Karen Siune (eds) Electronic Media and Politics in Western Europe: A Euromedia Research Group Handbook of National Systems, Frankfurt: Campus Verlag.

Doulkeri, Tessa (1979). Radio and television, legal and social problems (in Greek). Athens: Papazisis.

Katsoudas, Dimitrios K. (1987). "The Media: the State and Broadcasting" in Kevin Featherstone and Dimitrios K. Katsoudas, Political Change in Greece: Before and After the Colonels. London, Croom Helm.

Mayer, Kostas (1957–1960). History of the Greek Press (in Greek), three volumes. Athens: Dimopoulos.

# 8

# Ireland

*Mary Kelly and Wolfgang Truetzschler*

## National profile

In area the Republic of Ireland is 70 283 km$^2$. With 3 540 643 inhabitants Ireland has the second smallest population of the twelve European Community (EC) countries. Following a decline by almost a half in its population since the mid 19th century, firstly by famine and then mainly through emigration, the population began to increase in the 1960s. In the decade ending in 1981, the population increased by 16%. This was in the main due to a high birth rate, but net immigration also contributed.

The country is not a densely populated one, with fifty inhabitants per sq. km., and 44% living in rural areas (i.e. in areas which have less than 1 500 inhabitants), however, urbanization has increased over the last two decades. The population is not evenly distributed, with more than half the population living in the eastern region. The high concentration in Dublin (29% of the population lives in the city and its environment), particularly contributes to this regional imbalance. The second largest city, Cork, has less than 4% of the population.

There are two official languages in the State, namely Irish and English, but English is the mother tongue for the vast majority of the people. Only 2% of the population live in the Gaeltacht, the native Irish-speaking areas situated mainly on the west coast of Ireland. According to the 1986 Census results, just under 30% of the population can understand Irish, although this figure includes those who can only read but cannot speak Irish.

Although Ireland has traditionally been seen as a predominantly agricultural country, continuing industrialization is changing this. The percentage of the employed labour force in agriculture has declined from 35% in 1961 to just over 15% in 1988. The proportion employed in industry is 28% and in the services sector 57%. The share of women in the workforce in 1988 was 32% (the counterpart figure for the EC Twelve is 39%). The unemployment rate of around 18% (1990) is one of the highest in Europe. Ireland's industrial development is that of dependent rather than indigenous industrialization, and Ireland's economic structure is similar to that of other peripheral European countries, such as Greece, Spain and Southern Italy (Wickham 1986). Central to the state's industrial strategy since 1960 has been the attraction of export-oriented foreign companies to invest in Ireland.

In comparison with other European countries, Ireland is relatively poor, due to such factors as late and dependent industrialization, a high birth rate until relatively recently, and high unemployment.

Despite this relative poverty, Irish families have been willing to invest quite heavily in buying their own homes and in buying or renting broadcasting equipment. Around 80% of all adults live in owner-occupied homes and of the 1 044 800 households, 96% have a television set, 32% have cable television, and 38% have VCR-equipment.

Regarding the political system, the Irish Constitution (1937) declares Ireland to be a "sovereign, independent, democratic state". Ireland's political culture is a predominantly Catholic and a rather conservative one, a fact illustrated at every general election when approximately 80 to 90% of the electorate vote for one of the three conservative political parties Fianna Fail, Fine Gael and the more recently formed Progressive Democrats, an off-shoot of both Fine Gael and Fianna Fail. The two more left-wing parties, the Labour Party and the Workers Party, usually receive around 10–15% of the votes. Subsequent to the last election, Fianna Fail and the Progressive Democrats formed a coalition government. There are no substantial differences between the Government's policies and those put forward by the main opposition party, Fine Gael.

Traditionally, there is no strong left or agrarian political party as political debate in Ireland has tended to be in nationalist rather than class terms. All parties are committed to promoting industrialization, even dependent industrialization, "in the national interest", in particular in the hope of economic regeneration and a consequent reduction in unemployment and emigration. The predominant mode in public policy decisions since the 1960s which has emphasized economic and commercial rather than cultural criteria has also influenced decisions regarding the development of the new electronic media. Thus while cultural nationalism was the main thrust in the establishment of Irish radio (1926) and television (1961), decisions on the new media in the 1980s and 1990s are characterized by a strong commercial bias.

## Development of the press and broadcasting since 1945

The three major national newspapers, as well as the major regional paper and most local papers, are legacies from the late 19th and early 20th centuries. The three major dailies are the *Irish Times*, the *Irish Independent*, the *Irish Press*; while the major regional daily is the *Cork Examiner*. When initially established each was aligned with a particular political tradition and party: the *Irish Times*, established in 1859, represented the Unionist tradition; the *Irish Independent*, established in 1905, represented the constitutional   Nationalist tradition and Fine Gael; while the *Irish Press*, established in 1931, represented the Republican and Fianna Fail traditions.

Since the 1960s, in the Irish newspaper industry some gradual changes may be noted. One trend is the move away from party partisanship as newspapers seek to increase circulation. The *Independent* and *Press* newspaper groups are now less clearly identified with a political party. They articulate a mainly conservative socio-political and economic consensus which reflects the lack of a strong left-wing tradition in Irish society. The *Irish Times*  takes an independent political stance, and is more liberal on moral issues than either of the other two dailies. Left-wing, Republican and Irish-language weekly newspapers are published (the latter, *Anois*, is subsidized by the State), but sell to only a small readership.

A second trend is the growth in the circulation of some papers and the curtailing of others. While Irish newspaper readership is high by European standards, it is differentiated by class and region. The *Irish Times*, which caters for an upmarket readership, has gained considerable ground with the growth of a professionalized and urbanized middle class, especially in Dublin. At the beginning of the 1980s the *Sunday Tribune* was launched to serve the same market, and in 1989 the *Sunday Business Post*. Both continue.

The *Irish Independent* group has shown considerable skill in continuing to serve not only the middle and lower classes with its existing titles, but also in developing new titles attractive to, among others, the working class. The *Sunday World*, launched in the mid 1970s, is a popular, brash and downmarket tabloid. In the late 1980s, working with Express Newspapers (UK), the *Independent* group brought out an Irish edition of the *Star*, to compete in particular with the highly popular *Mirror* imported from Britain.

While the *Press* group also serves the middle-class market, its readership has been more rurally based than that of the *Independent*. With rural decline the *Press's* circulation and advertising revenue also stagnated, leading to financial problems and providing the context for the selling of roughly half of the *Press* to an American newspaper publisher in 1989.

*Public service broadcasting*

Broadcasting began in Ireland with the establishment of an Irish radio service in 1926.

Radio was under direct state control until the passing of the 1960

Broadcasting Authority Act which established the state-sponsored (public service broadcasting) Radio Telefis Eireann (RTE) Authority. The Act also gave the RTE Authority control over the new Irish television service. Irish broadcasting has since its inception relied both on advertising revenues and licence fees to fund its public service broadcasting service. Monopoly state control of broadcasting was abolished in 1989, with the licensing of private commercial radio services.

The 1960 Act brought new life to Irish broadcasting. Not only did Irish television begin, but in 1972 Raidio na Gaeltachta was established, transmitting Irish-language programmes; in 1978 a second television channel began transmitting, and in the following year a second radio station. Both radio and television, however, faced the problem of fostering Irish culture and home-produced programmes in the context of openness to strong foreign broadcasting competition especially from Britain. In 1991 over 60% of all television homes are in "multi channel" areas, i.e. ones which can receive British television either off air or via cable.

The founding of a second RTE television channel (RTE 2, now known as Network 2) in 1978 was a direct result of demands by "single channel" areas to equalize the television services being offered in different parts of the country. This decision did not fully satisfy these demands, and after the operation over a period of ten years of illegal "deflector" systems enabling the reception of British television, the Government in 1989 awarded licences to install and operate a network of multipoint microwave (television retransmission) distribution systems (MMDS) in those parts of the country in which viewers are currently not able to receive cable television.

RTE, like many other small states, has traditionally relied heavily on foreign-produced programming. RTE has endeavoured to reduce the proportion of imported programmes to 50% of programming time, and through an increase in the production of cheap but popular programmes RTE has managed to achieve a reduction in its reliance on foreign-produced software from 65% in 1984 to, according to RTE, 53% in 1988.

*Private broadcasting services*

Until the end of 1988, Ireland's privately owned broadcasting services traditionally consisted of unlicensed or pirate radio stations (see Mulryan 1988). However, at the end of 1988, the Irish parliament, after many delays, passed the Radio and Television Act 1988. This Act enables the setting up of a private commercial broadcasting service. Events have been taking place very rapidly since the enactment of the new law. A new regulatory authority for private broadcasters, the Independent Radio and Television Commission (IRTC), was established in October 1988, and several licences for local radio were awarded by the IRTC during 1989. The franchise for a new national private television service, TV3, was awarded in April 1989. TV3 has stated that it expects to be operational by the end of 1991.

## The press

### Legal framework

The press in Ireland, unlike the broadcast media, is not subject to specific legislation, i.e. to a specific press law. The right to freedom of the press is derived from the express right of freedom of expression as enshrined in the Constitution. However, this right is subject to a number of restrictions arising out of considerations of public order and morality, the authority of the State, etc.

Furthermore, there are a large number of statutes with implications for press freedom, such as, for example, the Official Secrets Act. Overall, the right to freedom of expression, which encompasses the press, "is so heavily circumscribed by conditions and limitations as to virtually negate it" (Boyle and McConagle 1988:10). There is neither a press council nor a specific right to reply incorporated in the various statutes that are of relevance to the press. However, some newspapers have voluntarily appointed "newspaper ombudsmen" as a means of investigating complaints by the readers and of avoiding litigation which may result in the Courts awarding high damages for libel.

Monopoly formation in the press industry is subject to specific cartel legislation. This enables the Minister for Industry and Commerce to prohibit any changes in the control of newspapers of more than 30% of the shares in the respective newspaper. To date there have been no occasions on which these laws have been invoked in connection with the Irish newspaper press.

### Ownership

Even though Irish law does not explicitly restrict foreign investment in Irish media services, foreign ownership of the press in Ireland is, as yet, limited but growing. The main one is the 1989 acquisition of a controlling 50% share in the loss-making *IrishPress* Newspapers by the US company Ingersoll Publications. The remainder continues to be owned by the de Valera family. As well as that, Eurexpansion, a Belgian subsidiary of the French publishing Groupe Expansion, owns a 50% shareholding in the *Sunday Business Post*. The tabloid newspaper the *Star* is jointly owned by Ireland's Independent Newspapers and Express Newspapers (UK).

Regarding concentration in ownership of the press, the major media concern in Ireland is Independent Newspapers plc, a company headed by

Ireland's only "press baron", Dr Tony O'Reilly. Apart from the titles already mentioned, Independent Newspapers publishes approximately 20% of the provincial press. In November 1990 Independent Newspapers bought 29.99% of the shares of the *Sunday Tribune*. Thus this media concern now has control of, or a controlling interest in, 75% of the entire Irish Sunday newspaper market. The company also has numerous interests in several countries in the fields of outdoor advertising and publishing. The *Irish Times* is owned by the Irish Times Trust, established in 1973 when the existing directors sold their shares to it. The objective of the trust is to secure the long-term independence of the paper and its liberal and democratic journalistic goals. A board of Trustees was appointed drawn from academic, public, business and trade union backgrounds. The *Cork Examiner* was bought by the Crosbie family in 1872, and has remained in their hands since.

## Financing

Irish newspapers have two sources of finance: "over the counter" sales (rather than subscriptions) and advertising. The total amount of money Irish people spent on newspapers in 1990 amounted to approximately IR£ 135.5 million, the amount received from advertising in 1990 came to IR£ 96.7 million (94% of which was earned by the national and 6% by the provincial/regional press). There are no subsidies for newspapers in Ireland, although limited financial support is available for Irish-language newspapers.

## Structure of the press

Traditionally, Ireland has a very high readership and a fairly large number of newspapers for its population: net sales of national newspapers combined total around five million copies a week. There are five national dailies and two national evening newspapers, as well as four national Sunday newspapers. The Irish regional or provincial press consists of approximately forty newspapers which tend to be published on a weekly basis.

Nearly all Irish newspapers are politically conservative and, apart from Ireland's most successful newspaper the *Sunday World* (and the *Star*), there are no tabloid newspapers of the more sensationalist variety. This is probably due to the wide availability of British newspapers (especially the tabloid ones), which can be bought all over Ireland and which are cheaper than Irish papers, as, unlike the UK, Ireland imposes a 10% value-added tax on the printing of newspapers.

**Electronic media**

*Legal framework*

Broadcasting in Ireland is mainly regulated by three Acts (see Truetzschler 1991b): the Broadcasting Authority Acts 1960–79, which regulate the public broadcaster RTE; the Radio and Television Act 1988, which contains the regulations applicable to private commercial broadcasting; and the recently (July 1990) enacted Broadcasting Act 1990, which, inter alia, facilitates the implementation of the EC Directive on Television Broadcasting. The content of foreign satellite television relayed on cable or MMDS (multipoint microwave distribution system) is currently not subject to any specific regulations, apart from the fact that the relaying of all television channels requires a licence.

Cable television is governed by the Wireless Telegraphy (Wired Broadcast Relay Licence) Regulations 1974, as amended in 1988; the new MMDS is subject to the Wireless Telegraphy (Television Programme Retransmission) Regulations 1989. Apart from these specific Acts and Regulations, other statutes such as Contempt of Court, Censorship, Defamation, Copyright, Official Secrets Act, Public Order, etc. also apply to broadcasting.

The three Acts contain fairly detailed and explicit regulations for private and public broadcasters. The laws also enable censorship by the Government in relation to "the troubles" in Northern Ireland. Advertising on RTE is restricted to 7.5% of total programming time; private broadcasters may broadcast exactly double this amount.

In practice the main difference between private broadcasters and RTE is not so much in the regulations, but more in the monitoring (of the adherence to the regulations) of individual stations by the Government and by the IRTC. Thus the public broadcaster has always been subject to fairly close  regulation (and even closer scrutinization by politicians). In conrast, the IRTC, whose main function is to ensure the operation of broadcasting services other than those of RTE, has on occasions taken a very liberal interpretation of the adherence by private broadcasters to the existing regulations.

The most recent piece of broadcasting legislation, the Broadcasting Act 1990, was designed by the Government primarily in order to ensure a profitable private broadcasting sector. The Act limits the amount of advertising revenue the RTE can earn in any year to the same amount it receives in total licence fee revenue in that year. In effect this means that RTE's income has been reduced by 10%.

*Structure and organization*

RTE operates two national television channels (RTE 1 and Network 2) and four national radio services: Radio 1, with a traditional public service programming mix; FM 2, a 24-hour popular music channel; the Irish language Raidio na Gaeltachta; FM 3 with its classical music programmes. RTE has also embarked on a joint venture with Radio Luxembourg, namely the operation of a new radio station, Atlantic 252, since 1989. The station is a commercial wall-to-wall popular music station, financed by British advertising and transmitting its programmes from Ireland to Britain on long wave.

Regarding private commercial broadcasting services, currently there is one national radio station (Century 100) and 23 local or county radio stations. There is no local television in Ireland, apart from the occasional campus broadcasts of a Dublin university, and the local cable television programmes run by the Cork cable TV company.

Cable television relays the Irish and British national television channels as well as between 6 and 10 (mainly) English-language satellite television channels. Pay TV may be provided on cable TV, but to date only one cable operator relays a pay movie channel to its subscribers. MMDS is only being implemented in the first half of 1991. Annual subscription fees for cable TV/MMDS amount to just under IR£ 90.

*Ownership and economic aspects*

The public broadcaster is financed both by licence fees and by advertising. Due to the introduction of the ceiling on its advertising income, as outlined above, and due to the sale of 50% of its shares in Cablelink (Ireland's largest cable operator; see below), RTE's revenue probably decreased by around IR£10–12 million in 1990. The loss of a substantial proportion of its advertising income has forced RTE to implement a number of cutbacks in its staffing and services.

The national radio station Century 100 is owned by a number of well-known Irish business men, including James Stafford, who has a share in Atlantic Satellites, the company awarded the franchise for the Irish satellite (see below). In 1990 Century 100 was reported to have accumulated losses of IR£ 3–4 million since the start of its operations in mid-1989. Since then Capital Radio, London has provided the station with loan capital of IR£ 1.5 million as part of a management contract for Century Radio.

Ownership of private local radio is indeed "local" and diverse: it includes local business people, teachers, farmers and farming organizations, lawyers, accountants, Irish-language groups, former pirate radio operators, former RTE employees, in short, people from all walks of life. Some of the new radio stations have received the backing of Irish financial institutions and/or of successful Irish entrepreneurs.

Local newspapers are involved in seven of the 23 of the local radio stations; shareholdings by the respective local paper are restricted to 25% of the shares in local radio stations. The Churches are minority shareholders in five of the local radio stations. The national press has to date not become active in private radio.

It is in no way certain that all of these new broadcasting services will survive, let alone be profitable. It is likely, therefore, that a clearer and more distinct pattern of ownership of private broadcasting services may evolve over the next few years due to an amalgamation of radio stations or monopoly formation in the area of independent broadcasting.

The franchise for the national private television service TV3 was awarded in April 1989 to the Windmill Lane Consortium, a group which includes the independent film/video production company Windmill Lane and, as the main Irish commercial investor, the Jefferson Smurfit Group, Ireland's largest industrial concern (in terms of annual turnover). The initial funding needed to set up TV3 is IR£ 30 million, an amount that would suggest an involvement by foreign investors.

Cable TV in Ireland is provided by 43 cable TV operators, the biggest of which is the firm Cablelink with over 80% of all cable TV subscribers. Licences for MMDS were awarded by the Minister for Communications in October 1989. There are seven companies or "MMDS franchisees" each of which has been awarded exclusive licences for MMDS in specific areas within the state. The seven franchisees consist of five companies active in cable television, including the firm Cablelink, the other two are newspaper publishers which form part of Independent Newspapers plc.

*Programming and audiences*

The programming on RTE Television is one that is usual for public service broadcasters, i.e. one with a fairly strong emphasis on news and current affairs programmes (see CSO, 1990). RTE's scheduling of programmes is noteworthy in that RTE has always operated in a highly competitive environment and is therefore highly skilled in arranging programme schedules to compete with foreign stations. Irish-language programming on RTE television is currently estimated to amount to only 3% of programming time.

RTE radio programmes are discussed above. The  programming on private commercial radio stations is essentially music-led, i.e. with the exception of the community stations and a few of the rural radio stations, these stations broadcast wall-to-wall popular music, interspersed by advertising and by the occasional news bulletin and short, cheaply produced current affairs programmes designed to fulfil the legal requirement that

20% of programming time be devoted to news and current affairs. There are very few Irish-language programmes on private radio.

Concerning listenership to radio, the latest survey data are summarized in the statistics section. The figures show that RTE radio is still the most popular radio station in the state, although local stations have made some inroads into RTE's listenership. The figures for local radio are the national average and hide the fact that some local stations have an even smaller listenership. The two RTE stations Radio na Gaeltachta and FM3 are not included in the usual audience surveys. The national listenership of these stations is estimated to be in the region of only 1–2% of adults (but around 26% in the Gaeltacht for Raidio na Gaeltachta).

*Satellites*

The franchise for the Irish direct broadcasting by satellite (DBS) service was awarded in 1985 to Atlantic Satellites, a company which was originally owned by the Irish entrepreneur James Stafford, but of which 87% of the shares were sold to the US company Hughes Communications subsequent to the awarding of the franchise. Very little has been heard of the company and its plans since 1985. What is known is that Atlantic Satellites was involved in negotiations with British Satellite Broadcasting (BSB) prior to the latter's merger with Sky Television.

The company is now actively pursuing the telecommunications side of the satellite, especially the establishment of a privately owned telecommunications link between Europe and the US. With the increasing deregulation of telecommunications in Europe, this has now become a more realistic option than in 1985.

*Telematic media*

The only Irish teletext service available is RTE's Aertel. (The British services Oracle and Ceefax can also be viewed in Ireland.) Approximately 15% of TV households (up from just under 2% in 1987) can receive Aertel, and the latest (1990) survey data suggest that 79% of these use Aertel at least once a week. The service carries information on news, finance, sports, weather, and farming, but no subtitling of television programmes as yet.

Irish videotex services have been undertaken primarily as private business ventures and are aimed at specific interest groups. As well as that a company formed by Telecom France and Telecom Eireann is introducing 5000 Minitel terminals from March 1991 onwards. This will be the first service aimed not only at the business market, but also at the general Irish consumer market.

Finally, Telecom Eireann (TE) is actively pursuing the development of an Irish ISDN service. Currently, the company has started a trial of ISDN within Dublin, and it intends to provide a commercial ISDN service by 1992–93. The company is also planning a trial (in 2–3 years) of a broadband ISDN.

## Policies for the press and broadcasting

### Actors and issues

The main actors in the press include the two associations of newspaper owners: the more powerful National Newspapers of Ireland  (NNI) and the somewhat less significant Provincial Newspapers Association of Ireland. Two other important actors are the press concern Independent Newspapers, especially its chairman and main shareholder Ireland's Dr Tony O'Reilly, and the chairman and owner of Ingersoll Publications, Mr Ralph Ingersoll.

Over the last few years these actors have been concerned repeatedly with a number of issues. One of these is the size of damages awarded by juries in libel actions against newspapers. The two representative bodies have therefore called for a reform of the defamation law, the main provisions of which are seen to be archaic. Currently the Irish Law Reform Commission is preparing a report on the updating of the relevant legal provisions, a report which is expected to be finalized in July 1991.

Other issues of concern to newspapers include the introduction of new technology in the printing of newspapers, such as direct input by journalists and the resulting job losses primarily amongst printers. Some of the daily newspapers have attempted to resolve this issue with some success, others have had to face occasional industrial unrest.

Another technological change, namely the development of colour printing in Irish daily, Sunday and in some provincial newspapers, has been a very successful innovation in that it has led to an increase in advertising revenue of just under 30% in the period 1987–90. This increase in revenue may have been aided by the curbing of RTE's advertising revenue as detailed above. In fact newspaper proprietors have called over years for the restriction of RTE's (in their view) dominant position on the Irish advertising market. The 1990 Broadcasting Act is partially a result of continuous lobbying of the Government by the newspaper owners.

As was outlined above, some newspapers have become active to a limited extent in other media activities, including local radio. The introduction of private commercial radio to date has not greatly affected the press. The national newspapers have remained completely unaffected and the provincial newspapers remain a viable alternative to local radio for advertisers.

Three major actors are involved in the formulation of broadcasting policy at present: public broadcasters, the Government and private operators. Over the last few years the Government has aligned itself with private broadcasters, as exemplified in the curbing of RTE advertising revenue. The extent to which the Government may further curb RTE in order to redirect advertising income from RTE to TV3 is a possible issue for the future. The possibility of TV3 getting into financial difficulties is a very real one given the limited advertising pool available in a country with a population of but 3.5 million.

In the light of financial constraints, private radio operators are beginning to form networking groups. Thus they have formed an advertising sales network, there are preliminary signs of programme networking, and two neighbouring stations are merging. These patterns are likely to continue. Another pressure group on the local radio scene, community radio, continues to press for the licensing of neighbourhood radio.

Another quite influential actor is the group of Irish-language speakers. Speakers of Ireland's first official language are fairly well served in terms of radio, but the same cannot be said for television. As a result of pressure exerted by this actor, there are Government plans to set up a television service that would broadcast programmes in Irish for two hours a day, seven days a week. A decision on this, however, has yet to be announced.

Multinational actors, although on the increase over the last two years, are still quite limited in terms of their overall number (see Truetzschler 1991a). The advent of TV3 may change this (see above). The licences for private radio services are mainly in the hands of Irish companies. In fact, the broadcasting contracts between these companies and the Independent Radio and Television Commission, IRTC, specify that any change in ownership must be referred to the RTC, whose decisions in turn are subject to approval by the Minister for Communications.

An actor with great interest in television broadcasting is the Irish film and television programme industry.

Other actors include the advertising industry, which is mainly in the hands of the multinational advertising agencies and which was one of the main pressure groups in favour of the introduction of private radio and television services. The Churches are also showing an increasing interest in the broadcast media, and in October 1989 set up an Irish Churches Council for Television and Radio Affairs. Political parties and trade union groups are not directly involved in any of the groups which have received local radio licences, although a number of licence holders are known to have connections with political parties, especially the main Government party, Fianna Fail.

*Policy trends*

The legislation outlined above shows that Ireland has no explicit or coherent national broadcasting policy. Similarly, Ireland does not have any overall media policy, one that encompasses all mass media. The wider cultural and social implications for Irish society of changes in broadcasting are rarely debated; decisions tend to be made (and justified to the public) in line with economic and commercial criteria.

National broadcasting policy is fairly consistent with European tendencies. Generally there is much emphasis on the economic and financial benefits of EC membership for Ireland, even though Ireland has fared rather badly within the EC over the last fifteen years in comparison to every other EC country (NESC 1989). The licensing of private broadcasting operations and the regulation of broadcasting in Ireland reflect current European trends, such as abolition of state monopolies, privatization of state enterprises, commercialization of broadcasting. In fact it can be argued that Ireland has simply copied its European partners and has privatized the airwaves without developing a specifically thought-out policy appropriate to a small state like Ireland. Concerning the recent EC Directive and Council of Europe Convention on Television Broadcasting, existing Irish media law is broadly in line with these, and those elements of the Directive not yet provided for in the law are contained in the Broadcasting Act 1990 outlined above.

*Telecommunications policy*

Basically, Telecom Eireann (TE) is used by Government as an instrument of industrial policy, especially with the intention of attracting foreign investment by offering advanced technology facilities. TE has no input into broadcasting other than in the provision of certain technical facilities. Most of the transmission facilities in the state are in fact owned and operated by RTE, but their use is subject to approval by the Department of Communications, and must comply with the relevant laws and regulations. However, TE's role may change in future, considering that it now owns 60% of the shares in Cablelink, Ireland's largest cable television operator.

## Statistics

(IR£ 1 = 1.3 ECU)
Population
Inhabitants                                                          3.5 m.
Households (estimated)                                               1.0 m.
Inhabitants/land area                                            50 per km$^2$

Broadcasting
Television household penetration (estimated)                         96%
Cost of licence fee March 1991
Black and white                                                   IR£ 44
Colour                                                            IR£ 62
Number of national television channels
Public channels                    2              (RTE 1, Network 2)
Private channel                    1        (TV3 planned for 1991/92)
Number of hours of television broadcast (1988)                      7 163

Number of national radio channels
Public              Radio 1, Network 2, FM 3, Radio na Gaeltacht
Private                                               Century 100
Number of local radio stations
Public                                                                1
Private                                                               23

Shares of national radio listenership in %

| Channel | Weekdays | Saturdays | Sundays |
|---|---|---|---|
| RTE Radio 1 | 44 | 38 | 36 |
| RTE 2 FM | 23 | 23 | 23 |
| Century 100 | 8 | 10 | 7 |
| Local stations | 24 | 30 | 34 |

(Source: JNLR 1990)

New electronic media
% of TV households with:
Video cassette recorders                                             38
Teletext                                                             15
Cable television                                                     32

Advertising
Market Shares of Television Channels in Ireland

| Channel | Market share in % |
|---|---|
| RTE 1 and Network 2 | 48 |
| BBC 1 | 16 |
| UTV | 14 |
| Others (BBC 2, Channel 4, satellites) | 22 |

(Source: RTE, January 1991)

The press
Newspaper circulation of 10 largest newspapers in 1990

| National dailies | Circulation |
|---|---|
| Irish Independent | 149 620 |
| Evening Herald | 100 220 |
| Evening Press | 99 467 |
| Irish Times | 93 187 |
| Star | 76 752 |
| Irish Press | 60 635 |
| National Sundays | |
| Sunday World | 327 104 |
| Sunday Independent | 225 468 |
| Sunday Press | 207 852 |
| Sunday Tribune | 102 261 |

Media economics
Analysis of Ireland's media revenue (IR£ million)

| Media groups | 1988 | 1989 | 1990 |
|---|---|---|---|
| National press | 64.7 | 80.2 | 90.6 |
| Regional press | 4.7 | 5.9 | 6.1 |
| Consumer press | 10.1 | 10.9 | 11.2 |
| RTE TV | 47.9 | 51.8 | 51.2 |
| RTE Radio 1 & 2FM | 14.3 | 18.0 | 16.2 |
| Outdoor | 11.6 | 12.4 | 13.3 |
| Totals | 153.3 | 179.2 | 188.6** |

(Source: Advertising Statistics Ireland)
** + appr. IR£ 5–9 million for private radio

# References

Boyle, K. and McGonagle, M. (1988) Press Freedom and Libel. Dublin: National Newspapers of Ireland.

CSO (Central Statistics Office) (1990) Statistical Abstract 1990. Dublin: The Stationery Office.

Curtin Dorgan Associates (1990) The Irish Film and TV Programme Production Industry. Dublin: Curtin Dorgan Associates.

JNLR (Joint National Listenership Research) (1990). Dublin: Market Research Bureau of Ireland.

Mulryan, P. (1988) Radio, Radio: The Story of Independent, Local, Community and Pirate Radio. Dublin: Borderline Publications.

NESC (National Social and Economic Council) (1989) Ireland in the European Community: Performance, Prospect and Strategy. Dublin: NESC.

RTE (Radio Telefis Eireann) (1991) The Television Market in Ireland. Dublin: RTE.

Truetzschler, W. (1991a) "Foreign Investment in the Media in Ireland", Irish Communications Review, 1(1).

Truetzschler, W. (1991b) "Broadcasting Law and Broadcasting Policy in Ireland", Irish Communications Review, 1(1).

Wickham, J. (1986) "Industrialization, Work and Unemployment'" in P. Clancy et al. (eds), Ireland: A Sociological Profile. Dublin: Institute of Public Administration.

# 9

# Italy

## Gianpietro Mazzoleni

### National profile

Among Europe's largest countries, Italy is also one of the most heavily populated. In 1990 the number of inhabitants was about 57.6 million over an area of 301 280 km$^2$, with a density of 189 inhabitants per km$^2$. About 30% of the population live in 49 towns with more than 100 000 inhabitants. Four metropolitan cities (Rome, Milan, Naples, Turin) have a population of over 1 million.

The natural population growth is steadily declining: 2.2 per thousand in 1990, compared to the 7.4 of 1951. The structure of the population is characterized by a high percentage of people in the middle and high age groups. The increase in the high age group is common to other European countries.

Around the country's borders there are a few French, German and Serbian minorities with a total of less than half a million people. Despite their limited numbers, these language minorities enjoy privileges such as special radio and TV broadcasts, besides newspapers and schools in their own languages.

Geographically, Italy is surrounded in the North by the Alps and in the centre and South by the Mediterranean Sea. The reception of foreign TV broadcasts only recently overcame these natural obstacles. The mountainous character of large areas (one third of domestic territory) and the long distances (more than 2 000 km from Milan to Palermo) have had an impact on the development policies of the mass media in the country.

Since the late 1940s, Italy has been governed by coalition governments, mostly led by the Christian Democratic Party (DC), the centre-moderate biggest party. The opposition has never succeeded in gaining executive power. The long lasting dominance of the same parties favoured their penetration into almost all sectors of daily life especially in the economic sectors (banks, finance, industry) and the information industry (newspapers, radio and TV, culture).

A further feature of the Italian political system is the *lottizzazione*, i.e. the partitioning of power among all parties, opposition included. The TV network RAI UNO and radio Channel RADIO 2 are considered to be under the control of the DC, RAI DUE and RADIO 1 are allegedly in the hands of the lay and socialist parties and RAI TRE in communist hands. The parties' influence is also extensive in press organizations, even if not as formally as in the public broadcasting company.

Italy's economic system is characterized by an extensive State participation ranging from banking and finance to agriculture. In the field of media and electronic communications, the State no longer holds a radio and television monopoly; this was rescinded in the 1990 Broadcasting Act. However, it still controls telecommunications and the postal services. The running of the public broadcasting channels is contracted to RAI and the telephone service to SIP. The postal service is still directly managed by the Ministry of PTT. The press sector as a whole is independent of State participation and works in a competitive environment. Following a long economic crisis in the early 1980s, negotiations between the government and the publishers led to Parliament passing Law 416/1981 which opened the way for special financial help by the State. For the first time in Italian press history the same Law prohibited concentration of ownership. Beside the special subsidies, all daily newspapers, weeklies and periodical magazines are subsidized indirectly by low VAT, low postal distribution and telephone rates, and the like.

### Development of the press and broadcasting since 1945

*The press*

The postwar history of the Italian press can be divided into four periods:

— The decade immediately following the Second World War (1945–54) was a period of rebirth and normalization of the entire media system. The main dailies (*Il Corriere della Sera, La Stampa, La Nazione, Il Resto del Carlino, Il Messaggero, Il Mattino*) consolidated their traditional leadership. During this decade the daily press upheld dominant social values and "the opaque paint of officialdom" (Aiello 1985:111). This endured for another decade, with certain exceptions.

— The years from 1954 to 1970 were years of great internal migration, of the so-called "economic boom" and of the race towards the affluent society. It was a stagnant period for the press, with regard to ownership patterns and circulation figures. The two most notable exceptions were the launching of the progressive (and aggressive) newsmagazine *L'Espresso*, and the daily *Il Giorno*, both breaking new ground in the news-making domains. The daily circulation remained stable around the 5 million copies that had been a constant pattern for decades. In contrast, the weekly press registered high penetration peaks reaching in the mid-1960s the highest European figure (33 copies pro capita).

— From 1970 to 1985 the media went through an "ordeal by fire", as witnessed by rapid changes in customs, technology, and political outlooks. Especially the daily press showed signs of awakening and was in fact in the vanguard of the country's political and cultural evolution. The old dailies inaugurated a journalism more keen on monitoring the social dynamics. New, prestigious newspapers were established (*Il Giornale Nuovo, La Repubblica*). This was also a period, however, of financial difficulties for the whole press sector, which opened the way for powerful interest groups to seize control of the major newspapers. The Press Law of 1981 attempted to rescue the ailing press by introducing legal barriers to the concentration of ownership in the hands of industrial trusts. While the financial subsidies worked, helping the publishers to get over the crisis, the antitrust measures were unable to uphold the cherished pluralism: a group of industrialists led by Fiat established the RCS Rizzoli-Corriere della Sera trust, a giant with assets in all publishing areas (books, periodicals, dailies).

— During the late 1980s the Italian press sector did well. The crisis of the previous years was fully overcome. The marriage between marketing and advertising and the news industry became very strong. The expansion of advertising investments, thanks mostly to the revolution in the television domain, drew a large amount of financial resources to the press, easing the process of transition to new technology and opening the way to sales promotion operations. By resorting to bingo, gadgets, prizes, folders etc. in order to increase the entertainment value of the news, the daily press circulation reached the peak of 7 million copies in 1989. The sporting dailies and the small, local newspapers were the ones that registered the highest growth rates. This has led to growing fears concerning the close relationship between information and commercial interests: and that the press was being conditioned by commercial interests.

## *Radio and television*

RAI was created after the war in 1946. In 1947 Parliament appointed a committee to control the objectivity and political independence of radio broadcasts. The three national radio networks began broadcasting in 1950.

Regular television broadcasts began in January 1954, with a coverage of 36% of the national territory. In November 1961, RAI inaugurated the second television channel, covering 52% of Italy. The diffusion of television in Italy, as in other countries, has been very rapid. In 1960 there were 2 million subscribers, in 1971 10 million, and in 1984, 14 million.

Regular colour television service (PAL system) began in 1975. In the same year Parliament approved an important reform bill (Law n. 103) that conferred exclusive broadcasting rights on RAI and that re-organized the entire industry, allowing the establishment of private cable TV. The pressure of private interests was so strong that they succeeded in attaining a ruling from the Constitutional Court (n. 202/1976) that acknowledged their right to broadcast in a limited area.

From that moment on about 600 local television stations and more than 2 500 radio stations were set up all over the country, a phenomenon that totally changed the traditional electronic mass media scenery in Italy.

In 1979 RAI, in an extreme attempt to counteract the explosion of local private broadcasting, inaugurated its third television channel, a network of regionally-based production centres.

In 1981–82 four nation-wide commercial networks were established by private entrepreneurs (businessmen such as Silvio Berlusconi, and publishers like Rizzoli, Mondadori and Rusconi). Due to financial difficulties the Italia Uno and Rete 4 networks, owned by the publishers, were sold to the Berlusconi trust in 1983–84.

Since 1976 the radio-TV situation in Italy has been so chaotic that it has been compared to the Wild West, with unregulated competition, births and deaths of hundreds of broadcasting enterprises, skyrocketing programme costs, and above all the consolidation of a private broadcasting industry monopolized by a single trust.

The policy-makers appeared unable (or unwilling) for more than a decade to approve a bill that would put some order in the broadcasting sector. Finally, in August 1990, Parliament passed the long-awaited Broadcasting Act that, even if critics see it as a "legalization of the status quo", introduced positive norms that will influence the further development of the public and private broadcasting system in Italy.

**The press**

*Policy framework*

Several laws and codes were enacted in the years following the end of the Second World War relating to information conveyed by the print media.

Of course, the Constitution guarantees "freedom of expression" to all citizens (art. 21), but the legislation foresees a series of conditions (and restrictions) to be met in order to exercise that freedom. The Press Law

n. 47 of 1948 is the first legislative body regulating the complex matter. It has undergone obvious and continuous updating. This Law provides basic norms dealing with the journalists' profession: it regulates the right to secrecy, safeguards moral standards, the right to reply, defamation and libel, the penal responsibility of the editors and reporters and the like.

Law 416 of 1981, better known as the Law on Publishing, (with updates in 1984 and 1987) contains the more detailed legislation aimed at regulating the information industry. It introduced a series of subsidies that helped Italy's press out of financial and structural crisis. Beside the subsidies chapter, the Law represented a true turning point in both the policy making and in the development of the entire sector.

The most significant innovations it inaugurated refer to:

— the transparency of ownership of publishing companies (ownership must be made public and owners may not be active outside the publishing field)

— the Guarantor (a sort of high authority of publishing with several enforcing powers and supervising tasks; must be chosen from former magistrates)

— the National Press Register (all daily newspapers, periodicals, press agencies and advertising selling companies to the press must register in order to be operational)

— the transfer of shares (should be communicated to the Guarantor)

— the concentration of the daily press (the acquisition of newspapers leading to a dominant position in the market is blocked by a series of detailed norms)

— the establishment of cooperatives of journalists (in case of cessation of publication of a newspaper by the former owner)

— the publication of accounts (all newspapers have to file standard forms and publish them)

— the price of newspaper copies (formerly fixed by Government, liberalized in January 1988).

Not all the new norms have worked in the implementation process, especially those concerning the concentration of daily newspapers. The binding legal devices could not block the birth of a huge trust such as the one commanded by Fiat, which (directly) controls the daily *Stampa*, one of the top national newspapers, and (indirectly – that is through a financial branch) the publishing giant Rizzoli-Corriere della Sera. The Guarantor took the case to Court and Parliament tried to tighten the norms in

1987, but unsuccessfully. The Supreme Court ruled (against the Guarantor's thesis) the formal non-existence of a Fiat trust, and (against Parliament's action) the retroactive effect of the 1987 new legal measures.

*Ownership and finance*

In Italy in 1989 there were 91 daily newspapers, most of them owned or controlled by a small number of publishing trusts including:

Mondadori-L'Espresso   (1988 turnover: 2 400 bn lire) hit the headlines in 1990–91 as it was the object of an unending war between the financier Carlo De Benedetti and the television tycoon Silvio Berlusconi, each trying to seize control. Mondadori-L'Espresso, in addition to owning 23% of the periodicals market, publishes the daily *La Repubblica* (one of Italy's top papers) and 9 provincial newspapers, reaching 13.5% of the total circulation.

RCS  Editori (Rizzoli-Corriere della Sera, 1988 turnover: 1 489 bn lire) considered independently of the Fiat-controlled press, controls 17% of the periodicals' circulation and publishes the two dailies *Corriere della Sera* and *Corriere dello Sport*, together accounting for 16% of the total circulation.

Fiat (1988 turnover in publishing activities: 195 bn lire) directly owns and publishes two dailies *La Stampa* and *Stampa Sera*, which together have 7% of the national circulation. Adding this figure to RCS's, according to the Guarantor's viewpoint that considers Fiat-RCS a trust controlled by Mr Agnelli, the sum is 23% of the circulation, thus exceeding the 20% threshold imposed by the law.

Monti-Riffeser  (1988 turnover 200 bn lire) controls 5 regional dailies, with a share of 9% of the total circulation.

Ferruzzi (1988 billing of publishing activities 143 bn lire) publishes Rome's daily *Il Messaggero*, with a circulation share of 4.5%.

There are also a series of minor groups publishing other dailies. The oil company ENI owns *Il Giorno,* a national newspaper; the ex-Communist party controls the daily *L'Unità* which enjoys a good circulation share; the Industrialists' Association prints the economic paper *Il Sole-24 Ore*, also scoring high circulation figures.

The traditional publishing houses that made their money out of printing activities (Mondadori, Rizzoli) have in recent years given in to the pressure of financial capital coming from non-publishing business. So, Berlusconi (a tycoon who made his fortune in real estate), Agnelli (the automobile mogul), Ferruzzi (the food and chemical giant), De Benedetti (an internationally known financier) and other less famous private entrepreneurs all manifested concrete interest in the old and new media fields, seizing relevant stocks of shares in publishing corporations. The main reason for their inroads in the media business is financial: unlike in the early 1980s, the sector is a gold mine (thanks also to the connection with the booming advertising industry). A further reason, at times even stronger than the financial one, is the wish to influence public opinion and the political establishment. In this latter case the buying and selling of dailies by private interests often takes on the character of "exchange-money" with the political powers, which are traditionally sensitive to the information issue.

## Characterization of the newspapers

Italy's daily press is usually defined in terms of two parameters: geographic coverage and content. Table 1 shows the typology of the press in 1989:

Table 1 Italian press by geographical coverage and content 1989

| Type | Number of papers | Circulation share |
| --- | --- | --- |
| Economic | 3 | 4.49% |
| National | 17 | 48.05% |
| Political | 6 | 4.46% |
| Provincial | 37 | 11.92% |
| Supra-regional | 2 | 3.56% |
| Regional | 15 | 10.28% |
| Sports | 3 | 16.47% |
| Other | 8 | 0.73% |

If one adds to the press of "national" importance the economic and sporting dailies, themselves distributed nationwide, the data would show that 25% of the papers (N=23) account for 69% of the total circulation. The sporting dailies represent a very strong sub-sector, accounting for most of the recovery of the Italian daily press from the setback of the late 1970s. The positive trend is also due to the increased commercial aggressiveness and the keen competition between the two "battleships" of Italy's newspaper industry: *Il Corriere della Sera* and *La Repubblica*. The century-old *Corriere*, whose primacy went unchallenged for decades, for a short period in 1988 was beaten by the young (born in 1976) and bright *La Repubblica*, which achieved a greater circulation, due to a lottery.

In the period 1987–89 the "national" press seems to have reached a sort of saturation, scoring an increase index of 3.7% in number of copies sold. By contrast the "provincial" press registers a much higher growth rate (11.2%), unveiling a surprising liveliness in a market traditionally dominated by the "big" press.

Italy does not have typical yellow-press newspapers. The only attempt, in 1981, to establish a tabloid imitating *The Sun* failed within weeks. This is mainly due to the existence of a successful weekly press of genuine popular character, which scores Europe's highest circulation figures. The daily press is instead, in the collective imagery of Italians, synonymous with elite information product. The real popular dailies in Italy are undoubtedly the sporting papers, vis-à-vis the remaining types which are more like the so-called "quality" papers.

As far as political allegiance is concerned, it is quite difficult to pinpoint exactly the position of Italian newspapers in relation to different sub-cultural areas. Only 6 newspapers are clearly political, most of them house-organs of political parties. There is one daily belonging to the Catholic Church (*Avvenire*) and two representing linguistic minorities (*Dolomiten* and *Primorski Dnevnik*).

In 1973 39.7% of the Italian population read a newspaper at least once a week; the figure reached 54.2% in 1984. Despite the significant increase, 45.8% of the population never take a newspaper in their hands.

The profile of the average reader is "male, employed, less than 45 years old with a higher education, belonging to middle-high social status, living in urban areas of North-Central Italy". The most preferred topics by readers are (in descending order): Local news (81.5%), Political events (66.3%), Sports (58.2% [82.1% males]), Entertainment (53.3%), Cultural (44.7%), Economy (31.0%).

**Electronic media**

*Legal framework*

Italy's broadcasting sector is regulated by two major bodies of law, no. 103 of 1975 and Law 223 of 1990 (the Broadcasting Act). The former, with some updating introduced in 1990, is still enforced and regulates public broadcasting. For more than a decade this law provided the only legal framework of the broadcasting field. One of its key features was the ban on private initiative in radio and television activities. It was clearly unfit to handle the tremendous pressures that led to the rise of commercial television. The situation of non-regulation favoured a chaotic development of the sector, eventually stabilized in the division of the field between RAI, the public company, and a private trust, Berlusconi's Fininvest. The road to this duopoly system is strewn with tens (hundreds, counting radio) of casualties, victims of the "law of the marketplace" otherwise called "television war" between cumbersome giants.

The 1990 Broadcasting Act froze this situation, basically acknowledging the territorial conquests of RAI and Berlusconi, each commanding three channels. However, the new law introduces a series of measures that should guarantee a more coherent evolution of Italian broadcasting:

— broadcasting is no longer a State monopoly, private enterprises can apply for licences to run stations;

— private companies may broadcast live, nationwide, by means of technical link-ups;

— the Guarantor for Broadcasting and Publishing is established as the high authority over both fields;

— programmes may have advertisement breaks, with a number of limitations, according to the EC directive no. 89/552;

— advertising should not exceed 15% of the daily transmission time and an hourly quota of 18%;

— contents and programme schedules may not be influenced by sponsors;

— the norms in the 1947 Press Law regulating the right of reply apply also to broadcasting;

— a National Register of Broadcasting Organizations is established;

— cross-ownership of media must meet the following conditions:

> — Anyone controlling over 16% of the total daily newspapers circulation may not hold any licence to run a national television network;
> — Anyone controlling 8 to 16% of the daily circulation may hold only one licence;
> — Anyone controlling less than 8% of the daily circulation may hold two licences;
> — Anyone with no shares in the daily press publishing companies may hold up to three licences;

— private licensees broadcasting nationwide are obliged to transmit a daily news service;

— 40% of the yearly transmission time has to be covered by programmes produced in Europe in the first three years following the granting of the licence, 51% in the following years; no less than 50% of these have to be of Italian production;

— the household licence fee is maintained in favour of the public broadcasting company (RAI) [142 000 lire in 1991];

— a Committee of Viewers is appointed as a consultative body to the Guarantor;

— a series of penal and administrative sanctions are introduced for the first time.

As far as cable television is concerned, the old Law 103 of 1975 actually suffocated it by limiting it to a mono-channel option and restricting its diffusion to small local markets. Those constraints provoked the private entrepreneurs' attack on the radio and television monopoly that led to the Constitutional Court's ruling of 1976 which opened broadcasting to private companies. The 1990 Broadcasting Act briefly deals with cable television, stating that it may be multi-channel and that it is regulated by similar norms to broadcasting.

Pay-TV has not been the object of any particular policy. The Minister of PTT, questioned about the legislation gap on this matter vis-à-vis several private initiatives about to be launched, stressed that the Broadcasting Act norms (e.g. limiting the ownership of channels) fully apply to what is considered a further outlet of traditional television.

The market for home video, VCRs and recorded cassettes, is expanding rapidly, but it is never mentioned as such in laws or decrees. The few norms regarding (indirectly) the field are those concerning the protection of copyright.

The "mass telematics" sector, videotex and teletext, enjoys more attention from policy-makers. Especially the videotex service, Videotel, run by the public telephone company SIP, has been the object of specific ministerial decrees in 1982 (when it was introduced experimentally), in 1984 (when the access was liberalized), and in 1986 (when it was established as a public service and norms, distribution standards and tariffs were fixed). The Italian teletext service, Televideo, given its technical nature as a by-product of television has not been the object of substantial policy-making by government. Producers of television receivers must include SCART plugs to all new models, allowing all sorts of telematic use of the monitor, teletext included. The editorial regulation of the service is issued by RAI, which runs the Televideo service.

As with Direct Broadcasting Satellite Television (DBS) and High Definition Television, the existing policies focus on the technological and financial aspects, for the simple reason that these services are not yet available to the consumer. Several experimental services are operated by the publicly owned electronics industry, in connection with European consortia such as ESA and EUREKA. Italy's government has joined the European partners in the development of a unique HDTV standard, abandoning the former interest in the Japanese standard.

*Map of the system*

Italy's radio and television system changed from a monopolized structure to a mixed system. The spontaneous and uncontrolled "revolution" in the mid-1970s imposed commercial broadcasting and forced public radio and television to give up its traditional monopoly. The 1990 Broadcasting Act finally gave political legitimation to this de facto situation.

The television networks' map looks like this:

| | |
|---|---|
| Public channels: | RAI UNO |
| | RAI DUE |
| | RAI TRE |
| Commercial networks: | |
| (owned by Berlusconi) | CANALE 5 |
| | RETE 4 |
| | ITALIA 1 |
| (owned by others) | ITALIA 7 |
| | CINQUESTELLE |
| | RETE A |
| | ODEON TV |
| | TELEMONTECARLO |
| | RETEMIA |
| | VIDEOMUSIC |
| | JUNIOR TV |

At the beginning of 1991 the structure of the entire system has undergone some "re-styling" as the Ministry of PTT, according to the dictates of the reform law, had to assess the compliance of the applications for licences with the legal requisites. Nevertheless major changes are not expected in the key features of the channel distribution.

Some of the commercial networks are actually syndicates and associations of local stations that maintain a fairly large autonomy in programme schedules, advertising collection and financial structure. The "pure" networks are those owned by Berlusconi; the local stations are just repeaters of the signal sent from the centre.

In addition there exist a few hundred small and medium-size independent private local televisions. These are clearly the weakest links of the system as they have to compete for the few licences that the Ministry can grant due to the limited availability of terrestrial frequencies. Many of these stations will eventually be forced to close, while almost all networks will survive.

The radio sector has a structure analogous to that of television. The public broadcasting company, RAI, runs three AM/FM nationwide channels and two stereo channels as shown in Table 2:

Table 2  Listenership of RAI radio

| Service | Listeners on an average day |
|---|---|
| RADIO 1 | 7 655 000 |
| RADIO 2 | 7 532 000 |
| RADIO 3 | 858 000 |
| RAI STEREO 1 | 792 000 |
| RAI STEREO 2 | 1 027 000 |

Altogether the RAI channels have a 52.4% share of the national audience. The number of commercial networks changes all the time: there were only a handful in the mid-1980s, more than two dozen in 1991. This growth witnesses the networking trend that characterized the field at the turn of the decade, when many of the about 3 000 local commercial stations felt compelled to merge in order to stay in the business. The major commercial radio channels reaching significant national audiences are shown in Table 3:

Table 3  Listenership of commercial radio

| Service | Listeners on an average day |
|---|---|
| RETE 105 | 2 102 800 |
| RADIO DEEJAY | 1 475 500 |
| MONTE CARLO | 1 166 800 |
| RADIO ITALIA S.M.I. | 848 800 |
| DIMENSIONE SUONO | 842 500 |
| RADIO ITALIA NETWORK | 723 700 |
| MILANO INTERNATIONAL | 528 700 |
| RADIONORBA | 441 300 |
| RADIO KISS KISS | 436 300 |
| GAMMA RADIO | 403 100 |
| (Source: Audiradio 1990) | |

Network ownership is scattered among different companies. The largest slice however is controlled by the Mondadori-L'Espresso publishing group. The Berlusconi Trust entered the radio business late and now has a stake in a couple of networks. The commercial radio stations, depending exclusively on advertising, offer mostly music, heavily packed with spot advertisements, and very little news.

Other features that complete the overall map of Italy's broadcasting system are in the areas of advertising, programme production, audience monitoring and copyright levies.

Advertising was in the RAI's monopoly years a secondary source of income, the main source being the household licence fees. Since the arrival of private radio and television channels, advertising has become "the" resource par excellence of the domestic broadcasting market. The tumultuous growth of television and its enormous ability to grab substantial slices of available resource, blew up the traditional balances that privileged the press, thus provoking dramatic shock waves in the entire mass media system. The main "villain" of such uprising was Berlusconi (see below) who inaugurated defiant techniques that disconcerted the traditional market leaders.

In 1974 65% of the total advertising spend went to the press, only 15% to television (RAI); in 1989 the press got about 45% while television took 48%. In absolute terms, however, the press has not suffered much, as the total advertising investment has simply exploded since the mid-1970s (from 300 bn lire to 8 000 bn lire!) The marriage between advertising and commercial television, unavoidable since the private channels depend on advertising revenues, has also brought deep changes to the traditional patterns of the programme output and development of this medium. RAI programmes were never "sliced" with spot ads: advertising was concentrated in a few slots before and after. The commercial stations imported the American pattern with an excessive number of breaks that annoyed the viewers. The number of spot ads shown in 1981 was 260 000 but reached 1 m. in 1990! Despite these enormous figures, the actual concentration in an hour-span is not as excessive as earlier. In fact, the advertisers' associations, fearing a boomerang effect on their investments, reached a gentleman's agreement with the major commercial channels that cut the previous 25–28% concentration down to a more reasonable 16%. The Broadcasting Act has now imposed new ceilings on all broadcasting organizations (see above).

The explosion in the number of commercial stations has increased the total daily transmitting time immensely. This led broadcasters to buy programmes on foreign markets. With 71% of programmes being imported, Italy was in the mid-1980s the country airing the highest proportion of foreign television programmes (compared with 60% for Kenya, 17% for France and 2% for the United States). The keen competition between public and private networks and between big and small stations in the international market places led to a skyrocketing of prices, even for low quality material. In the past few years the situation has changed somewhat, as the major networks increased their home-production quotas. All imported programmes are regularly dubbed on Italian television.

The following table depicts the trend from 1987 to 1990 of the audience ratings in prime time:

Table 4  Prime time audience ratings in percent from 1987–90

| Channel | 1987 | 1988 | 1989 | 1990 |
|---|---|---|---|---|
| RAI | 45.0 | 46.7 | 48.4 | 52.0 |
| FININVEST | 44.9 | 39.2 | 37.7 | 36.3 |
| Other | 10.1 | 14.1 | 13.9 | 11.7 |
| | 100.0 | 100.0 | 100.0 | 100.0 |

(Source: Auditel)

The issue of the copyright levies has been a thorny problem for years. Several stations, especially the smallest ones, and mainly radio, evaded the payment, both because they could not afford it, and because they claimed dispensation as no law explicitly obliged private radio and TV stations to pay the levies. This led to a strong action by SIAE (the public association of authors) that even succeeded in a few cases in having courts close down the stations. RAI had an agreement with the association to pay 4.75% of its advertising budget, while Berlusconi in 1985 negotiated 2.50%. Recently SIAE, vis-à-vis the huge increase of the advertising revenues of Berlusconi, asked for a substantial increase of his quota, receiving a sharp refusal. The controversy ended up in the Supreme Court that in 1990 upheld the legitimacy of the television tycoon's stance.

Oddly, the Broadcasting Act's norms never mention the issue of copyright levies, thus leaving a large margin for further controversies.

### Organization of the two major broadcasting groups

RAI is a public-owned company, governed by a board of 16 members appointed by Parliament. It enjoys the financial privilege of getting its income from both the household licence fee (52%) and advertising (32%). Sales of programmes and other commercial activities accounted for the remaining 16%. Its turnover of 2 985 bn lire (1989) makes RAI Italy's prime communication group. Beside broadcasting, through a number of subsidiary companies RAI undertakes a series of related activities: publishing, records, advertising, programme sales. RAI employs about 15 000, and transmits 23 000 hours of television broadcasts and 59 000 hours of radio programmes (1988). The contents of the public company's transmissions have the structure shown in Table 5.

Table 5  Structure of RAI transmissions

| Programme type | Radio (%) | TV (%) |
|---|---|---|
| Entertainment | 22.2 | 45.7 |
| Cultural | 54.6 | 16.8 |
| Educational | 0.8 | 4.5 |
| Information (News & Sports) | 18.9 | 26.8 |
| Advertising | 1.8 | 2.5 |
| Other | 1.7 | 3.7 |

(Source: RAI, 1988)

As far as the production figures of television programmes are concerned, RAI has consistently had very high levels of home-production, in contrast to the commercial channels that are heavy importers of foreign material. The situation changed in the 1980s, when the public broadcasting company, in order to counteract the fierce competition from the private networks, increased its import rates. Lately, things have again changed, this time in the direction of a larger home-production quota by both RAI and the commercial outlets. In 1988, the RAI quota was 74%. The new Broadcasting Act, as observed, will drive toward even higher figures in the coming years.

The Berlusconi broadcasting empire epitomizes the deep changes in Italy's television system. When speaking of the commercial networks, one automatically thinks of Berlusconi's channels. Of course, there exist many other private enterprises, but their influence is marginal. Fininvest (Berlusconi's company) and RAI control 90% of the domestic television market, which explains why the term duopoly is currently used by analysts.

The 1989 turnover of the entire group was 6 677 bn lire, 40% of which was in television, cinema, publishing and advertising. Less than 2 500 employees worked in the television divisions. The Fininvest-owned channels aired a total of 20 300 hours in 1988, quite close to RAI's. The home-production quota however was much lower than RAI's, being only 23.1%. Table 6 shows the range of the whole offer by the three nationwide networks:

Table 6  Content of programmes offered by RAI

| Programme type | % of total |
| --- | --- |
| Entertainment | 76.1 |
| Cultural | 3.3 |
| Educational | 0.2 |
| Information | 3.4 |
| Advertising | 13.7 |
| Other | 3.3 |
| (Source: RAI, 1988) | |

Compared to the variety of the programming of the public channels, the offer of the commercial ones appears quite biased towards entertainment and advertising and private television is perceived as such by the viewers.

The issue of advertising cannot be separated from the phenomenon of commercial broadcasting and above all from the Berlusconi phenomenon. The fortunes of this tycoon began when he understood in the late 1970s the importance of a strong symbiotic relationship between television and advertising. Berlusconi established the company Publitalia to secure as many advertising outlets as possible. The aggressive methods used by the company became famous and were soon imitated by RAI and other channels. Its success in the past decade earned this the company title of the "safe" of the Berlusconi empire. In fact Publitalia has a turnover of 2 200 bn lire in 1990, that is about 60% of the money spent on television advertising, and 30% of the entire market.

The fall in Berlusconi's quota is mostly due to the growing ag-gressiveness of RAI, very much engaged in launching a highly diversified programme offer, particularly qualified in the information and current events sectors.

### *The "new media"*

The abundance of television channels made available by dozens of nationwide networks and hundreds of local stations restrained the demand for different outlets for more than a decade. This accounts for the limited growth of the "new media" and the "telematic media", compared with other countries.

The first casualty of the channel surplus was cable television. It simply does not exist in Italy, not even on a small scale.

Television satellites have fared better. Italy took part in the L-SAT project of the European Space Agency. RAI was assigned the use of one channel of the Olympus Satellite. It became operational in November 1990 as RaiSat. It transmits 15 hours of educational programmes, sport, music and news in three languages daily. The number of subscribers has reached 2 000 in 2 years, with parabolic antennas getting more sophisticated and cheaper all the time. RAI employs the same transponder to beam part of the regular scheduling of the terrestrial network RAI UNO and, above all, to experiment with HDTV and transmission standards.

A new, all-Italian DBS, named Sarit, is expected to be launched in the near future. There is a proposal by RAI and the public electronic company Selenia Spazio to activate two transponders for direct television broadcast on the telecommunications satellite Italsat launched in the autumn of 1990 by the Italian Space Agency.

Experts and analysts predict a bright future for DBS as there are no technical problems hampering the diffusion of such new outlets. The market projections, however, are more pessimist, as almost all European television satellites have been quite unsuccessful. It is a classic example of an overheated offer unable to inflame a rather icy demand.

Consumer responses to videotex and teletext have been less than satisfactory from a marketing perspective.

The RAI teletext service, called Televideo, became operational in 1985. It employs the UK Teletext Level 1 standard and 4.5 million TV sets were equipped with decoders in 1990, with a potential audience of 13 million.

Of the 1 000 pages available, the most popular are those carrying the latest news, the weather forecasts, soccer results, and the TV programme guide. Televideo provides subtitling in English, French and German to the Italian programmes beamed from RaiSat. A special feature offered by the service is "telesoftware", allowing educational computer programs to be distributed to personal computers equipped with a Televideo interface.

The videotex service Videotel is operated by the public telephone company SIP. Following a prolonged period of testing (from 1982 to 1986) the service became operational in 1986, based on the CEPT standard, level 3. To boost the consumer take-up, SIP set low tariffs, rented the terminals at a cheap rate (7 000 lire a month), and established link-ups with the French Minitel. In 1990 Videotel registered 1 500 information providers and about 100 000 subscribers (the old forecasts expected 250 000 by 1990!) Recently SIP put significant investments in the business hoping to reach 600 000 users by 1993.

Pay-TV is about to be introduced in Italy, but not via cable. The service will be broadcast like the French Canal Plus. The three channels that are going to offer pay-TV services are the newly established Tele+1, Tele+2, Tele+3. As soon as they get the licence from the Ministry (expected in 1991) each will have a different viewer profile and scheduling: the first channel will feature recent films, the second will specialize in sports, the third will mix culture, information and education. In order to receive the signal, the subscriber must have a decoder.

Market projections made by the managing company of Tele+ speak of 200 000 subscribers by the end of 1991 and of 1 200 000 in two to three years.

Finally, home video is catching on at the outset of the decade. The sector in a few years achieved very high growth rates, following a slow start due to the proliferation of broadcast outlets. In 1988 there were 6.2 million owners of VCRs in Italy ; two years later (July 1990) the figure had doubled, reaching 29% of all households.

## Policies for the press and broadcasting

After more than a decade of delays and tottering steps by government and political forces in the broadcasting and new media fields, the policy-makers have in the early 1990s at last been activated. New laws have been passed and new decrees have led to a less "sloppy" handling of the domestic electronic media world, a "high authority" has been established in the publishing and broadcasting fields, in a word the system seems to have finally plugged in to the mainstream of Europe's media policy. The undertaking has not yet finished, but the right direction seems to have been taken by policy-makers.

The rationale behind Italy's eccentric complexity in the media domain lies in its unique political environment.

Economy, media and politics are closely associated in Italy. On one side, most fortunes and misfortunes of domestic industrialists can be interpreted in terms of the intensity of their connections with political circles. Moreover the domestic media are connected with the political establishment and the parties have always been extremely sensitive on communication issues. Domestic tycoons must blandish some political party, even one not in power, in order to do business.

The political parties worked out at least three modes of conditioning the communication domain: running their own media, influencing the editors and editorial boards of the press and broadcast media, and using the reform bill proposals as pressure tools. In recent years this interaction pattern showed some cracks, due to the shifting of traditional political balances and to the greater independence of the economic actors. Politics has gradually lost the previous central and "necessary" character it possessed in the country's life.

In the mass communication precincts this new wave takes the features of "market logic". Between industrialists, parties and communication institutions new balances are being established.

The basic model is however still that of "imperfect exchange" but now the politician is losing primacy to the economic entrepreneur, and the media see their role revalued. This transition is not painless. The perception by the political establishment of losing control of communications has pushed parties and governments in the past decade to take contradictory stands. They immobilized themselves in a policy stalemate and, fearing the further loss of citadels still under their influence, majority and opposition forces clung to them by partitioning RAI between themselves. The wild "deregulation" in broadcasting that characterized the late 1970s and the 1980s quickly exposed the sector to political blackmail.

The mostly defensive strategies by political parties vis-à-vis the developments in the media marketplace do not appear to be winning. Their inability to work out positive regulations weakened the political dominance: tycoons and trusts met only weak legal opposition when they moved into electronic mass media. They have gained enormous influence and are practically beyond any political control.

The recent Broadcasting Act shows this political acceptance of the market-originated revolution.

Italy's media policy's stage of the 1990s will probably feature an intriguing match between the supporters of the "market logic" and the fans of the "political logic". The serious risk in a game like this is that the consumers will continue to play the role of powerless "spectators".

# Statistics

(1 ECU = 1 450 lire)

| | |
|---|---:|
| Population | 57. 6 m. |
| Inhabitants per km$^2$ | 189 |

Daily press

| | |
|---|---:|
| Circulation | 6 764 000 |
| Price per copy | 1 200 lire |

Public broadcasting

| | |
|---|---:|
| No. of household lic. fees | 14 851 310 |
| Cost of household lic. fee | 142 000 lire |

Television

| | |
|---|---:|
| Number of channels | 3 |
| Number of hours | 23 000 |

Radio

| | |
|---|---:|
| Number of channels | 5 |
| Number of hours | 59 000 |

Commercial broadcasting

| | |
|---|---:|
| Number of TV networks | 11 |
| Number of local TV stations | 700 |
| Number of radio networks | 20 |
| Number of local radio stations | 3 800 |

Television audience shares (prime time) 1990 in %

| | | |
|---|---:|---:|
| Public television | | 52.0 |
| RAI UNO | 25.6 | |
| RAI DUE | 15.2 | |
| RAI TRE | 11.2 | |
| Commercial networks | | |
| (major) | | 36.3 |
| CANALE 5 | 18.3 | |
| ITALIA 1 | 10.6 | |
| RETE 4 | 7.4 | |
| (minor) | | 11.7 |

New electronic media
Video cassette recorders

| | |
|---|---:|
| Number of owners | 13 000 000 |
| Penetration | 30% |
| No. of prerecorded cass. | 9 760 000 |

| | |
|---|---:|
| Videotex Subscribers | 100 000 |

Teletext

| | |
|---|---:|
| Number of sets | 4 500 000 |
| Potential audience | 13 000 000 |

DBS

| | |
|---|---:|
| Number of subscribers | 2 000 |

Advertising investments (1990)

| | % | sum % | bn. lire |
|---|---|---|---|
| Press | | | |
| Daily | 23.0 | | |
| Periodical | 20.6 | | |
| Total | | 43.6 | 3 480 |
| Television | | | |
| Public | 13.8 | | |
| Commercial Networks | 30.1 | | |
| Local TV | 2.5 | | |
| Foreign | 1.3 | | |
| Total | | 47.7 | 3 799 |
| Radio | | | |
| Public | 1.4 | | |
| Commercial | 2.0 | | |
| Total | | 3.4 | 270 |
| Cinema | | 0.2 | 19 |
| Outdoor | | 5.1 | 404 |
| TOTAL | | 100.0 | 7 972 |

Statistical references:
RAI, Documentazione e Studi, 1987–1990
UNIVIDEO, 1989
ISTAT, Compendio Statistico Italiano, 1990
ISTAT/AIS, Immagini della società italiana, 1988
ADS, 1990
Relazione Semestrale Garante Editoria 1989, 1990
UPA, 1990
AUDITEL, 1990
AUDIRADIO, 1990

## Reference

Aiello, Nello (1985) Lezioni di giornalismo. Garanti: Milano.

# 10

# Luxembourg

## *Mario Hirsch*

### National profile

On a tiny area of 2 586 km$^2$ some 380 000 people live in Luxembourg. Out of these some 104 000 inhabitants are of foreign origin, mostly Portuguese and Italian. Furthermore some 32 000 people from the neighbouring regions of France, Belgium and Germany commute daily to work in Luxembourg. Foreigners account for over 43% of the working population of 180 000. The Luxembourg economy has undergone dramatic structural changes over the last decade with the rapid decline of the steel industry (in 1970 close to 30 000 people were employed in that sector, in 1991 only some 9 000 were left) and agriculture. On the other hand the services sector experienced a relentless expansion over the same period, expanding from 4 000 employees in the banking field to well over 16 000. The gross national product came close to 6 billion ECU in 1990.

Officially Luxembourg is a trilingual country (Luxembourgish, French, German). While French is the administrative language, German is the language of the media, both as far as the printed press is concerned and as far as viewing preferences of TV and radio audiences indicate.

### Development of the press and broadcasting since 1945

Media activities have always been exclusively the domain of private initiative. This not only applies to the press, but also to the audiovisual media. With the exception of videotex and satellite broadcast the government never had any stake in media developments.

#### *The press*

As opposed to the broadcasting landscape, the Luxembourg press situation is extremely diversified. No less than five dailies with a total circulation of over 100 000 copies are published, alongside three weeklies and a large number of monthly publications. The Luxembourg press presents the peculiarity that it is affiliated (with one exception) to the main political parties. Because most publications could not subsist on their own, four out of the five dailies (the fifth one is a local edition of a French regional newspaper *Républicain Lorrain*) and the three weeklies benefit from considerable public subsidies, both direct and indirect.

*Broadcasting*

Broadcasting in Luxembourg started at the end of the 1920s when French financial and industrial interests (Havas, Paribas, CSF etc.) founded Compagnie luxembourgeoise de radiodiffusion (CLR), the fore-runner of Compagnie luxembourgeoise de télédiffusion (CLT). The need to look for a new home base that left freedom of initiative to private entrepreneurs became obvious following the nationalization of broadcasting in France and other European countries at that time. In 1930 the Luxembourg government choose to grant CLR a de facto monopoly in broadcasting despite the fact that such an exclusivity is mentioned only in the franchise agreement between the government and the company and not in the broadcasting law of 1929 which refers to broadcasting authorizations to be granted by the government to private operators. CLR used this privileged position to start multilingual programme activities aimed at neighbouring countries and beyond.

The drawback of this very special approach was of course that broadcasting aimed specifically at Luxembourg audiences, which also falls, according to CLT's reading of the franchise agreement, under the company's monopoly, was not among the first priorities and remains up to today underdeveloped both as far as radio and television are concerned (CLT devotes only a few hours per day to its Luxembourg radio activities and not more than three hours per week to its Luxembourg TV activities aimed specifically at local audiences) for the obvious reason that it does not make commercial sense to devote specific programming to a native audience of some 270 000 people.

CLT's monopoly came under fire in 1984 when the government initiated the GDL satellite project (eventually known as the Astra system). Not only was CLT not involved in this project, but it also fought openly against it together with the French government, arguing that the Luxembourg government was breaking unilaterally the franchise agreements and their exclusivity clause by granting a franchise to use fixed-satellite service frequencies attributed to Luxembourg to the then GDL operating company Coronet. CLT even started a court action against the government and Coronet in August 1984.

The government choose to go ahead with the project and in early 1985 it gave in to pressures from its European partners who complained about Coronet being too much under American influence and it set up a new operating company, Société Européenne des Satellites (SES), comprising only European shareholders together with a governmental stake of 20%. The government offered also a state guarantee in 1986 to SES that covered most of the satellite procurement costs and that was extended to 100 million ECU in 1987. SES launched successfully its first satellite late 1988 and its second one in February 1991 offering some 24 channels (April 1991) to audiences all over Europe.

Meanwhile CLT was plagued by a series of misfortunes in its attempt to make friends with the French authorities. In November 1985 and in January 1986 the French government disregarded CLT's application for the new commercial fifth and sixth TV channels. This followed the non-implementation of an earlier governmental agreement (October 1984) between France and Luxembourg to give to CLT two out of the four transponders on the French DBS satellite TDF1 with a commercial exclusivity. This declaration of intent appears in retrospect as an attempt to get rid of the GDL/Coronet threat or at least to delay it sufficiently so as to make sure that TDF1 would be up in orbit first.

Following the 1986 change of government in France, CLT was able to make up some of the lost ground by getting a stake of 25% in the sixth TV channel M6, which was however only a small compensation for its ambitious plans to become the leading commercial television in France. The company was more successful in Germany with the launch of RTL Plus together with Bertelsmann. This channel was first launched in 1986 making use of terrestrial frequencies out of Luxembourg. It achieved its breakthrough and break-even point in 1990 after its penetration had been considerably extended following its distribution via a Eutelsat satellite and Astra since 1989. In French-speaking Belgium as well the company was able to retain its strong position on cable networks by obtaining in 1987 for RTL-TVi the exclusive commercial licence. This achievement was however short-lived following the entry on Belgian cable of the new French commercial channels. In early 1990 CLT launched a new and very successful Dutch TV channel, RTL Véronique (now called RTL 4), that was able to circumvent the strictive Dutch media legislation by the fact that it is being broadcast out of Luxembourg via Astra and labelled as a Luxembourg channel. This strategy led increasingly to a dislocation of CLT's programming activities away from Luxembourg, the company maintaining in Luxembourg only the group headquarters. Apart from a considerable loss of revenue for the state, this implied also a stagnation of the personnel employed in the broadcasting field in the country, compensated only partially by the advent of SES.

The needs of Luxembourg audiences were covered by all these initiatives out of Luxembourg only indirectly. The government is aware of the need to do something for its own population especially since pirate radio activities started transmitting in the early 1980s. It presented in May 1990 to Parliament an ambitious liberalization scheme that envisages the authorization of up to 40 local radio stations, four regional networks and one public-service radio network. This scheme is expected to be adopted by Parliament in 1991.

**The press**

Press legislation is rudimentary. The constitution establishes the freedom of the press without any limitations whatsoever. An antiquated law from 1869 deals with infractions committed by the press and regulates the right of reply. A 1976 law introduced direct state aid to press organs in order to safeguard diversity. There are no ownership rules nor limitations. No particular content rules apply to the press except for offending comments dealt with by the 1869 law.

The press is entirely in the hands of private interests, linked, however, closely to political parties or trade unions as far as ownership and editorial policy are concerned. The largest newspaper, *Luxemburger Wort , belongs to the catholic bishop of Luxembourg and it has close links with the dominant political party, the Christian-social party (CSV). This group controls also the largest weekly, Télécran* (circulation: 30 000), plus a number of other periodical publications as well as extensive book publishing activities. The second newspaper, *Tageblatt,* belongs to the socialist trade unions OGB-L and FNCTTFEL and has close relations with the socialist party (LSAP). The newspaper *LetzebuergerJournal* is owned by the Liberal party (DP). Finally the newspaper *Zeitung vum Letzebuerger Volk* (circulation:4 000) is owned by the Communist party (KPL). The two weeklies *Revue* (circulation: 20 000) and *d'Letzeburger Land* (circulation: 8 000) have no direct affiliations with political groupings. They have however links with CLT which is a shareholder through subsidiaries.

Broadcasting in Luxembourg is totally advertising-financed, owing to the commercial nature of CLT which makes a licence fee superfluous. There are no limitations on advertising, either quantitative or qualitative, except for some forbidden sectors (tobacco, pharmaceuticals) and some regulations concerning the protection of children. The new media law will however introduce some regulations and restrictions. The advertising CLT/RTL draws from its purely Luxembourgish broadcasting activities is estimated to be in the region of 3 million ECU. The total turnover of the CLT group oscillates around 200 million ECU.

The advertising market in Luxembourg amounts to some 25 million ECU. The press has a share of close to 80% of total advertising revenues, whereas audiovisual media (CLT/RTL plus commercial pirate radios such as RFM) account for less than 20%. Despite this situation, which is enviable at first glance for the press, the new media law envisages doubling direct state aid to the press up to 1 million ECU in order to compensate for possible loss of revenue following the liberalization of the radio landscape. The law contains also a provision that submits the level of state aid to periodic review.

This carving-up of the market is likely to change to the disadvantage of the press once the radio liberalization has produced its results. The 4 regional radio networks to be authorized under the new law will be entirely advertising-financed and the local radio stations at least partially.

**Electronic media**

*Legal framework*

The legal situation of the media is extremely simple when compared to most European countries. The basic legislation is a law from 19 December 1929, which submits the operation of a radio station to the authorization of the PTT minister. The conditions to be respected by the operator are outlined from case to case in a separate document called *cahier des charges* Following this general principle, the Luxembourg government concluded on 29 September 1930 a franchise agreement with CLR. Over the years, these franchise agreements together with the corresponding *cahiers des charges* have been extended and whenever CLT wanted to make use of new frequencies or to introduce new services like TV (CLT started its TV activities in 1954), new franchise agreements were negotiated and new *cahiers des charges* elaborated. Today, nine of these documents apply to CLT's operations. They follow the lines of the 1930 agreement which introduced a de facto broadcasting monopoly for CLR/CLT. The present franchise regime will expire in 1995.

CLT operates under the general rules of a commercial company with some loosely worded public service obligations. The government is represented by a commissioner.

For the time being no specific regulations exist for distribution via cable or satellite. The franchise under which SES operates follows the general lines applicable to the CLT scheme. Transponder lease arrangements between SES and its customers have to be approved by the government. The new law on electronic media, likely to be adopted by Parliament in the course of 1991, introduces a greater degree of complexity into the legal framework governing broadcasting in Luxembourg. Apart from the fact that it is likely to diversify broadcasting outlets considerably (under the terms of that law up to 40 local radio stations, four regional networks and one public radio station could see the light of day), the law hardly mentions television, except for the fact that it eases considerably the access to cable networks for programmes other than over-the-air programmes. It introduces a complicated authorization procedure, supervisory organs, content specifications, advertising rules, technical specifications and ownership limitations (no single shareholder can hold more than 25% of the stock of a radio station). The law proposes also to incorporate into Luxembourg law the provisions of the 1989 EC directive on transfrontier television.

### Organization and ownership

CLT is a commercial company but it operates under a franchise agreement (*concession de service public*) and under the limitations of a *cahier descharges*. Because of this peculiar status the government retains some important controlling rights and, in particular, 75% of the shares have to be nominal ones that can change ownership only with the approval of the government. The government can impose its veto in case a change of ownership threatens the political neutrality of the company or in case a competitor tries to acquire a stake. The statutes of the company prescribe also that the board has to be made up of a majority of Luxembourg citizens and that both the director general and the chairman have to be Luxembourg citizens.

CLT is owned by Belgian and French interests while Luxembourgish shareholders play a negligible role with less than 6% of the shares. Effective control lies in the hands of a holding company, Audiofina, that holds 56% of the shares and corresponds to an alliance between the two major shareholders' Groupe Bruxelles Lambert (Albert Frére) and French multimedia group Havas.

SES is organized also as a commercial company operating under the provisions of a franchise agreement. Luxembourg involvement is however much more important than in the case of CLT, owing to the difficulties the company encountered in the early stages to raise seed money. Two state institutions, the national savings bank and the national industrial credit organization hold 20% of the stock and one third of the voting rights. The other shareholders are financial institutions from Scandinavia, Belgium and Germany plus some media related interests such as Thames Television plc and two smaller ITV companies. Besides its role as largest shareholder, the Luxembourg government exerts similar controlling rights over SES to those over CLT plus the requirement that transponder lease agreements have to find its approval.

*Programme policy*

There are no public prescriptions as far as programming is concerned, except the general formula contained in CLT's *cahiers des charges* that the company should broadcast "programmes of a high intellectual level". Programmes should furthermore be "objective" and not "offend" foreign governments. The programme commission that is supposed to supervise CLT's programmes exists on paper only and is at best concerned only with the domestic activities of the company on the rare occasions it is convened. CLT/RTL has to provide air time on request by the government for political or cultural programmes aimed at Luxembourg audiences.

The new media legislation is likely to change this situation because of the introduction of European regulations, the establishment of a public radio service and the creation of supervisory organs with considerably more influence than at present.

*New electronic mass media*

For the time being no comprehensive legislation exists for electronic media other than broadcasting. Public regulation limits itself to certain procedural rules as far as the operation of cable networks and the reception of satellite signals is concerned. For cable, the PTT gives its authorization provided certain technical criteria are respected. The new media law will however bring some order into this situation by establishing criteria for cable and satellite television. Its provisions are however extremely liberal and should hardly affect present practice in these fields.

New developments in electronic media are predominantly in the hands of private operators. The 106 existing master antenna cable networks, which connect some 70% of all households, are either entirely run by private companies or involve municipalities. The PTT is, however, concerned about the relative dispersion of cable-TV networks, their differing technical capabilities and their diverging pricing policies. It senses the need to introduce a greater coherence, so as to be able to prepare the ground for the eventual introduction of ISDN systems. A lingering conflict, which still is not resolved, opposes SACEM (in charge of collecting authors' rights) to many cable networks and the consumers' association ULC has called for an open boycott against attempts to collect a flat sum at subscribers' level. Videotex has been introduced at the end of 1986 by the PTT and despite bridges with systems in neighbouring countries has failed so far to attract much more than 250 subscribers.

## Policies for the press and broadcasting

Since most of Luxembourg's broadcasting activities are internationally oriented and since the two companies in the field, CLT and SES, are dominated by foreign shareholders, the role of national actors and notably that of the government in media policy-making is by necessity marginal. In order to defend the interests of these two export-oriented companies in the European framework, the Luxembourg government has however played a very active role in formulating European rules both at the Council of Europe (CoE) and at the European Community levels, softening down the two instruments, the CoE convention and the EC Directive on transfrontier broadcasting, and making them much more liberal than originally intended.

The formulation of a genuine national media policy has however gradually emerged over the last 10 years, leading to the elaboration of a comprehensive media law that was tabled in Parliament in May 1990 and that is going to be adopted in the course of 1991. While its primary aim is to liberalize at long last the national radio landscape by multiplying the outlets and by breaking up the de facto monopoly enjoyed by CLT/RTL over the last 60 years, it proposes to regulate also some other activities such as cable and satellite television.

The need to liberalize Luxembourg broadcasting has been felt ever since the early 1980s when pirate radio stations emerged (over the last 10 years some 25 illegal radio stations have been launched; most of them offer programmes for the large foreign communities living in Luxembourg, but some, notably RFM, proved to be very successful commercial competitors to CLT/RTL).

The need for an orderly process became obvious because of frequency interference problems caused by some of these illegal operations. At the 1984 Geneva ITU meeting Luxembourg managed to obtain and coordinate some 40 local radio frequencies (limited to 100 Watt). The PTT drew up a plan that enables the establishment of four regional networks (through the interconnection of local frequencies) that provide for a national coverage. Two supplementary national FM frequencies were also secured and shaped so as to improve the technical quality of some RTL programming activities (the Luxembourg radio programme of RTL still has not achieved a national coverage with good quality).

These technical prerequisites were supposed to provide enough leeway to envisage a thorough liberalization. CLT/RTL tried to delay liberalization attempts, threatening repeatedly to sue the government in case it was going to break unilaterally its monopoly. In order to prevent competition, CLT proposed to the Luxembourg press a joint venture under the form of a "window-solution" on its existing Luxembourg radio programme.

These negotiations failed however primarily because CLT was eager to keep prime time programming for itself.

The press, pushed by its political sponsors, is of course eager to seize the new opportunities and it is likely that the four regional networks will be attributed to consortia involving the four national dailies. The apprehension is however that, in view of the fact that advertising revenues are likely to be limited, one of these consortia will prevail at the end of the day. All indications point to the likelihood that it will be the consortium involving the *Luxemburger Wort*, the daily which enjoys already now a position of quasi monopoly.

Many observers, and especially the main opposition party, the Liberal party, feel therefore that the whole exercise in liberalization will end up with a mere extension of that monopoly to the field of radio and perhaps television, after a "Darwinian" selection process.

## Statistics

(1 ECU = 42 Lfr)

| | |
|---|---|
| Population | 380 000 |
| Population density pr. km$^2$ | 147 |
| | |
| Number of TV channels | 1 |
| Number of radio channels | 1 |

| Newspapers | |
|---|---|
| Title | Circulation |
| Luxemburger Wort | 80 000 |
| Tageblatt | 20 000 |
| Letzeburger Journal | 6 000 |
| | |
| Advertising market | 25 m. ECU |

# 11

# The Netherlands

## *Kees Brants and Denis McQuail*

### National profile

The Netherlands are small and densely populated – 15 m. people inhabit
41 000 km$^2$, or 440 per km$^2$. The highest point is just over 300 metres above
and the lowest a few metres below sea level. All parts are easy to reach by
broadcasting or cabling and, being approximately 240 km. long and 190
km. wide at its broadest points, the country as a whole is very accessible
(or vulnerable) to cross-border broadcasting with (or without) satellites.
To the south it borders with Belgium, whose northern half is Flemish
(Dutch)-speaking and to the east and southeast with Germany. Over-the-
air broadcasts from both countries can be seen in a fair part of the country,
but with a cable density of around 80% there seem to be more borders
crossed than just these two. There are two official languages, Dutch and
Frisian, the latter only spoken in the province of Friesland, which has just
over half a million inhabitants. Almost one million people of non-Dutch
nationality live in the Netherlands, some 7% of the population, the largest
groups being the Turks (175 000) and the Moroccans (140 000).

The Netherlands is one of the richer countries of Europe, both economically and communication-wise (shipping and road transport) linked
to Germany. With a gross national product of Dfl 432 billion (1987; ECU
186 bn.), a positive trade balance, a per capita income of Dfl 27 210 (ECU
11 700; 1988 figure), a private consumption of Dfl 333 billion (1987; ECU
143 bn.) and a low rate of inflation (3%), the Netherlands counts as one
of the more successful OECD stories. On the other hand, unemployment
is relatively high (425 000 in 1989, or just over 6%) and double that figure
for those on a more or less permanent sick benefit. The extensive (and expensive) social security system is under scrutiny and revision.

The political system, with three large and five small(er) parties and
never a clear majority for one party, has created a situation of permanent
coalition governments. The 1980s were characterized by centre-right
governments with both a Christian Democratic media minister and prime

minister. Since 1990 the PvdA (Labour) and the CDA (Christian Demo-crats) have been in power, the former party providing the media minister, the latter the prime minister. The Netherlands is a constitutional monar-chy.

## Development of the press and broadcasting since 1945

The recent history of press and broadcasting is closely intertwined with the socio-political developments of the past ninety years, summarized in that one word for the kind of social system almost unique to the Nether-lands: "pillarization". Dutch society between the beginning of the 20th cen-tury and the mid-1960s (and notably the first 20 years after World War II) was a principal example of "segmented pluralism", with social movements, educational and communication systems, voluntary associations and poli-tical parties organized vertically (and often cross cutting through social strata) along the lines of religious and ideological cleavages. Unlike the two religious groups – Calvinists and Catholics – the Socialists incor-porated only one class on the basis of a clearly class-bound ideology. From a social-economic point of view, the liberal "pillar" was the mirror-image of the socialist one.

The press in those years had strong links with political parties, both for-mally – the editor of the newspaper often being the party leader as well – and informally – political journalists getting their news from party officials of the same "pillar". About two thirds of the press had interlocking direc-torships with one of the four pillars, creating a fairly closed political com-munication system in which the press functioned as the platform for the pillarized elite. Next to these was a politically more neutral press with, however, a rather conservative undertone.

The origin of Dutch broadcasting lies in the 1920s, when radio amateurs and the telecommunication industry (Philips) found each other. But it was not long before representatives of the pillars quickly moved in. In 1930 the Government made special rules for radio in which only broadcasting cor-porations with strong ties to these "streams in society" were allowed on the air: the VARA for the socialists; the KRO for the catholics; the NCRV and the VPRO for the protestants. The AVRO, originally born out of com-mercial interests, aspired to be a national broadcasting corporation, but in reality had strong links with the bourgeois-liberal sphere.

This pillarized structure changed dramatically towards the end of the 1960s with the loosening of religious and ideological ties; both party press and broadcasting systems were "de-pillarized". While political parties had to change their campaign politics, press and broadcasting engaged in a struggle for as big a public as possible, while radio and TV pirates disturbed the tenuous balance of the system by broadcasting from the North Sea.

## *The press*

The newspaper situation at the beginning of the 1970s was dominated by tendencies to press concentration, affecting both partisan and more neutral papers. The socialist *Het Vrije Volk* – shortly after the war the largest daily – was reduced to a Rotterdam local paper and in 1991 merged with another Rotterdam paper (to keep its own name but lose its independence). *Het Parool*, emerging as a socialist underground paper during the war, dropped its radical tone at the end of the 1960s and is now struggling to hold its major position in Amsterdam. The communist *De Waarheid*, originally another resistance paper and for a long time supported financially by the party, first became a weekly, but ceased to exist in 1991.

Of the two catholic dailies, *De Volkskrant* changed its tune, to successfully become the paper of the better educated liberals, while the more conservative *De Tijd* first changed into a weekly (1974), to merge fifteen years later with another weekly, *HP*. *Trouw*, Dutch reformed and also set up as a resistance paper, is holding its ground, but its publisher merged with that of *De Volkskrant* and *Het Parool* to form a new Perscombinatie NV. Partly as a reaction to the gradually more liberal line of *Trouw*, orthodox christians started in 1975 the conservative *Reformatorisch Dagblad*.

Of the neutral newspapers *DeTelegraaf* is the largest, in spite of it being closed for four years after the war because of its collaboration with the German occupiers. The *Algemeen Dagblad* filled the gap originally left by the *DeTelegraaf*. Both papers grew in circulation in the 1970s. The liberal–conservative *Nieuwe Rotterdamse Courant* and *Algemeen Handelsblad* merged in 1970, to become the largest and fastest growing evening paper *NRC Handelsblad*.

## *The 1969 Broadcasting Act*

In broadcasting, advertising had already been an issue before the war, but particularly in the late 1950s and early 1960s financial and press interests had lobbied for advertising-financed media. One Cabinet had proposed a dual system based on the English model but this was successfully resisted by supporters of the broadcasting status quo. A Cabinet fell in 1965 because of the broadcasting issue, two years later a catholic–socialist Cabinet produced a Broadcasting Act which bore all the marks of a compromise. In 1969 the Act came into effect introducing the following rules:

— Blocks of advertisements (outside the actual programme) were allowed, commercial broadcasting companies were not. A special non-profit foundation (STER) was set up to handle advertising, the proceeds of which went proportionally to the broadcasting organizations and partly to compensate newspapers for their losses in advertising revenue due to the coming of STER.

— The Act did not do away with the "pillar" system, as the 5 original organizations remained on the air, but the system was opened up to new licensees as long as they aimed "at satisfying cultural, religious or spiritual needs felt among the population" and added to (not duplicated) the existing pluriformity within the system. The allocation of broadcasting time remained based on the number of members and/or subscribers to the broadcasting magazines produced by the different organizations.

— A Dutch Broadcasting Foundation (NOS) was founded alongside the existing organizations which was to have a much more independent position than the previous cooperative bodies. The NOS was to provide coordination and technical services, but also so-called "meeting point programmes" and programmes which are explicitly suited to a collective approach (national occasions, sports, news). The Board of the NOS has government-appointed members, including the Chairman and representatives from the broadcasting organizations.

This neat setup, designed to open up and, at the same time, to protect the existing order turned out to favour a concealed form of commercialization and also those opting more for entertainment than for culture, information and education, four elements which, according to the Act, were supposed to characterize broadcasting in a "reasonable ratio". The ideologically neutral TROS (originating from a TV pirate station and aiming at a more general public) and, later, the ex-radio pirate Veronica (VOO) entered the door opened by the Act and grew explosively in audience and number of members. On the other hand, a new evangelical broadcasting organization (EO) showed that not everyone had "de-pillarized".

*Commercial pressure*

Foreign stations, sometimes with advertising explicitly aimed at a Dutch audience, were relayed via cable and had in fact made an end to the scarcity of channels. A new centre-right government, and particularly the conservative coalition partner VVD, seemed to be more in favour of commercial developments, but at the same time tried to protect the old system. Some argued that the end of scarcity made publicly regulated broadcasting obsolete. Moreover, commercial interests and particularly the publishers felt unjustly excluded and public demand seemed to be pressing for more entertainment than the system could provide.

A Government White Paper in 1983 exposed the split between the Christian Democrats favouring the existing public system and the conservative VVD, which was all for commercial free enterprise in broadcasting. The new 1986 government, with the same centre-right coalition partners, agreed in principle that there should be room for commercial television, but surrounded its potential introduction with so many if's that a plan made by three of the public broadcasting organizations together with four publishers was quickly aborted. As a means of protecting the national market and the existing system, the same government banned satellite advertising in Dutch and subtitling of foreign programmes transmitted via cable, but the European Court ruled this ban discriminatory and in violation of the Treaty of Rome.

In 1988, while starting a third public TV channel to strengthen the position of the existing organizations vis-à-vis the growing number of foreign (commercial, satellite) channels, the government introduced a new Media Act. Many considered it a typical product of "Hans Brinker" policy making: putting a finger in the dike to prevent the flood from coming in. Commercial television was not mentioned but a deregulatory trend was set in motion.

Besides privatizing part of NOS, the Act introduced a new Commissariat for the Media which is responsible to the Minister for Culture. It controls the finances of broadcasting, the issuing of licences and the division of air time. It can impose sanctions on public organizations that do not uphold the law, e.g. through product placing or blatant sponsoring. The rules for the latter are, however, relaxed.

At the end of 1989 the tenuous balance was shaken again. From Luxembourg a commercial, Dutch-language, satellite station (RTL4) started broadcasting. Within one year it had attracted a quarter of the average audience and limited the chances of any other, national, commercial initiatives.

The present centre-left government, with a social democratic Minister of Culture, has now given up the resistance against commercial television and has even introduced advertising in local broadcasting. In line with the McKinsey research rapport and a NOS plan, the minister is now in favour of a dual system, alongside RTL4, with three competing channels, one of which (with TROS and Veronica) would be semi-commercial.

**The press**

The post-war years have seen an overall decline in the number of independent national and regional newspapers; of the present titles about half can be considered independent. Between 1946 and 1990 the number of independent publishers declined from 81 to 20 and the number of titles from 124 to 75, only 45 of these having their own editor in chief, the rest being editions with different titles but shared editorial content. The partisan tradition, with interlocking directorships between parties, unions and media, has come to an end too, albeit papers still have an editorial political stand.

The total circulation of newspapers is 4.9 m., covering 90% of Dutch households. There are nine national dailies combining 43% of the total circulation of Dutch newspapers (see statistics section) and 65 regional papers, ten of which have a circulation of over 100 000. The one-paper city is a common feature in the Netherlands, with almost half of the more than 700 communities being served by only one paper. Some of the national papers are very small, like the two orthodox christian ones, while *Het Parool*, although claiming to be national, draws 90% of its readership from Amsterdam and relies partly on local news. The *Telegraaf and Algemeen Dagblad* mirror the socio-economic pyramid of the population with a strong lower middle class readership, while *De Volkskrant* and particularly *NRC Handelsblad* are strong in status class A.

Although there are 74 titles and about 45 editorially independent papers, the market is controlled by only a few publishers (see statistics section). The four largest control two thirds (63%), with concentration continuing. With the growing possibilities for TV advertising, there is a marked decline of income for the press; however, family magazines have suffered most from commercial TV. The introduction of local TV advertising in 1991 is expected to affect the regional press, which has already seen a diminishing readership since 1980, to an even larger degree.

In comparison to German or British newspapers, Dutch dailies should be characterized as "quality press", since tabloids and their sensationalism do not exist in the Netherlands. The emphasis – also with the regional press – is on national and international news. Less than half of the news is local or regional. Especially the Friday and Saturday papers have several supplements; for *De Telegraaf* and *De Volkskrant* one hun-dred pages is not abnormal. The growth in size has meant strong competition for the weekly opinion press, which has shown a steady decline. Because of the weeklies and the extensive supplements, but also because traditionally the majority of readers (some 90%) subscribe, Sunday papers were considered to be unviable. The *Krant op Zondag* which started in 1990 so far has had only a marginal position.

All newspapers (and most broadcasting organizations) subscribe to the one national news agency ANP (Algemeen Nederlands Persbureau) which was founded in 1935. It also represents (and translates) foreign press agencies like Reuters, UPI, AP, Tass, AFP, DPA, etc. Associated Press has its own news agency in the Netherlands.

Diversity and media pluralism have for several decades been part of the state logic. Government interference with the press is limited to supportive measures for economically weaker papers, especially since the introduction of TV advertising in 1967. Papers with a financial loss can receive compensation or apply for subsidy from an independent (but government-financed) Press Fund. Until 1980 newspapers did not pay VAT; at present they pay 5% on subscriptions. In spite of union pressure, there is no press merger law in the Netherlands. A proposed law on commercial broadcasting limits ownership by publishers of commercial stations to 33.3%.

**Electronic media**

*Broadcasting*

Eight main broadcasting organizations, the NOS and a number of small organizations, share the three national TV channels, employing some 7 000 people. There are five radio channels with specific profiles: information, easy listening, pop music, classical music and services for particular groups.

The allocation of TV-airtime operates via a three-tier system based on membership levels. To become a member, a person either takes a subscription to a programme guide of the respective organization or pays an annual membership fee of Dfl 10 (ECU 4.30). The success of these magazines depends on their (still) having the monopoly on detailed programme information. Membership is made attractive with all sorts of extras, ranging from T-shirts to free entrance to TV-shows. Airtime is apportioned on a 5:3:1 ratio for the following respective groups:

— Class A: any broadcaster with over 450 000 members, of which there are 6 – VARA (socialist), KRO (catholic) and NCRV (protestant) until the end of 1991 provided the majority of programming for Nederland 1, and the popular and amusement-oriented AVRO, TROS and VOO (Veronica), with each more than 800 000 subscribers, shared Nederland 2. Each gets some twelve hours' television airtime per week and 65 hours' radio.

— Class B: any broadcaster with between 300 000 and 450 000 members gets seven hours' weekly TV time and 39 hours' radio time. There are only two B-organizations: the liberal/progressive VPRO, which evolved from a Dutch reformed to an avant garde station, and the EO.

From 1992 the allocation of the organizations between the three channels will be reshuffled.

— Class C: any broadcaster with between 150 000 and 300 000 members. At present there are no stations in this category. Any organization with 60 000 members which thinks that it differs from the present organizations and will contribute to the existing diversity – to be judged by the Commissariat – can become an aspirant broadcasting organization with limited airtime for two years in which it must grow to at least 150 000.

By law all corporations are obliged to present in their programming a reasonable ratio of information (25%), culture (20%), amusement (25%) and education (5%). The EBU ESCORT-system is used for the operationalization of this "full (balanced) programme" obligation, but the fact that airtime is determined by the number of members usually means that the organizations all have different definitions of these categories, according to what attracts enough viewers. The pattern of television consumption still shows a sizable and even growing attention to information (particularly because of NOS programmes), while drama and entertainment combined attract fewer viewers than ten years ago (table statistics section). Home-produced, Dutch-language programmes are the most successful. Until recently the public broadcasters deemed the language barrier sufficient protection against loss of audience to foreign commercial stations.

Alongside these organizations there is the NOS with no membership but twice as much broadcasting time (23 hours' TV and 86 hours' radio per week) as an A-corporation. It provides news, sports and cultural programmes and uses the Nederland 3 channel. Viewer ratings for the third channel are low, except for sports programmes. The channel also provides airtime for some twenty small non-member (religious, humanist, etc.) organizations and for school, party political and minority programmes. Mainly due to NOS programming, domestically produced output for TV is around 70%, for which a total programme budget is available of some Dfl 900 m. (ECU 387 m.) annually for all corporations; an amount that excludes costly (drama) productions by the individual organizations.

For national broadcasting there are three revenue sources: licence fee (65%), advertising (35%) and membership dues, which mainly finance the organization and the colourful listings magazines. Advertising comes in short blocks before and after news bulletins and with "floating" blocks adding up to 6% (with, from 1992, a rise to 15% for a reorganized second channel and probably advertising during programmes). This generated an annual revenue of around Dfl 577 m. (ECU 248 m.) before the coming of RTL4, in 1988. There is a fierce competition with RTL4, but there has been for a long time an unmet demand for advertising access. Money spent on TV advertising is 15% below the European average. However, in the coming years, a deficit of Dfl 100 m. (ECU 43 m.) is expected for the public broadcasters, due to diminishing STER revenues.

Commercial broadcasting was legalized in 1990, but no service has been launched yet. Publishers can participate with a maximum of 33%; however they will lose their STER-compensation money if they join.

Local and regional television has been waiting for further development of cable and a definite government ruling. On a regional level there is no television but there are 13 radio stations, since the Media Act of 1988, set up as independent foundations. They are paid via the national licence fee based on three hours' airtime. Some of these stations, however, broadcast up to twelve hours per day. Since 1991 both advertising and soft sponsoring are allowed.

Local cable television started experimenting in 1970 with six stations and has since grown to 90 and another 270 radio stations. Broadcasting time ranges from a few hours per week on some of the TV-stations to 24 hours a day on some radio stations. Until 1991 they were paid through local means, contributions, donations and extra cable subscription. Sometimes (as e.g. with Super Channel in Utrecht) a satellite station is asked to pay for entry on the cable and part of that money is spent on local programming. Although not yet put down in law, local advertising and participation of publishers, hitherto forbidden, were introduced at the beginning of 1991. That will also probably mean the end of commercial pirate stations, which, in their thousands, filled the air in the 1980s. Advertising is expected to amount to Dfl 5 m. (ECU 2.1 m.) in the first year and to rise to 70 m. (ECU 30 m.) in 1995.

*New electronic media*

Since the early 1970s cable has been a hot issue in media policy. National discussions mainly concentrated on distribution of TV-programmes via cable, since the laying of cable networks was initially encouraged in order to improve reception quality, especially of foreign television channels; and to rid the environment of the numerous antennas.

The development was facilitated by a change in the Telegraph and Telephone Law of 1904. This provision, established in 1969, allowed bodies other than the PTT to install and operate cable systems. This meant a considerable growth in larger cable systems, usually covering a whole town or city. At the present time, around 80% of all Dutch households are connected to a small (MATV) or larger cable network (CATV). The most densely cabled areas are the cities of Amsterdam, Rotterdam and The Hague; the areas least likely to be further cabled are the Eastern corner of the Netherlands and the thinly populated Northern areas. A penetration of 85% is expected to be the maximum.

Most cable viewers have a choice of up to 19 public channels, including 3 Dutch, 3 German, 2 Belgian, 2 British and usually one local, and up to 19 satellite stations. Some of the latter have a very low reach; CNN is, since the Gulf War, included in most cable networks. There is a "must carry" rule for Dutch public TV channels. Although in principle five channels for DBS are available, no plans are expected within the next five years. The bulk of the viewing time is shared by Nederland 1 and 2 and RTL4, which after two years of broadcasting has managed to surpass the public stations (see table in the statistics section). The extension of channels has so far not resulted in more time spent on viewing television: with just over two hours (122 min) per day, this is somewhat low by international standards.

The local press and TV stations are allowed to provide cable text, of which there are more than 100 with a penetration equal to that of cable in households and a revenue, in 1987, of Dfl 20 m. (ECU 8.6 m.). Information is presented in a fixed, teletype way and advertising, in text form with still images, is allowed. Cable text providers pay the cable companies an entry fee of around one guilder for every household.

Operating cable is always a local matter and the operating area can be no greater than that of a local authority area, of which there are just over 700 in the country. Would-be operators must acquire an authorization from the PTT for a specific area. Most of these authorizations are assigned to local governments; the rest are in the hands of building firms, cooperative associations, pension funds, etc. The initial investment costs are met by the operators and costs are covered by charging an entry fee and subscription. The charges vary a good deal, but the national average for the combined monthly fee is about Dfl 15 (ECU 6.45), but will rise slightly in the coming years, due to copyright costs and extension of cable net and new technologies.

The diversity and localization of cable management is reflected in the technical diversity of its systems. There are at least 14 different kinds of networks in operation, the majority being of the "mini-starnet" kind. Many of the original systems were "tree" networks, with later developments of "branch-off" nets. Most of these networks now have combinations of two or three of these systems. Advanced optical fibre networks are being laid in Amsterdam and Rotterdam, mainly however for professional subscribers (large industries). In 1988 the Dutch Government decided that in 15 to 20 years' time PTT and cable TV networks should merge at the local level.

At present, there exists only one subscription TV-channel, Filmnet, which uses the Belgian transponder ECS-1 and provides mostly movies.

When it was still owned by the Swedish Esselte and the Dutch VNU, the break-even point was supposed to be at 300 000 subscribers. When they pulled out, this was reduced to 100 000, a figure reached after five years in 1990. Subscription costs are between Dfl 40 and 50 (ECU 20) and an extra Dfl 95 (ECU 40) for the installation of the decoder. Decoding of the signal, which is first scrambled at the cable station, takes place at the residence of the subscriber. There is a small scale experiment with pay-per-view in the province of South Limburg (Cinema- TV).

*Video and telematics*

Video recorders are today found in every second Dutch household. Although the main reason for acquisition is for "time-shift" viewing, renting films is also very popular and not very expensive. However, the total turn-over of rented tapes has decreased with the extension of satellite stations (notably RTL4); research indicates that it is only a relatively small number of consumers that accounts for the majority of rented tapes. The sale of prerecorded cassettes – a hitherto unexploited market in the Netherlands – is expected to grow rapidly.

High Definition Television (HDTV: D2-Mac) is expected to be available from the mid 1990s and will have an impact on the sale of TV sets. This technique offers a transport service for digital video and audio signals that can be used for different kinds of tele information services like video telephone or the consultation of video libraries. The upgrading of present cable networks is necessary for HDTV transmission, but this will postpone the implementation of fibre optical cable networks or the introduction of a Dutch broadcasting satellite.

The penetration of teletext and videotex is slow but steady. Especially Teletekst , a non-commercial service provided by the NOS and transmitted together with broadcasting signals is growing. Over 40% of Dutch households now have a TV set with receiver, with the average user consulting the service about ten minutes a day. Teletekst provides information on news, weather and sports and a subtitling service for the deaf and hard of hearing. Access to Teletekst is free and there is no advertising.

Videotex has much less general public interest; the majority seems to be for commercial and professional use. The Government provides only a limited subsidy for technological developments; development of the consumer service is considered to be a task of private initiative.

Three major public videotex systems are in operation at the moment. Viditel, started in the early 1980s, is a telephone-based service provided by the PTT and about 27 000 subscribers. Videotext NL, a private company partly owned by the PTT, is comparable to the French Télétel system and started in 1989. Some 15 000 terminals have been sold (there is no subscription), but so far little use has been made of it. Finally, there is RITS, a hybrid system with some 8 000 subscribers using a combination of telephone and cable networks. It is limited in its possibilities, but relatively cheap and on offer in most big cities.

## Policies for the press and broadcasting

The commercialization issue has pitted the adherents of a market-led media system against political parties (several have during recent years become market adherents however) and the majority of the broadcasting organizations. The regulation issue follows the commercial demarcation lines and also covers the issue of press concentration, cross-ownership and diversity. In broadcasting however, most issues centre round the focal point: the prolongation and protection of the existing public broadcasting system. How far should the Government go in order to maintain or reassert the principles of public service and diversity which the system was intended to serve?

Part of the discussion about the issues and problems surrounding cable and satellite centred around the possible threat which these potentially commercial and lucrative media might pose to the existing broadcasting system. When, as expected, the programme guides published by the public broadcasters lose their copyright on programme information, subscription will drop and so will membership, on which allocation of broadcasting time is based. A concession for a longer period is proposed, but will mean the end of the openness of the system with members and possible new entrants. The financial blood-letting from the STER, particularly to RTL4, might endanger part of the financial basis of the system, especially since raising the licence fee is a politically sensitive issue and a substantial rise not likely.

Publishers are eager to profit from cable and commercialism, but are equally afraid of losing the STER-compensation if they join a national commercial station. Furthermore no-one really knows what this will mean to press and magazine advertisements. In 1989 the gross advertising expenditure for the media amounted to over Dfl 4 billion (ECU 1.7 bn.), which was 6% more than in the previous year (see table in the statistics section). The expectation is that in 1991 RTL4's advertising revenues will be Dfl 200 m. (ECU 86 m), while STER will drop to about Dfl 400 m. (ECU 172 m.).

Government policy has been characterized by constant hesitations and decisional hiccups. On the one hand, the government was aware of financial possibilities and the chance that advertising money would otherwise cross the border, on the other there was a traditional hesitation about advertising in general and commercialization in particular and, also through traditional ties, it tried to stay put in preserving both the existing system and the principles it was supposed to embody. The coming of RTL4 shook the shaky pillars of Hilversum, so to speak. The Government reacted with several plans and actions:

— The introduction of a third channel, which until mid-1991, however, was attracting a minimal audience.

— Giving up its resistance to advertising on Sundays, commercial broadcasting and to local advertising. More efficient collection of licence fees and more privatization are other suggestions by McKinsey which are likely to be followed.

— The introduction of a special fund to stimulate Dutch cultural productions by the public broadcasters. It is paid for by STER means, 6% of its revenues, some 40 to 45 m. guilders (ECU 17 m.) per year.

The discussion about protective measures, in which opponents and adherents seem evenly dissatisfied though for different reasons, points to two, at first sight opposing, issues: deregulation and regulation. The centre-right Government which proposed the Media Act in 1988 had long been sympathetic to deregulation; it should improve the business climate which is darkened by an abundance of rules and regulations. The privatization of the NOS technical facilities (NOB) and removing the PTT monopoly on the provision of "terminal equipment" (telephone sets, etc.) are results of this policy and lively examples of the often stated adage "government keeping its distance".

The PTT however retains its monopoly with regard to cable, and a government-commissioned advisory body even suggested a stronger hold. Broadcasting has, since its introduction, been subject to rules and regulations, partly due to its supposed intrusive nature. The "full programme" formula and the necessity of representing a particular "stream" in society, which already featured in the 1969 Broadcasting Law, are now being re-emphasized in the new Act and even supplied with minimum percentages. Moreover, there are an advisory Media Council and a new Commissariat for the Media with strong regulatory powers. Regulation of the media is of a selective nature, as regulation of press concentration or rules on cross-ownership have so far not come off the ground.

*Conclusion*

The Netherlands stands in a similar position to other smaller West European states, whose media systems are vulnerable to cross-border flows and whose economies have less to gain from liberalization than those of some larger countries. In adapting to change, Dutch media policy has been guided by a cautious following of irresistible trends and by the objective of maintaining coherence and a degree of balanced interdependence between the main elements of the system – broadcasting, new media and the press. At the time of writing, this aim seems to have been achieved in reasonable measure.

## Statistics

(1 ECU = Dfl 2.33)

| | |
|---|---|
| Number of inhabitants (m.) | 15.0 |
| Number of households (m.) | 6.1 |
| | |
| Number of national TV channels | 3 |
| Number of TV-hours daily for the national public (combined average) | 14 |
| Number of national radio channels | 5 |
| Number of hours on radio | Ranging from 13 (Radio 5) to 24 hours (Radio 1) |
| Number of independent national dailies | 9 |
| Number of independent regional dailies | 45 |
| TV penetration | 97% (colour 80%) |
| TV licence cost Dfl | 156 (ECU 67) |
| Local TV channels | 83 |
| Local radio channels | 228 |
| Number of hours on local TV: from a few hours per week to a few hours per day | |
| Number of hours on local radio: from a few hours per week to 24 hours per day | |
| Number of video cassette recorders (m.) | 3.5 |
| Number of teletext decoders (m.) | 2.5 (40%) |
| Number of videotex subscribers | 50 000 |
| Number of cabled households (m.) | 4.9 (80%) |

TV offer and viewership

| Programme type | Broadcasting share (%) | Viewing time (%) |
|---|---|---|
| Information | 38 | 31 |
| Art | 4 | 1 |
| Drama | 22 | 27 |
| Entertainment | 6 | 13 |
| Sports | 13 | 12 |
| Children's | 14 | 9 |

(Source: NOS Research Department, 1988)

Reach and audience share of the most important TV stations

| | Reach in % | Audience share % |
|---|---|---|
| Nederland 1 | 100 | 20 |
| Nederland 2 | 100 | 19 |
| Nederland 3 | 100 | 12 |
| RTL4 | 84 | 26 |

National daily press in the Netherlands

| Title | Circulation | Orientation |
|---|---|---|
| De Telegraaf | 725 000 | conservative |
| Algemeen Dagblad | 417 000 | conservative |
| De Volkskrant | 334 000 | progressive |
| NRC Handelsblad | 234 000 | liberal/conservative |
| Trouw | 120 000 | progressive/christian |
| Het Parool | 100 000 | progressive-/Reform. |
| Dagblad | 52 000 | conservative/christian |
| Financieele Dagblad | 39 000 | conservative |
| Nederlands Dagblad | 26 000 | conservative/christian |

(Source: De Journalist, December 1990)

Market share of publishers (1990)

| Group | % market share | No. of papers |
|---|---|---|
| Holding De Telegraaf | 18 | 33 |
| Elsevier/NDU | 16 | 55 |
| VNU | 16 | 37 |
| Perscombinatie | 12 | 3 |

(Source: De Journalist, December 1990)

Gross advertising expenditure (in Dfl. m.)

| Medium | 1986 | 1989 |
|---|---|---|
| TV | 317 | 476 |
| Radio | 72 | 94 |
| Newspapers* | 1 308 | 1 517 |
| Free sheets | 602 | 670 |
| Consumer magazines | 441 | 523 |
| Trade publications | 338 | 397 |
| Cinema | 12 | 12 |
| Outdoor | 434 | 600 |
| Total | 3 524 | 4 289 |

(Source: VEA)

* Local and classified ads not included

# References

A lot of data can be drawn from (Dutch language) specialized magazines like Adfor-
matie, Informatie & Informatiebeleid, Mediaforum, Media Markt and special publications by NOS. Harry Bouwman was very helpful in collecting some of the data.

Arnbak, J., van Cuilenburg, J. and Dommering, E. (1990) Verbinding en ontvlechting in
de communicatie. Amsterdam.: Otto Cramwinkel:.

Brants, K., Huizenga, M. and McQuail, D. (1986) "The Netherlands", in H.J.
Kleinsteuber, D. McQuail and K. Siune (eds), Electronic Media and Politics in
Western Europe. Frankfurt/New York: Campus Verlag: pp.202–219.

McKinsey & Co (1990) Herwinnen van aantrekkingskracht door versterking van
televisieprogrammering: Samenvatting van eindrapportage aan NOS-bestuur. Hilversum.

Manschot, B. and Rodenburg, M. (1990) "Broadcasting in the Netherlands", Medien
Journal 3:133–142.

# 12

# Norway

*Helge Østbye*

## National profile

In some respects, Norway is a monolithic country. With the exception of a small Lapp population, the population comes from one ethnic group. The state school system is dominant, and the Lutheran State Church includes more than 90% of the population. On the other hand, geographical conditions do not favour internal communication in Norway. Total area is larger than e.g. Great Britain and Germany, but large parts of the country are uninhabitable, and the population is only 4.2 million. High mountains, deep fjords, tough climate and long distances between populated areas make all kinds of communication difficult. Geography has divided the society into a lot of small units with strong regional differences in political and religious orientation, cultural traditions etc.

During the union with Denmark from 1400 to 1815, Oslo became the cultural, political and commercial centre. Nationalist opposition against the union with Sweden (1815–1905) got much of its strength from the periphery. One lasting outcome of this periphery protest is two official languages: *bokmål* (literary Norwegian) based on the dialect of the upper class in Oslo and strongly influenced by Danish, and *nynorsk* (new Norwegian) which is based on countryside dialects from the western parts of Norway (Haugen 1966 and 1968). *Bokmål* is now used by 80–90% of the population as their written language.

The industrial revolution reached Norway later than most Western European countries, but the industrialization process went very fast. Now, less than 7% of employment is in the primary sector and 25% in the secondary sector. Norway has a mixed economy where private capitalism is combined with a few nationalized industries, and a lot of public regulations in the economic sphere.

Norway is among the richest countries in the world (GNP per capita), but a process of transformation is taking place in several sectors, and the unemployment rate is higher than before, though lower than in most

European countries.

The largest political party, the Labour Party (Arbeiderpartiet), is a social democratic party of the Northern European type. Labour was in government almost continually from 1936 until 1965, most of the time with a majority in the Parliament. Since 1965, Labour has been in and out several times. There are three parties to the left of Labour, but only one of them, the Left Socialists (Sosialistisk Venstreparti), is represented in the Parliament.

The non-socialist block has traditionally consisted of four parties of which the Conservative Party (Høyre) is the largest. Important changes in Norwegian media structure took place after the formation of a Conservative minority government after the election in 1981. The basis for the government was broadened in 1983, when the Christian People's Party (Kristelig Folkeparti) and the Centre Party (Senterpartiet) joined. The Christian People's Party represents the interests of the fundamentalistic, Lutheran type of Christianity. The Centre Party is an agrarian party. The Progressive Party (Fremskrittspartiet) is a right wing party which represents an anti-tax and anti-bureaucracy protest, with a substantial support in the population. For 50 years from 1880, the Liberal Party (Venstre) had a dominant position, but since 1985 it has not been represented in the Parliament.

In 1986 the coalition government was replaced by a Labour minority government. A new bourgeois government was formed after the 1989 general election, but it lasted only one year, and in November 1990 Labour took over again.

A referendum on Norwegian entry into the Common Market took place in 1972. The two major parties, the leadership of the trade unions and the employers' associations were in favour of joining the EC. A coalition between the periphery and urban radicals resulted in a defeat for the power elite. In 1990 this has again become an important political issue.

## Development of the press and broadcasting since 1945

*The press*

World War II represents an important point of change in the development of the press system in Norway. Before the war, all the major political parties had their own, small newspapers in most cities and towns. During the war more than 60% of the newspapers were stopped by the authorities (Hjeltnes 1990:15). Some of these papers never restarted. Most of the Labour press never regained their pre-war strength, especially on the advertising market.

The post-war years are characterized by monopolization (Høyer 1974).

The largest newspaper in each town has survived, and increased its share of local advertising and circulation. Smaller papers often have a downward trend, and some of them have been closed down. New newspapers have appeared, but only papers started in smaller places with no previous paper have had any success. The total number of newspapers has been reduced in the post war period, but the number of towns with their own paper has been slowly increasing. The combined effect of these trends has been a dramatic reduction in local competition. On the other hand, national tabloid newspapers have had a considerable increase in their circulation outside the capital.

The close links between the newspapers and political parties continued during the first post war period. As a result of competition and monopolization, most non-socialist newspapers have declared their party-political independence, partly in order to attract readers from all parties. The Labour press, which is owned by trade unions and the Labour party, has retained a formal affiliation with the party, but it is acting much more independently than in the 1950s and 1960s.

## The electronic media

The 1933 Broadcasting Act established Norsk Rikskringkasting, NRK, as a national, public service broadcaster in the BBC tradition.

After the liberation in 1945, NRK immediately continued the well established programming from the 1930s. Many of the voices from the London war-time transmissions continued in NRK, giving the broadcasting company a strong legitimacy and popularity. The first aim was to build new transmitters in order to reach all parts of the country. In the 1950s, 1960s and beginning of the 1970s there was a widespread acceptance of NRK's role, although some specific programmes created some minor moral uproars.

The first experiments with television took place on the initiative of NRK in 1954. There was a lot of discussion concerning if and when Norway should establish a television channel, but no one objected to the idea of NRK running the service. Norway was the third last European country to establish a national television service (only Iceland and Albania were later). The service was officially opened in 1960.

From 1933 on, NRK invested its limited resources to create a national network. Small regional offices produced programmes for the national network. In 1957, these offices were given permission to transmit regional broadcasts, but for 10 years few resources were allocated to this task. Since 1970, NRK has increased the number of regional offices, and each office has got more time (in particular for regional broadcasting) and more staff (5% of the staff worked in regional offices in 1970, almost 25% in 1990).

Until 1982 NRK had a monopoly position, in television as well as radio. Then, the new Conservative government introduced three new elements in the broadcasting system: local, independent radio; local, independent television and cable distribution of satellite channels. Formally, local radio and television were introduced on a preliminary basis, but everyone knew that the process could not be reversed.

The most successful part of the liberalization of broadcasting was the introduction of local radio (*nærradio*) in 8 communities. In 1984, the number of permissions exploded, and local radio is established as a permanent part of the Norwegian media system. From 1988 the stations are allowed to carry commercials, but they must have a local basis.

In 1981, the Conservative government also gave permission for a few community antenna companies to produce local television for cable distribution (some cable networks were already in operation, most of them in order to extend the area where reception of Swedish television was possible). The number of licences for local television increased dramatically in 1984, and some stations were licensed to have terrestrial transmission. Commercials were not permitted in the local channels, and local television has had severe economic problems (Nymo 1984). Most of the stations closed down. Audience ratings show that local programmes are popular, in particular when they cover smaller areas (Werner et al. 1984: 38).

Retransmission on cable of television programmes via satellite was also introduced in 1981–82. The use of direct broadcasting satellites had been on the political agenda since the early 1970s. The Nordic Council (which consists of parliamentarians from Denmark, Finland, Iceland, Norway and Sweden) regarded transmission of the national channels to all five countries as the most efficient way to improve cultural exchange between the countries. An investigation and discussion on the possibility of using direct broadcast satellites for this purpose started in 1972, but it was never possible to reach a decision (NU A 1979:4E). After the Danish decision to withdraw from these Nordsat discussions in 1981, the original plan was more or less dead. A Swedish company developed a DBS satellite called Tele-X, and for some time this vitalized discussions of a mini-Nordsat, but the satellite is now used for transmission of the private Swedish channel TV4 and NRK's radio and television programmes to oil rigs in the North Sea and Norwegian settlements in Spitsbergen. The Norwegian PTT transmits the two national Swedish television channels for redistribution on cable in Norway. Passing several stages of liberalization, cable distribution of satellite channels is now virtually unregulated, with the exception that the content must comply with Norwegian legislation (e.g. ban on advertisements for alcohol or tobacco). Sky Channel, which was the first channel to be transmitted, has disappeared from Norwegian cable networks, but a lot of other channels are now available. In addition to British,

French and German programmes, there is also one Norwegian satellite channel, TVN, which has some own production, but most programmes are imported and subtitled in Norwegian. TVN is aimed directly at Norway. Two Swedish channels, Scansat TV3 and TV4, also try to attract a Norwegian audience and advertisers. The closest any has come to a fulfilment of the culturally based Nordsat idea is the pan-Scandinavian, commercial satellite channel Scansat TV3. Most of its content is imported, and the only possible, positive cultural effect is a marginal improvement in the mutual understanding of Scandinavian languages. It is interesting to note that a commercial company may have achieved more for Nordic mutual understanding than the politically and culturally more ambitious Nordsat idea, which was opposed by intellectuals and artists.

Video represented the first challenge to the Norwegian broadcasting monopoly, but it had a slow start before a breakthrough in 1980 and 1981 (Werner 1982; Høst 1983; Hultén 1984). In October 1988 more than 40% of the population had access to video (Haraldsen and Vaage 1988). When video was introduced, it was less regulated than the more established branches of the media industry, and the first batch of pre-recorded video cassettes on the market was dominated by pornography and violence. From 1985, video is regulated by the Film and Video Act. Local authorization of cassette dealers and a central registration of all cassettes for hire in order to ease content control and to reduce the distribution of illegally copied cassettes were introduced (NOU 1983:9). According to a survey in 1983, the average viewing time for video was 6 minutes per day (37 minutes for households with video, 2 minutes for those without) (Høst 1983). The number of video cassette players is now several times higher than in 1983, but the average time spent on video viewing is almost at the same level. Also the pattern (with youth as the heavy consumers) has remained unchanged (Haraldsen and Vaage 1988).

**The press**

*Structure*

There are approximately 180 newspapers in Norway. Most of them are small, and have a local orientation. The larger papers have a broad coverage of national and international news, but with the exception of two tabloids and a few party political organs, distribution is mainly regional or local.

Norwegians read a lot of newspapers. Each household buys 1.8 papers per day on the average (excluding Sundays – Sunday newspapers were prohibited in 1919, but reintroduced in 1990). Subscription is the most common form of buying newspapers.

*Legal framework, ethical rules and policy framework*

Broadcasting, film and video are regulated by specific legislation, but there is no press law in Norway. The Constitution grants a basic right to print. The Norwegian press legislation specifies that the principal editor has the legal responsibility, that there is a limited right to reply and a limited protection of sources. There are some restrictions on communication in general: prohibition of dissemination of state secrets, libel, racial discrimination, etc., but no legislation gives the journalists any special protection. On the other hand, every citizen has the right to look into letters and documents in the civil service, and this is an important tool for the journalists.

The press is divided on several policy issues, such as press subsidies, restriction of foreign ownership and the development of newspaper chains. The introduction of new technology has, in most newspapers, united the owners, the editors and the journalists against the typographers.

*Ownership and finance*

Most of the press and other print media are organized in private stock companies. Some newspapers and publishing houses have a very limited number of stockholders. Ownership of the press has traditionally been local, and very few owners control more than one paper. Labour newspapers are owned by local trade unions and party branches. There has been strong technical, economical, and editorial cooperation between the Labour newspapers, and for some purposes, they can be regarded as a newspaper chain. This is about to be formalized, as almost all Labour newspapers are merging into one company. Twenty percent of the circulation comes from the Labour press.

One newspaper group is larger than this, the family-owned Schibsted group. In 1860 *Aftenposten* was founded by Amandus Schibsted. During most of this century, *Aftenposten* has been the largest newspaper in Norway, with two separate papers each day (morning and afternoon). In 1966, the Schibsted group bought *VG*, a small evening paper, with serious economic difficulties and a circulation of less than 30 000. The new owners developed *VG* into a modern tabloid, and had great success on the market. *VG* became the largest newspaper in Norway in 1981, and the daily circulation in 1989 was 360 000. The Schibsted group also owns a minority of the shares in three of the largest regional newspapers (*Fædrelandsvennen, Stavanger Aftenblad* and *Adresseavisen*). The group is also engaged in book publishing. Plans to expand by acquiring some local newspapers has been called off, and companies for video production, local radio and television, and a new newspaper in Oslo have all failed. But the group accounts for more than half of the total Norwegian newspaper circulation and almost

40% of the newsprint comes from their papers.

A recent development in the Norwegian newspaper structure is a chain of non-socialist newspapers, mostly with local monopolies. The Orkla group (based on mining, timber and paper production) has bought 6 newspapers, and the group is also closely linked to *Dagbladet* (a tabloid newspaper, the third largest paper in Norway, which also controls 6 local papers). The Orkla group also publishes several weekly magazines, owns cable networks and is involved in book publishing and a satellite television channel (TVN).

Until recently, the newspaper industry was the territory for idealists. During the post war period, a lot of the papers have made a loss most years. Some newspapers, however, made a substantial profit, but most of the surplus was reinvested in the paper. Recent changes in ownership have led to an increased focus on profit in some parts of the industry.

Several newspapers had to close down in the 1960s, and the industry's organizations turned to the government for subsidies. Labour's and the Centre Party's press would gain most from the press subsidies, and these parties backed the proposition, while the Conservative Party opposed. Newspapers were already exempted from VAT, and from 1969, some newspapers have received money directly from the state. Several kinds of subsidies were introduced, but the most important is production subsidy where the papers receive a certain amount per sold copy. Rules were made in order to channel the subsidies to papers with the weakest structural position on the market (the smallest papers and papers with a minority position on the local market – no. 2 papers), but with preset rules so that there should be no fear of state interference with editorial policies.

In total, the subsidies account for less than 2% of the industry's total income. But it means survival or death to a lot of newspapers, especially the no. 2 newspapers. The system is important in the protection of local competition. Since 1981 the Conservative Party has proposed a reduction in the subsidies, but it has met opposition from its coalition partner, the Centre Party. In real terms, there was a small reduction in subsidies from 1983 to 1986, and an increase in 1987–88 during the Labour government. In 1989 and 1990 the press subsidies again became an issue in media politics because the Conservative government announced that it wanted to scrap the whole system of press subsidies along with reduction of subsidies to other industries.

Advertising revenue is the major source of income for the Norwegian press. It accounts for 52% of the total income, compared to 37% from circulation.

## Electronic media

### Structure

After 8 years with regional, independent, private broadcasting, the Broadcasting Act of 1933 established a national broadcasting company, NRK (Norsk rikskringkasting, Norwegian Broadcasting Corporation) in the public service broadcasting tradition. The company was owned by the state, and was given exclusive rights to broadcast oral messages, music, pictures, etc.. The monopoly lasted for almost 50 years. Now, NRK transmits one television channel and two radio channels. Regional broadcasts are transmitted for several hours per day on one of the radio channels.

Transmission of satellite television channels via cable, and local, independent radio and television was allowed in December 1981. Local radio has become a success. More than 400 stations have been on the air. Local television, however, has found it difficult to survive, and only a handful of stations are transmitting on a regular basis. Some of these are owned by foreign companies.

Norwegians listen to radio for approximately 2 hours per day and watch television for 1 hour. Since the monopoly was broken in 1982, NRK has not lost any substantial part of its audience. Local radio is popular, especially among young people, but NRK's share of the radio consumption is approximately 90%. Satellite television reaches at least 1/3 of the population, and this represents the major challenge for NRK. So far, NRK is still dominating, but amongst those with access to satellite channels, its share is 65–70% of the time spent on television.

### Legal framework

The Constitution secures everyone a right to print, but according to a Supreme Court decision, the same right does not apply to broadcasting. The general criminal laws put the usual limits to the journalistic freedom: libel, blasphemy, some kinds of pornography and portrayal of violence etc. are prohibited.

In 1988 NRK was granted a more independent position vis-à-vis the government. Only the director general was to be appointed by the government, and NRK was freed from the strict rules of appointment procedures and wages which apply to civil servants. To what extent these changes will give NRK more real autonomy, remains to be seen. Parliamentary debates in 1990 give no cause for optimism – the parliament is still interested in details in appointment of officials and content of specific programmes.

The Broadcasting Act made it possible for the Conservative government which came to power in 1981 to allow private, local radio and television stations on a temporary basis. In 1987 the Broadcasting Act was changed in order to make local radio permanent. Local radio is regulated by the Local Broadcasting Act (Lov om nærkringkasting) of 1987 (Ot.prp. nr. 47 1986–87; Innst. O. nr. 3 1987–88). This act made local radio permanent and accepted advertising in local radio, but introduced a tax on revenues from broadcasting advertising. The income from this tax will be used to subsidize local radio stations in areas where the economic foundation is too weak to support a station. So far, this procedure has been undermined or boycotted by most rich local radio stations (Ryland 1990). The introduction of advertising seems to favour stations with music and local news at the expense of stations with a more idealistic basis. The Act states that local radio should, as a general rule, not cover an area larger than one commune (Norway has 450 communes, the smallest have a population of less than 1000), and the municipal councils are authorized to issue licences for transmission. The Act also established the Local Broadcasting Council which is appointed by the Ministry of Cultural Affairs and has an independent secretariat. This council can withdraw licences to transmit for both local radio and local television.

The Local Broadcasting Act treated local television in the same way as local radio, with one major exception: local television was not allowed to transmit commercials. This was changed by the Advertising in Broadcasting Act (Lov om reklame i kringkasting m.v.) of 1990 (Ot.prp. nr 55 1989–90).

*NRK's organization*

NRK is a hierarchical organization with 2 600 employees. In economical, administrative, and technical matters, the director general shares the overall responsibility with NRK's board of governors, but nobody (except in the case of a court decision) can overrule him in matters concerning programmes and programming policy. The director general is appointed for an 8-year period, and he cannot be renominated for the position.

The Ministry of Cultural Affairs is the most important policy-making body outside NRK. Especially in periods with bourgeois government since 1981, the Ministry has been active in media policy issues. Before 1981, NRK had a lot of influence on the broadcasting policy. The ministry also handles major changes in the structure of NRK's organization and new services. The appointment of the director general is regarded as an important question which involves the political leadership in the Ministry as well as the rest of the Cabinet.

The board of governors is also appointed by the Cabinet. The board has the final word in matters concerning economy, administration, personnel etc., and it can influence the selection of director general. In periods when there is a conflict between the Ministry and the NRK, the board is more politically important.

The Broadcasting Council is appointed by the Parliament (14 members) and the Ministry (11 members). The Council has changed from an expert group to a reflection of party politics. The Council discusses programmes and programming policy. Its decisions have the form of advice to NRK, and there are several examples where the broadcasting company has disregarded its advice (Østbye 1977). The Council also takes part in the nomination of the Director General.

There are two radio channels and one television channel. These channels are run independently of each other, but they share some resources. Regional programmes are produced by 17 regional branches, each with a head office and substations located in other parts of the region. One branch produces programmes in Lapp for distribution in the northern region and for the national networks. The other 16 branches also divide their attention between regional radio programmes and productions for national radio and television. For some years, there have been trials of regional television, but neither personnel nor equipment allows for more than small scale experiments.

*Ownership and financing*

NRK is owned by the state, but was in 1987 given a more independent position vis-à-vis the Ministry.

Advertising is banned in NRK's radio and television broadcasting. NRK is financed from two sources: a TV licence and a special tax on radio and television equipment. The licence fee accounts for more than 4/5 of the revenue (NRK 1989: 44). Before 1987, the Parliament voted on NRK's total budget; since 1988 only the licence fee is decided by the Parliament, and it is up to NRK (the board and the Director General) to decide on how the money is spent.

Local radio is financed by the owners and by advertising. Commercials are allowed on local television from 1991. The introduction of advertising may lead to an expansion of local television.

*NRK's programming policy*

Like other public service broadcasting institutions, NRK is trapped in a triangle of influences: the political authorities, the audience and the journalists all represent challenges to ideas like balance, relevance, quality and independence. To rely heavily on only one of these bases will easily transform the broadcasting company into a political commissariat, a purely commercial company, or a paternalistic institution. For NRK, autonomy is an important goal. The Broadcasting Act abandons external censorship, but a lot of external institutions try to influence NRK's programming policy. The Parliament is one of these. The Parliament has the authority to change the Broadcasting Act and e.g. impose objects clauses on NRK, introduce censorship, reduce NRK's budgets etc. Until now, the Parliament has done little of this kind. Some discussions in the Parliament may, however, be understood as warnings. In order to avoid interventions, NRK is possibly practising self-censorship with more narrow limits in the programming than an external controller would be able to exert in an open, democratic society.

NRK broadcasts 3 000 hours of television. One third is news and information. In the early 1980s, between 55 and 60% was Norwegian productions, but this has been reduced to 50%. Almost all the Norwegian productions are produced by NRK itself. Most of the imports come from the USA and the UK. Imported programmes are subtitled. Dubbing is used only in children's programmes.

*Telematic media*

The development of new telematic media increased the interest in mass media issues in Norway towards the end of the 1970s. The first issue to raise the interest in media politics was satellite television: plans for a Nordic exchange of television programmes by means of direct broadcasting satellites. The second issue was home video.

The Norwegian PTT (Televerket) has been operating a videotex system (Teledata) since 1978. Private use was mainly tested in a pilot project in one area, Bergen, where the largest newspaper played a leading part by delivering general news (Mathisen 1982). The pilot project was closed down in 1981, and indicated that private households were not likely to become heavy users of videotex. The permanent system is mainly for commercial information.

For some time, there have been plans for an integrated telecommunication network for telephone, data and video transmission. A Royal Commission has proposed that the Telecommunication Administration should have the responsibility for the development of the national network, but that private companies should compete with an independent branch of the PTT for the local networks (NOU 1983:32 and NOU 1984:29). Almost all the present cable networks are only transmitting television pictures. But the telephone system is gradually upgraded to ISDN standards.

**Policies for the press and broadcasting**

The traditional struggle between the national centre and the periphery in Norway could be extended to include conflicts along a local–national–international dimension. A second range of issues concern the conflict between monopolies and de-monopolization. An underlying dimension in most media politics is a conflict between a focus on economy or technology vs. a focus on cultural factors or media content. A fourth dimension is latent rather than manifest: a conflict between media as commodities or as public goods. If media are regarded as commodities, private ownership, deregulation and free market competition is a sensible policy. If, on the other hand, the media are regarded as means to reduce gaps between different segments of the population (information gaps and differences in the supply of culture and entertainment), then state ownership and regulation can be justified in order to avoid the consequences of free competition.

*Main actors*

The political parties are one group of important actors. The parties are often working in cooperation with other associations like Christian organizations, trade unions, etc. The parties and some of the organizations are interested in a broad spectrum of issues in media politics. Along the centre–periphery dimension, the Progressive Party and the Conservative Party represent one pole, with the Centre Party and probably the Christian People's Party at the opposite pole. The Progressive–Conservative alliance represents one pole on the remaining three dimensions, but there with the Labour Party and the Left Socialists at the opposite pole. The conflicting location of the parties along different dimensions has made it difficult to make a broad coalition in media politics.

A second important group of actors are the media themselves. The formation of conglomerates makes the picture difficult to read. In general the existing media, with the exception of NRK, have favoured the introduction of new media. The press was important as owners in the early stages of local radio and television and cable networks, and some of the larger newspapers also planned to involve themselves in the second television channel. The press also wrote a lot about these new media, trying to create a public pressure supporting advertising in the local broadcasting media and to have a quick decision on the second television channel. Conflict of interest was hardly discussed as an ethical theme in these matters.

The Norwegian electronic industry used to play an important role as a pressure group in media politics, often acting in cooperation with trade unions and employers' associations. But now almost all radio receivers,

TV sets, video recorders, etc. are imported, and the industry plays a minor role. Film producers and associations for advertising agencies and advertisers have tried to influence decisions on advertising in local media and national television.

## Main issues – integration or disintegration?

The broad coalition behind the broadcasting policy in the 1950s, 1960's and beginning of the 1970s has disappeared. The Conservative Party proclaimed in the election campaign in 1981 that it promoted a second television channel financed by commercials and organized outside NRK (Høyres arbeidsprogram 1981–85: 89). Since the formation of the Conservative government in 1981, most decisions on broadcasting politics by non-socialist governments can be interpreted as steps towards this goal. The decision to allow local radio, cable transmission of satellite programmes and local television broke the monopoly and put the question of financing on the agenda. At the same time, the government weakened NRK by allowing only insignificant increases in the licence fee leading to cuts in NRK's budgets, rather than allowing a strengthening of the institution in order to meet the new competition. The Labour party has tried to strengthen the NRK.

A broad coalition has emerged in support of the local media. But no such unity emerged on two major questions concerning the organization of a second television channel: organization inside or outside NRK; and financing: commercials or increased licence fee (Vaagland and Østbye 1986). In 1990, the TV2 question appears to have been solved. A broad coalition, including the Labour Party, but excluding the Progressive Party, accepted the establishment of a private, second channel, financed by advertising. In order to secure some of the PSB goals, there are a lot of regulations on form and content of both programmes and commercials. It is far from certain that a station with these restrictions on advertising will make it financially possible for the company to produce and distribute a national channel.

The press subsidies represent another topical theme. The Conservative Party would like to abandon most of the subsidies. The Labour Party is the strong defender of the subsidies, usually with some support from the Centre Party when it is not in government with the Conservatives. Labour and Centre Party newspapers would be likely to suffer most if the subsidies are abandoned. Estimates show that local competition would remain only in a few cities. Also most of the smallest newspapers (circulation less than 2–3 000) would be likely to disappear (NAL 1990).

Other themes present in the media debates in the early 1990s were: regulation of advertising in television, new technology (ISDN etc.), and media questions related to the 1994 Olympic Games in Lillehammer.

Technical innovations, results of competition and import of new media and new ideas create the challenges to the Norwegian mass media system. The solutions are affected by the Norwegian traditions and political culture.

## Statistics

(1 ECU = 8.07 NOK (January 1991))
(The following figures are from 1989)

| | |
|---|---:|
| Population | 4.2 million |
| Number of households | 1.7 million |

Public broadcasting

| | |
|---|---:|
| Number of national, terrestrial television channels | 1 |
| Number of national radio channels | 2 |
| Number of local television permissions (very few operating) | 129 |
| Number of local radio permissions | 455 |
| Television penetration | 97% |

Size of television licence fees

| | | |
|---|---|---:|
| Black-and-white | 600 NOK | 75 ECU |
| Colour | 1 100 NOK | 135 ECU |
| Number of hours on national television | | 3 500 |
| Number of hours on national radio | | 13 000 |
| (including short-wave international services, | 550 hours | |
| and regional programming, | 7 467 hours) | |

New electronic media

| | |
|---|---:|
| Video cassette recorders penetration | 40% |
| Cable penetration | 30% |
| Satellite connection | 35% |

Advertising revenue (estimated see Ot.prp. nr 55 1989–90)

| Medium | m. NOK | m. ECU |
|---|---:|---:|
| Newspapers | 3 600 | 450 |
| Weekly magazines | 300 | 40 |
| Journals | 400 | 50 |
| Cinema | 55 | 7 |
| Local radio | 50 | 6 |
| Satellite television (TV3, TVN) | 60 | 7 |
| Free sheet newspapers | 50 | 6 |
| Non-mass media advertising | 4 750 | 590 |

Newspapers
Number of independent newspapers:

| | |
|---|---:|
| 6 days per week | 63 |
| 4–5 days per week | 21 |
| 2–3 days per week | 64 |
| 1 day per week | 4 |

The Norwegian Newspapers' Association (NAL) has in addition 35 smaller, local members, of which most publish 1 or 2 issues per week.

Circulation of the 10 largest newspapers

| Title | Circulation |
|---|---|
| VG - Verdens Gang (indep., Oslo, national tabloid) | 360 331 |
| Aftenposten (indep. Cons., Oslo, national/regional) | 267 278 |
| Dagbladet (indep, Oslo, national tabloid) | 214 637 |
| Aftenposten aftenutgave (indep. Cons., Oslo, regional) | 193 932 |
| Bergens Tidende (indep., Bergen, regional) | 99 408 |
| Adresseavisen (Cons., Trondheim, regional) | 88 722 |
| Stavanger Aftenblad (indep., Stavanger, regional) | 67 490 |
| Arbeiderbladet (Labour, Oslo, national/regional) | 55 707 |
| Fædrelandsvennen (indep., Kristiansand, regional) | 45 820 |
| Drammens Tidende og Buskeruds Blad (Cons., Drammen, regional) | 42 827 |

# References

Haraldsen, Gustav and Vaage, Odd F. (1988) Radiolytting og fjernsynsseing høsten 1988. Oslo: Statistisk sentralbyrå (Rapporter 88/27).

Haugen, Einar (1966) Language Conflict and Languaage Planning. Cambridge, Mass.: Harvard University Press.

Haugen, Einar (1968) Riksspråk og folkemål (translation of Haugen 1966). Oslo: Universitetsforlaget.

Hjeltnes, Guri (1990) Avisoppgjøret etter 1945. Oslo: Aschehoug.

Høst, Sigurd (1983) Videobruk i Norge vinteren 1983. Oslo: Institutt for presseforskning.

Høyer, Svennik (1974): Norsk presse mellom 1865 og 1965 (del I og II). Oslo: Institutt for presseforskning.

Høyer, Svennik (1982) Pressen – økonomisk utvikling og politisk kontroll, in NOU 1982:30 Maktutredningen. Massemedier. Oslo: Universitetsforlaget.

Høyres arbeidsprogram 1981–85. Oslo: Høyre.

Hultén, Olof (1984) Video i Sverige. Stockholm: Sveriges Radio.

Innst. O. nr. 3 1987-88. Innstilling frå kyrkje og undervisningskomiteen om lov om nærkringkasting

Lund, Sissel (1985) Billedmedier i Norge. Oslo: NRK/Forskningen.

Mathisen, Kjell Olav (1982) Teledata brukererfaringer. Kjeller: Televerkets forskningsinstitutt.

NAL (1990) 10 teser om pressestøtte, Oslo: Norske Avisers Landsforbund

NOU 1983:3 Massemedier og mediepolitikk. Oslo: Universitetsforlaget.

NOU 1983:9 Lov om film og video. Oslo: Universitetsforlaget.

NOU 1983:32 Telematikk. Oslo: Universitetsforlaget.

NOU 1984:29 Organisering av televirksomheten i Norge. Oslo: Universitetsforlaget.

NRK (1989) Tall + Fakta Beretningsåret 1988. Oslo: NRK.

NRK (1990) Programregler. Oslo: NRK.

NRK årbok 1983 (1984). Oslo: NRK.

NU A 1979:4E Nordic Radio and Television via Satellite. Copenhagen: The Secretariat for Nordic Cultural Cooperation.

Nymo, Birger (1984) Publikum og fjernsyn over kabel. Kjeller: Televerkets forskningsinstitutt.

Østbye, Helge (1977) Norsk rikskringkasting. Bergen: Senter for medieforskning.

Østbye, Helge (1982) Norsk rikskringkasting – ett monopol, to medier in NOU 1982:30 Maktutredningen. Massemedier. Oslo: Universitetsforlaget.

Østbye, Helge (1988) Mediepolitikk. Oslo: Universitetsforlaget.

Ot. prp. nr. 47 1986–87 Lov om nærkringkasting. Oslo: Kultur- og vitenskap-departementet.

Ot. prp. nr. 55 1989–90 TV2 – Lov om reklame i kringkasting m.v. Oslo: Kirke- og kulturdepartementet.

Rokkan, Stein (1975) "Sentrum og periferi, økonomi og kultur" in Sentrum og periferi i historien (Studier i historisk metode X). Oslo: Universitetsforlaget.

Rokkan, Stein and Valen, Henry (1962) "The Mobilization of the Periphery", Acta Sociologica.

Ryland, Stig (1990) Reklame i nærradio, Volda: Møre og Romsdal DH

Seip, Jens Arup (1959) "'Det norske system' i den økonomiske liberalismes klassiske tid", Historisk tidsskrift, 39.

Seip, Jens Arup (1975) "Modellenes tyranni" in Sentrum og periferi i historien (Studier i historisk metode X). Oslo: Universitetsforlaget.

Smeland, Sverre (formann) (1973) Tilråding fra nærkringkastingsutvalget. Oslo: NRK.

St. meld. nr. 84 1984-85 Om ny mediepolitikk. Oslo: Universitetsforlaget.

Syvertsen, Trine (1985) Forsøk med lokal radio og fjernsyn i Norge (utkast). Bergen: Senter for mediefag.

Tofte, Tor Jørgen (1985) Program 2 i NRK/radio. Kulturpolitikk eller lokaliseringspolitikk? Bergen: Senter for mediaforskning.

Vaagland, Olav and Østbye, Helge (1986) "Slutten på NRK-monopolet – og hva så?" in Pressens årbog 1985:2. Copenhagen: Reitzel.

Werner, Anita (1982) Ungdom og video vinteren 1982. Oslo: Institutt for presseforskning.

Werner, Anita, Høst, Sigurd and Ulvær, Bjørn Petter (1984) Publikums reaksjoner på satellitt- og lokalfjernsyn. Oslo: Institutt for presseforskning.

# 13

# Portugal

*Joel Hasse Ferreira*

## National profile

Portugal covers a territory of 92 100km$^2$, including the Atlantic Islands of Madeira and the Azores, and has a population of 10.4 million. The country is a language region in itself; the population has no significant minorities with a language or dialect of their own, the dialect *mirands* being spoken only by a few thousand people, usually as a second language, in Miranda do Douro, in the north-east of the country. General education standards are still low compared to the European average. Illiteracy, in 1990, stood about 17%.

The political system after 1976 is a semi-presidential democracy. The Prime Minister is appointed by the President based on the political results of parliamentary elections. The President is elected for a five-year period and the Parliament is elected for a maximum period of four years.

Though Portugal is considered a new industrialized country by international standards, extreme regional disparities prevail in the country's level of economic development. Industry is concentrated in the coastal region and particularly between Setbal and Braga. The Lisbon administration, correspondingly, is a centralistic one, even if the Constitution, approved in 1976, established administrative regions.

The country dates back to 1140, being one of the oldest States in Europe. It bordered on the Spanish Kingdoms of Leo and Castela and the existing borders date back to the thirteenth century when the Arabs were evicted from the country, two centuries before the fall of the Granada Kingdom, in the south of Spain. After playing a very important role in the discoveries of America, Africa and Asia, Portugal was occupied by Spain from 1580 to 1640, regaining independence after a civil war and a war against Spain.

The Republican system was set up in 1910, but was interrupted by a dictatorship from 1926 to 1974. In the course of the two year revolutionary period from 1974 to 1976, there were 6 governments, until the approval of the Constitution took place, in April 1976. Since then the two main parties, the PSD — the Social Democratic Party (a liberal party) – and PS — the Socialist Party – have ruled the country, individually or in coalition.

Being an Atlantic state, Portugal, until the 1960s, was not oriented towards Europe but towards the overseas world. Hence, Portugal has close relationships to her former colonies in Africa (Mozambique, Angola, Guinea-Bissau, Cabo Verde and S.Tomé and Princípe) and Brazil, all of them countries where Portuguese is spoken as an official language.

> Portugal is a country whose history reflects a determined independence in European affairs. Being both small and peripheral, it is not widely known to international policy analysts. Yet it represents a fascinating paradox: a former world power that yet remains economically underdeveloped. The dictatorship that ruled the country from 1926 to 1974 is not enough, by itself, to explain the slowness with which the country has developed. Loss of its overseas empire in 1974-74 led to Portugal's application for entry into the EEC in 1977; a 1985 treaty led to EEC membership effective in 1986. Since then Portugal has posed somewhat of a challenge for the Community, which through its various initiatives has been trying to bring the poorer EEC members closer to a level of economic development found in other areas of Europe. In the euphemism of the EEC, Portugal is decidedly a Less Favoured Region (LFR). (Case and Ferreira 1990)

## Development of the press and broadcasting since 1945

From 1945 to 1974, the newspaper press was under State censorship. During this period, many of the national daily newspapers were bought up by financial groups wanting to have some influence on the political and economical system through the media.

All this changed in 1975, with the nationalization of the main economic groups by the fourth Government of the April Revolution, led by Vasco Gonçalves. The main Portuguese daily newspapers have been taken over by the State and only in the late 1980s have some been privatized gradually. The last will be *Diário de Notícias*, in 1991.

The weekly newspapers began just before the end of dictatorship, in 1973. The first one was *Expresso*, owned and edited by Francisco Pinto Balsemão. This newspaper was linked with the liberal wing of the regime and also with the moderate liberal opposition. During the 1980s *Semanário* and *Independente* were launched.

In 1975 the weekly *O Jornal* was created by a group of professionals, trying to develop links with national and international groups. This journal is the only paper expressing mainly moderate left views.

The only television company working in Portugal, Radiotelevisão Portuguesa (RTP), began regular broadcasts in 1957. Created as a private firm, it was really controlled by the Government, through the censorship and special links with several private owners and the possession of some shares. The initial capital was put up by the Government, private radio stations, and some banks. RTP joined Eurovision in 1959.

Following nationalization after the 1974 revolution, control of the network has undergone many changes, culminating in a recent constitutional change allowing private television broadcasting in Portugal.

In 1975, television was established on the Azores. In 1978, the second channel (RTP 2) began broadcasting, and then colour television was introduced using the PAL system. Together, the two stations transmit about 200 hours per week. Not all locations in the country can receive the TV signal. RTP1 covers 95% of Portugal and RTP2 covers 75%.

The revenues of RTP have hitherto come from licence fees and advertising. In 1988 only about 1.7 million television sets were "legally" in service and many additional television receivers were not registered. Recently, the Portuguese Government announced that the licence fee will be dropped. Public service television (controlling two channels) should be able to compete with private television (that will have the other two channels).

## The press

### *Policy framework*

A press law was passed in 1975 and slightly revised in 1976, 1978 and 1988. It mainly concerning press crimes and trials. There are some subsidies, financing paper and distribution, but only under established conditions. There are no monopoly regulations, even though the press has voiced the need for anti-monopolist measures.

The press law guarantees the freedom of press, including the freedom to set up enterprises and free competition. No censorship can be allowed and prices must be determined by the managers of the press companies. Also the press law establishes the global statutes for professional journalism and defines the conditions for advertising.

### *Ownership and finance*

In Portugal, there are daily newspapers and weekly newspapers. The morning daily newspapers in Lisbon are *Correio da Manhã* (belonging to a press group led by Carlos Barbosa), *Público* (belonging to an economic group, SONAE, controlled by Belmiro de Azevedo) and *Diário de Notícias* (still State-owned). *Correio da Manhã* is the only one which is now very profitable.

The evening daily newspapers in Lisbon are *A Capital*, belonging to F.Pinto Balsemão and *Diário Popular*, where the majority of the shares belong to Horácio Roque, who has many other economic interests, mainly on the Madeira Islands and in South Africa.

In Oporto, the only profitable daily newspaper now is *Jornal de Notícias*. The others are *Comércio do Porto* and *Primeiro de Janeiro* which are also owned by economic groups.

There are other daily newspapers, namely in Coimbra, Aveiro and Braga, but they only have regional distribution.

The weekly newspapers are relatively new in Portugal, but they have increased their readership during the 1970s and 1980s. The most important weekly newspapers are *O Jornal*, centre-left oriented, owned by a group of journalists; *Expresso*, created in 1973, centre-right, but trying to be independent, belonging to the Pinto Balsemão group; *Independente*, irreverent right-wing, created in the late 1980s and *Semanário*, right-wing oriented, created in the early 1980s.

Most *Independente* and *Semanário* shares are in the possession of media economic groups linked with the press.

### Structure and organization

There are more than 100 local and regional newspapers, most of them linked to the Catholic Church and local or regional economic interest groups.

There are strong regional differences (see statistical section) The only daily newspaper with a national distribution is *Público*. This newspaper has simultaneous printing and distribution in Lisbon and Oporto, with tele-transmission of national texts and regional supplements for each one of those metropolitan areas.

Readers who are top and middle managers have *Público* as the first daily newspaper with 37.9% and *Diário de Notícias* as the second one with 25.3% (source: Marktest data).

## Electronic media

### Legal framework

The Portuguese Constitution of 1976 guarantees the freedom of expression and a pluralistic model. In July 1988 Parliament passed Law no. 87/88, regulating radio activities. The defence and promotion of cultural and educational values is left to the public sector.

Together with the Parliament the Government appoints the majority of the members of the "High Authority to the Media", the legal structure which rules in conflicts concerning freedom of the press and broadcasting media. The licence to operate private radio channels is controlled by a Consultative Committee of the Government.

The statutes of the public company Radiodifusão Portuguesa were established in May 1984. There are references to the promotion of Portuguese culture and musical production, integration of youth and children in society, patriotic stimulation and regionalization of broadcasting.

Television broadcasting is regulated by Law no. 58 of 1990. This law includes conventional hertzian television, cable TV and satellite TV. The conditions of broadcasting include a public service under State responsibility and the opening of television to private operators, through a State licence. The concession of public TV service is given for fifteen years to the enterprise Radiotelevisão Portuguesa.

Cabling has not happened in Portugal. Only a few municipalities (in tourist zones and new municipalities) have decided to retransmit satellite television programmes.

A Telecommunications Act passed in 1990 gives regulatory authority to the ICP, Instituto das Comunicações de Portugal (the Communications Institute of Portugal), a governmental body which is independent of the operators.

## Ownership and financial aspects

The public enterprise RTP is owned by the state and governed by a five-member board, typically composed of managers appointed from the various state-owned enterprises, lawyers or politicians. These members serve terms of three years but may be asked to step down following changes of government.

In early 1991, the Portuguese Government published regulations for new private TV channels in Portugal. The Government also created a firm to be owned by private and public partners to distribute the TV signal throughout the country. Private television channels must be advertising-financed.

Several groups have shown an interest in competing for the private television licence:

— SIC, controlled by Balsemão group, linked with several Portuguese press groups and some international economic interests.

— The Radio Renascença group, linked with the Catholic Church, sees an advantage in the addition of a television channel, especially if linked with other groups.

— Other candidates are mainly economic groups in the north of the country. Some of these groups could present a proposition together with Radio Renascença.

## Programme policy

Sports and soap opera (telenovelas), mainly Brazilian, are very dominant in the television programmes. Also programmes for children are increasing. There are several "telejournals" during the day on both channels and also round-table discussions with politicians and specialists in several fields.

The showing of feature films has increased strongly and also their average quality. On Madeira and the Azores, most of the information concerns regional problems.

In 1989, RTP1 transmitted 240 hours of advertising, corresponding to 4.1% of the total schedule. RTP2 transmitted 45 hours of advertising, corresponding to 1.1% of the total schedule.

There are no legal provisions for local TV. Some "free" or "pirate" transmissions have been made by local groups, but the quality is very low.

The local and regional radio stations have been developed in a very important way, in the late 1980s, after a special law concerning local radio was enacted. Many local radio firms applied for licences and several hundred stations are now transmitting in Portugal. In Lisbon, the most important is TSF, which now competes with the national stations. All over the country, local stations are very important local news media and facilitators of local, political participation. In the late 1980s local radio has been a big revolution in Portuguese society.

## Telematic media

The Correios e Telecomunicações de Portugal (CTT) has responsibility for the post, telephones (excluding Lisbon and Oporto) and European telecom. Telefones de Lisboa e Porto (TLP) handles the telephone network of Lisbon and Oporto urban areas. Companhia Portuguesa Radio Marconi operates in international telecom, excluding Europe.

The global strategy of telecom in Portugal includes the creation of a digital network with integrated services utilizing optical fibres as support. The project is orientated to the constitution of a multiservice network, permitting the access to cable TV and telecom services.

Joint-ventures between TLP and CTT have been created in recent years to operate new telecom services like:

— Telemovel (celular mobile telephone)

— TLM for paging, and

— Video conferencing.

These services are being developed mainly for business use.

*Foreign media availability*

In many towns, like Lisbon and Oporto and in the tourist regions, one can find French, English, German, Spanish and Italian newspapers. Also, the sales of parabolic antennas have grown strongly in the late 1980s adding the satellite programmes to the existing Portuguese ones.

## Policies for the press and broadcasting

*Main actors and interests*

The state is still the main actor, controlling television and having an important influence on radio, combined with control of a morning newspaper. But other actors are emerging gradually. The group Pinto Balsemão is a strong candidate for a private television channel and controls the weekly *Expresso* and the Lisbon evening newspaper *A Capital*. It is also strengthening links with other European media groups. The Carlos Barbosa group also competes for a private television channel. The group controls a newspaper in Lisbon, *Correio da Manhã*, and has shares in the weekly *Independente*. It is also into radio.

New groups, like SONAE (which owns the daily newspaper *Público*) and FNAC (which is associated with the Jornal group in local radio TSF), are becoming more active in these fields. SONAE has even shown its interest in having a private television channel, but seemingly the group has given up this project.

Journalists in national and regional media participate in local radio and even in some national newspapers such as *O Jornal*. And there are local and regional interests increasing their presence in local regional press and radio.

Direct press control by the political parties has seemingly come to an end. The Socialist Party influenced several daily newspapers like *Republica, Luta* and *Portugal-Hoje. Republica* ceased publication after being occupied by communist workers and journalists during the Revolutionary period and the others were closed down later due to financial problems.

The Communist Party supported *O Diário* for many years, but it also closed down during the 1980s.

The Catholic Church still broadcasts on Radio Renancença, and is trying to put a private television project together. The church also controls several regional and local newspapers.

Foreign groups are not yet very important in Portugal, even though the privatization of TV could fuel some of their interest in Portugal.

The multimedia groups are becoming more important, mainly those that are in television, radio and press. The Balsemão group will most likely increase its influence, and the links established between the economic cooperative group FNAC and *O Jornal* press group also signal the emergence of an important competitive multimedia group.

*Main issues*

The trend towards private interests in television is irreversible and accepted as the most important trend in public opinion in Portugal.

The illegal explosion of local radio stations obliged the State to approve new laws and now hundreds of private local and regional stations are on the air, encouraging the participation of local citizens and interests in social affairs.

The opening of two television channels to private interests could be a step in a direction that could reduce public service television to a single public channel.

However, since local press and radio are important, it is not clear whether the private television stations that are coming will be able to regionalize their channels.

European integration is being done through the gradual application of the main recommendations included in the general resolutions for liberalization and deregulation.

Local TV is practically non-existent in Portugal. Some programmes, often of bad quality, have been broadcast illegally in several places around the country, but with little success.

**Statistics**

(1 ECU= 178 Escudos)

| | |
|---|---|
| Population | 10.4 m. |
| Population density pr. sq. km- | 113 |
| Number of households | 2.2 m |

| Broadcasting | |
|---|---|
| Number of households with TV sets | 1.7 m. |
| Number of national television channels | 2 |
| Number of hours broadcast in 1989 | |
| RTP1 | 5 850 hrs |
| RTP2 | 4 090 hrs |
| Number of national radio channels: | 5 |
| Number of local radio channels: | several hundred |

Radio audience shares

| Channel | Audience share in % | Coverage |
|---|---|---|
| In the Oporto region: | | |
| Radio Renancença channel 1 | 34.0 | national |
| RFM (R.Renancença) | 24.0 | national |
| Radio Nova | 18.8 | local |
| Antena 1 | 18.8 | national |
| Radio Comercial (FM) | 18.6 | national |

Radio audience shares (cont.)

| Channel | Audience share in % | Coverage |
|---|---|---|
| In Lisbon urban area: | | |
| R.Ren.-channel 1 | 36.0 | national |
| TSF | 20.9 | local |
| R.Cidade | 17.6 | local |
| R.Comercial-FM | 14.0 | national |
| Antena 1 | 14.0 | national |

(Source: Marktest data/last week February 1991)

Shares of the advertising market (1990)

| | |
|---|---|
| Television | 44% |
| Press | 37% |
| Outdoors | 11% |
| Radio | 8% |

Total advertising expenditure 60 000 m.

The daily newspapers with the largest market shares (January 1991)

| Title | Market share Lisbon | Market share Oporto | Total |
|---|---|---|---|
| Correio da Manhã | 29.5% | - | 18.6% |
| Público | 16.8% | 16.8% | 16.8% |
| Jornal de Noticias | 0.2% | 53.5% | 15.2% |
| Diário de Noticias | 16.2% | | 11.7% |

(Source: Marktest data Feb. 1991)

Circulation of the main weekly newspapers (week 4–10 March 91)

| | |
|---|---|
| Expresso | 20.1% |
| O Independente | 6.2% |
| Tal & Qual | 4.2% |
| Semanário | 3.5% |
| Sábado | 3.4% |
| O Jornal | 3.1% |

Sábado is the most important week magazine, created two years ago and Tal & Qual is a weekly journal, independent, covering essentially sensational facts.

# References

Anurio RTP 1989, Lisbon.

Case, Donald Owen and Ferreira, Joel Hasse (1990) "Portuguese Telecommunications and Information Technologies: Development and Prospects", Telecommunications Policy, 14,4, 290–302.

Ferreira, Joel Hasse (1986), "Notas sobre algumas questões estratégicas ligadas às mudanças tecnológicas na comunicacão social portuguesa", Revista de Comunicacão e Linguagens, 4, December.

Lopez da Silva, M. and Ferreira, Joel Hasse Brauman, C. and Simes, G.R (1990), "Delimitacão e Perspectivas do Meio Audiovisual e da Telecomuncacão em Portugal" CECL-JNICT. Lisbon.

"28th European Telecoms Congress" (1989) Comunicaes September, special issue.

# 14

# Spain

*Rosario de Mateo and Joan M.Corbella*

## National profile

Spain covers an area of 504 782 km$^2$ and has a population of 38 473 000 inhabitants. Population density is 77 inhabitants per km$^2$. However, the population distribution is very unequal: at the periphery the density is 100 inhabitants per km$^2$, whereas in the interior of the peninsula it is only 25. The metropolitan areas Madrid and Barcelona, with about 4.5 and 3 million inhabitants respectively, are the main nuclei of population, though we find four more cities with more than half a million inhabitants.

Since 1982 the Spanish economy has undergone a slow but continual recovery, with a falling-off in unemployment rates (17% in 1989) and a constant increase of the gross domestic product. Nevertheless the yearly inflation rate, which was 5% in 1987, has increased again to 7% in 1989 and 1990.

The economic activity is focused in Madrid and Catalonia (service and industry), followed by the Basque Country (industry) and Valencia (industry and agriculture). However, the two regions with the highest income per person are the Balearic Isles and the Canary Isles. This is due to tourist incomes. Madrid and Catalonia are just behind the islands. The distribution of wealth is very unequal, and the south and the inner regions are among the poorest regions in Western Europe.

With the Constitution of 1978, Spain became a parliamentary monarchy. A regime was established which recognizes the existence of different regions and cultural particularities in Spain. Seventeen autonomous regions (Communidades Autónomas – CCAA) were established, each one having its own parliamentary and governmental system. The State Administration is distributed between the central and the regional governments. The regional governments handle issues concerning culture, health, urbanism, security, etc. with some variations. Defence and foreign policy are the prerogative of the central government.

The Constitution acknowledges the linguistic plurality of Spain.

Spanish (or Castilian) is the official language for the whole country. Catalan, Basque and Galician are official languages in their respective regions.

The Spanish Socialist Party (PSOE) has been in power since 1982. It now holds the absolute majority in the State Parliament and in most Regional Parliaments. In other CCAA the government is in the hands of conservative parties (Galice, Castile, Balearic Isles) or nationalistic parties (Catalonia and Basque Country).

With the socialist government (PSOE), Spain has joined the EC and participates in the NATO alliance. This has brought Spanish international politics in line with the rest of Western Europe. At the same time, Spain has been obliged to restructure its legislation in economic affairs, adapting it to the EC. The new situation in Europe has made it easier for foreign capital to enter most branches of production. This situation has also allowed Japanese companies to invest in Spain.

### Development of the press and broadcasting since 1945

Mass media in Spain in 1945 worked on the premises imposed by Franco's regime after his victory in the Civil War (1939). Until the beginning of the 1960s, the conditions for the development of the media were tightly controlled. From then till the dictator's death in 1975, they were, apparently, more liberal. In 1975 the transitional period to democracy started, and old and new values coexisted for a time. This gave way to the formation of the present structures in the mass media.

The main concern of Franco's government was the ideological function of information. Therefore, the State tried to control the mass media through laws and regulatory measures and in many cases through the ownership and management of the media.

The press, according to the law of 1938, was considered a national institution and its organization was under state control. Radio information services were also under strict control following the rules of 1939. The organization of this medium was set down in the law of 1934. These rules implied the reduction of the freedom of speech, because of imposed censorship of news. Private companies were required to apply for administrative licences in order to set up radio and press activities.

This control was strengthened when the State took over a great number of newspapers, magazines and radio stations. On 28 October 1956, the first official television broadcasting began. Television was constituted as a public state monopoly dependent on the Government. Its regulation was essentially based on the existing legislation for radio broadcasting.

At the end of the 1950s, the financial oligarchy and technocratic economists from the Opus Dei (a Catholic lay order) became strong in the political and economic scene. The Stabilization Plan of 1959 marked the beginning of an economic development which presupposed the existence of a European market. But this international opening was not possible as long as Spain continued with its dictatorship system. That is why an institutional reorganization was carried on. The reorganization had the appearance of a political liberalization of the Franco regime.

The Press and Printing Law in 1966 can be viewed in this context. The aim of this law was to liberalize the written press, though censorship and regulation of journalistic enterprises continued. Broadcasting own information was forbidden for radio stations, which were obliged to broadcast the official news bulletins of the public radio station, Radio Nacional de España. However, the bill of 1964 was important because of its rationalization of the Spanish radio sector. This bill fixed and defined the public and private broadcasting of national, regional (referring to the area formed by some townships) and local media. Afterwards the setting up of FM radio stations was relatively liberalized, and a pattern for the financing of radio companies was established.

Television continues to be a national public monopoly, lacking a legal entity of its own, since its management was under a general office of a ministry. Televisión Española (TVE) had its own technical network, while in the rest of Europe the broadcasting function was in the hands of the PTT. The financial sources of TVE were the General State Budget and advertising.

After Franco's death (1975), the State was removed from the management of the printed press. The existing restrictions in this field were abolished, mainly through the law of 1984 which also provided the press and the news agencies with economic State help.

In the radio sector public and private ownership and management coexisted, and freedom of information was introduced in 1977. However, all legal structures and the organization of radio were maintained until 1987, when the Telecommunications Act (Ley de Ordenación de las Telecomunicaciones, LOT) was passed.

Television reached adulthood in 1980, when the Radio and Television Statute was promulgated. This statute invalidated the previous television regulation, which was chaotic and partial. From this year onwards, management was progressively decentralized. First of all, the monopoly of the State administration ended with the approval of a law in 1983 which allowed the CCAA to have their own channels. Secondly, in 1988, the private television law was passed, and the public monopoly of television ended.

## The press

*Legal framework*

The press in Spain is not controlled by any specific legislation since the promulgation of the 1978 Constitution. Formerly, the law of 1966 was an impediment to the normal development of press activities. The activity of the press is now free, only subject to legislation protecting honour and individual privacy, as well as the respect of the Constitution. Therefore, there are no limitations to the ownership or the financing of publications. However, the participation of press companies in radio and television is regulated in order to guarantee the plurality of these two media and to avoid monopolization.

In 1986, the entry of foreign capital in Spanish press was liberalized, so as to adapt Spanish legislation to the regulation of the European Community. Since then many press groups have started activities in Spain, for example Bertelsmann, Hachette, Bauer, Springer, VNU and Hersant (most of them in the field of non-daily press). Other groups were established in Spain earlier, by taking advantage of some openings in law, like G+J.

Although the Spanish press is financed through advertising and sales, it became necessary in 1984 to establish a legal framework for State subsidies. This regulation had its origins in the crisis of the press sector during the early 1980s and it was based on the circulation of the newspapers, the consumption of Spanish paper and technological renovation. At first these measures were intended to make it easier for newspapers to survive during the crisis and only wholly-owned Spanish enterprises could receive support. This led to accusations of unfair competition by the EC, and subsidization was gradually reduced from 1988 onwards, in such a way that today there is no help from the State, directly or indirectly, to the press (only a reduction in post and telecommunication rates).

The governments of some CCAA with their own language (Catalonia, Basque Country) give economic help to the press (magazines and newspapers) to make up for the difficulties in keeping a press with a language different from Spanish.

*Press ownership and financing*

Until 1984 some newspapers in Spain were owned by the State and they competed in the market with the private press, which was mostly run by family-owned companies. Sales and liquidation of the newspapers created by Franco's regime (in all the main cities) have left the sector completely in private hands. At the same time, the Constitution sheltered the freedom of speech and free enterprise, so that the market was rearranged at the end of the 1970s and the beginnings of the 1980s.

During this period, the Spanish press went through a very severe crisis, along with a general economic crisis in Spain. This forced a number of well established old newspapers to close down, because they were not able to switch to new technology. At the same time, new newspapers, not run by family-owned companies, were created and they have become market leaders within a few years. These newspapers are for example *El País* (created in 1976 by PRISA, which is now one of the leader communication groups in Spain) and *El Periódico* (created in 1979 within Grupo Zeta, one of the leaders in the magazine market). Along with these new companies, only the main newspapers of great tradition survived, for example *ABC, La Vanguardia, La Voz de Galicia or Heraldo de Aragón*. These are all family-owned companies.

In 1986 the admission of foreign investment in the press sector was allowed. In this way, the most important European press groups started their activity in Spain, either by buying existing publications or by creating Spanish versions of the most popular magazines in their country of origin. The most important ones are Bertelsmann, Grüner und Jahr, Axel Springer, Bauer, VNU, Hachette and Agostini. These groups now have the largest non-daily press sales, together with some Spanish owned companies, such as Grupo 16, Hymsa or Grupo Zeta, which have also received foreign investment in recent years.

However, foreign capital has entered the Spanish daily press with much more difficulty. Only Hersant, Rusconi, Murdoch, Expansion and Springer have formalized their presence in newspapers by buying part of the capital in newspaper publishing companies. None have created their own newspapers. Only the deal between Prensa Española (publisher of *ABC*, with the second largest circulation) and Springer to launch a new popular newspaper, *CLARO*, in 1991, changes the transnational way of penetrating the Spanish press. At the same time, PRISA (owner of *El País*, the highest circulation newspaper, radio network SER, part of Canal+ etc.) in 1989 began expansion into foreign press markets, by taking over capital in some French and British companies.

Regarding the financing of press, newspapers and magazines, revenue comes from selling copies and from advertising. Advertising contributes 50% to 70% of the income in the main Spanish newspapers, and the rate is similar in magazines. So, this implies a great advertising dependence by the publishing companies, although advertising revenue continues to grow in the last years. On the other hand, the State press subsidies, created in 1984 to help newspapers survive the crisis, were deemed to be unnecessary in 1990, and were therefore stopped.

*Structure and organization of the daily press*

The reading rate of newspapers in Spain is among the lowest in Europe: 80 copies sold per 1,000 inhabitants. Only in the regions in the northern half is this rate 100 copies per 1 000 inhabitants. Low rates are in part due to the fact that Spain is a country with a poor reading tradition (including newspapers, magazines and books) and that there are not popular newspapers (yellow press) of great circulation, as in other countries.

In recent years, there has been a trend among the leading newspapers to seek new readers by printing specialized supplements and using a lot of graphics and illustrations intended to win over readers who are not used to reading. That is why sales of newspapers have slowly increased every year since 1986. Besides, there has been a remarkable increase in the sales of Sunday editions: by including magazines in full colour and other supplements in this way, the leading papers have increased their circulation by 70% and 100%.

The two newspapers with the highest circulation, *El País* and *ABC*, have national distribution, though in most CCAA they are exceeded in sales by the main regional newspapers. Among these newspapers we find *La Vanguardia* (Catalonia), *El Periódico* (Catalonia), *El Correo Español-El Pueblo Vasco* (Basque Country), *La Voz de Galicia* (Galicia)and *Diario Vasco* (Basque Country). Other newspapers with national distribution are *Diario 16* and two sports newspapers (*As* and *Marca*), all of them published in Madrid. Out of 90 to 100 newspapers published in Spain, only the main ones, either national or regional for Catalonia and the Basque Country have a daily circulation of more than 100 000.

In order to overcome the economic problems that this low circulation of newspapers created, a number of parallel strategies were evolved in the 1980s. Some of the national newspapers publish special editions in some CCAA (*El País* and *ABC*) in order to increase their sales regionally. Some publishing groups have collaboration agreements with local newspapers to exchange national and local news (Grupo 16). A third strategy is to establish new press groups, publishing regional newspapers in some CCAA and sharing news with other CCAA papers (Grupo Zeta, which publishes *El Periódico de Catalunya*, *La Voz de Asturias*, *El Periódico de Extremadura* and *El Periódico de Aragón*; Prensa Iberica, with newspapers bought to the State in 1984; COMECOSA, set up by *El Correo Espanol-El Pueblo Vasco* and regional newspapers).

Most newspapers are published in Spanish. Only six of them are in Catalan and one in Basque, and a few more are bilingual, Catalan/Spanish and Basque/Spanish. Newspapers printed in Catalan receive economic help from the government of Catalonia, in order to mitigate their economic difficulties.

*Structure and organization of the non-daily press*

In the wide field of non-daily press, Spain has an enormous quantity of journals; most of them have a small circulation, with only a few exceeding 500 000 copies. Contrary to newspapers, most magazines have a national reach. This fact makes it easy for them to survive. Only in Catalonia is there a local press written in Catalan, which is quite successful.

General information weeklies belong to groups whose capital is mostly Spanish. These groups often have publications in many fields. Grupo Zeta (the Murdoch Corporation has 25% of the capital) has the following magazines of general information: *Interviu, Tiempo* and *Panorama*, with circulation figures of about 100 000 and 200 000 copies each. Besides, it has travel, sports, economic and sex magazines. Grupo 16, also with foreign capital, publishes a weekly of general information, *Cambio 16* (with a circulation of 100 000) which competes with those belonging to Zeta and other ones with smaller circulation. Grupo 16 also publishes magazines on travel, history, cars, among other specialties.

## Electronic media

*Legal framework*

In the 1980s, there was an important change in the legal regulation of television, radio and the other electronic media.

In television, the 1980 statute established that RTVE had the monopoly in Spain. Under the control of Parliament, RTVE developed the State jurisdiction in television, including the control of the technical network, and also managed the public radio channels (Radio Nacional de España, RNE). RTVE had State funding until 1987, although its main source of income has always been advertising. In 1983, the changes started with the passing of the "third channel law". This law allowed the CCAA to create a channel for their geographic area to add to the two RTVE channels, and under the same charter as RTVE. The regional Parliaments were in control and should use the Third Channel broadcasting network of RTVE. But Catalan and Basque channels, which started broadcasting before the law was passed, have their own networks.

In 1988 the private television law was passed. The bill establishes that the State will allow private companies to run three national channels. Foreign participation is limited to 25% of share. The same limit goes for communication companies. The technical network is provided by the public company Retevision (controlled by Telefónica and RTVE among others). Retevision was created by splitting up the RTVE network into the management functions of television channels and the broadcast of signals.

In 1987 the telecommunication regulation law (LOT) was passed. This law establishes a relative liberalization for the non-basic services (value added services and some others) and keeps the fundamental position of Telefónica (semi-public company under the control of Government). The same law governs the radio broadcasting and establishes that public stations (State AM radio and State and CCAA stations in the FM band) must coexist with private ones (in both, AM and FM). Rules were established in order to avoid ownership concentration among privately owned radio stations, and foreign capital was accepted, but in a very limited way.

During the first years of the 1990s it is expected that cable and satellite television will be regulated (which depends on RTVE as the 1980 statute specifies). This is also the case for local television, with many viewers in some regions, but without any regulation, and about 400 municipal public radio (*radio municipal*). The Radio Municipal law was passed in April 1991.

## Television organization and structure

Until August of 1989 there were only television channels controlled by the central Administration (RTVE) and the CCAA Administration (third channels). Then the government gave management of three new national channels to three private companies. All these channels are broadcast by the terrestrial network owned by Retevision.

Until 1989, when private channels started to broadcast in Spain, there were the two television channels of RTVE which covered the whole country. These two channels were managed for TVE S.A., a public company owned completely by RTVE. The regional third channels are also managed by public companies and dependent on the CCAA Parliaments. In 1983, Basque (Euskal Telebista) and Catalan (TV3) channels started broadcasting, and the Galician channel (Television de Galicia, TVG) started in 1985. In the last two years some other third channels have started: Andalusia (Canal Sur), Valencia (Canal 9), Madrid (Telemadrid, TM3) and Murcia. Also, at this time, the Basque Country and Catalonia created their fourth channels, without a clear regulation. The rest of the CCAA are negotiating with RTVE in order to set up their own third channels in 1991.

In 1989, private television began competing with public channels. Antena 3, Tele 5 and Canal+ are the three licensees broadcasting nationally, although their introduction has been gradual, starting in the bigger urban areas. Canal+ broadcast is a pay-TV channel.

So, in the whole of Spain, there are today two public channels and three private ones, one of which must be paid for whereas the others are financed by advertising. It is important to remember that TVE is no longer on the General State Budget in 1990. In the Basque Country and in Catalonia viewers can also watch regional channels in their own language (one in Basque, and two in Catalonia). Five CCAA each have a regional channel. These channels are financed by advertising and the CCAA Budgets. The other ten CCAA do not have regional channels at present, so they only receive the five national channels. However, regional channels often cover adjacent CCAA partially.

The 1980 legislation specified cable- and satellite television to be used by RTVE. For this reason, TVE had two channels available through Intelsat that broadcast part of their programming to Western Europe and to Latin America (in 1990, there is a unified channel, TVE Internacional). RTVE has not taken any action in the cable television field, and the existing experiments have been carried out by small municipalities, waiting for a regulation on this sector. Some important towns like Barcelona have also made projects for cable television, but these are not installed yet.

*Radio organization and structure*

The structure of radio in Spain has to be studied from two different points of view: ownership and coverage. Radio channels with local coverage can be publicly owned radio stations (*radio municipal*) or private stations (small companies); some regional radio stations are owned by public companies, which belong to regional corporations of radio and television; others are private radio stations which have established regional or national networks. There is also the public national network of Radio Nacional de España (RNE), in the corporation RTVE.

In 1983 and in 1990, the central Government and the regional Governments (where they have jurisdiction) have increased the number of licences for radio stations. This fact has led to a strong growth in radio programming in Spain. The main enterprises and corporations in this sector are the following:

— RNE (RTVE ownership) has one AM network and four FM networks, one of which broadcasts different programming in each region (in Catalonia in Catalan language).

— SER (the oldest private radio network in Spain) has one AM network and one FM network, with about 150 radio stations (owned by SER or associated to networks). SER owns also the Cadena Dial (7 stations in FM) and Radio Minuto (18 stations). The most important share is held by PRISA (publisher of *El País*). SER is the leading network in audience ratings, with its standard programming and its "formula radio" channel (classic, folk, rock and other music genres, news, health information etc.).

— Antena 3 (created in 1982, and owned principally by press companies, as the publisher of *La Vanguardia*) has almost 90 FM radio stations in 1990, either associated or owned directly. Besides, it has an affiliated network, Radio 80 (19 FM radio stations).

— COPE (created by the Catholic Church radio stations in most towns) has over 80 stations in AM and FM, either associated or their own.

— Onda Cero Radio (created in 1990 by merging the RATO network and acquiring new concessions) has 104 stations in AM and FM. It is owned by the ONCE (the Spanish organization for the blind).

— Cadena Ibérica (created in 1988) has 19 radio stations in AM and FM in the main cities of Spain.

Apart from these networks with national coverage, there are regional radio networks in FM connected to the CCAA radio and television corporations and some private networks in Catalonia and elsewhere. We also find some private stations (AM and FM) with local coverage that are not syndicated to networks, and more than 400 local *radio municipal*, depending on municipal councils.

## Ownership and economic aspects

Regarding financing of radio and television, the public and private companies base their income on advertising. There are no radio or TV licence fees. However, public broadcasting corporations can receive funds from the State and CCAA Budgets. All regional television channels are supported by the CCAA, because they do not receive enough income from advertising to finance themselves. In the last years, TVE has not received any State funding because of its high advertising revenue.

Public radio stations are financed via transfer of funds from the radio and television corporations, as they do not get sufficient revenue from advertising.

Public media are organized in Corporations of Radio and Television, which combine the activities of both media, either nationally or regionally, in accordance with the laws of 1980 and 1983.

The private media are integral parts in the setting up of multimedia groups. This is due to market dynamics and the facilities given by legisaion. So, the three private television channels have among their main shareholders communication groups, which represent the 25% of capital that the law allows:

— Antena 3 has among its shareholders Antena 3 Radio, the Godó Group (publisher of *La Vanguardia*) and Prensa Española (publisher of

*ABC* ). Antena 3 Radio is owned by the Godó Group and a large number of regional newspapers.

— Tele 5 has the following shareholders: Berlusconi, 25% and ONCE (national blind organization, with lots of investments in many sectors, such as banking, radio, television and newspapers), 25%. The third investor is the financier J. de la Rosa.

— Canal+ has as main shareholders French Canal+ and PRISA group (publisher of *El País* and one economic newspaper, books and also owner of radio network SER; it also invests in foreign press).

As has already been mentioned, the most important radio networks are integrated in multimedia groups, but there are also some national, regional and local radio stations or networks not related to multimedia groups.

## Programming policies

Television programming is highly dependent on advertising income. This fact forces private and public enterprises to choose programmes likely to attract a large audience, light entertainment (talk-shows, shows), films, series and sports competitions. We hardly find cultural programmes and never in prime time. There is no difference between the public or the private programming policies. The only exception is the pay television channel Canal+, which does not rely on advertising and broadcasts basically films and sports.

In the radio field, programming has two different trends: public and private radio stations in AM and some radio stations in FM base themselves on informative programmes, informal talk-shows with people, shows and competitions and programmes with telephone participation from part of the audience. The other way is represented by the FM radio stations which are specialized in "formula radio" (classic, folk, rock and other music genres, news, health information, etc.).

## Reception of foreign programmes

Spain, because of its geographic position, has some difficulties in receiving satellite television. This can be overcome by using larger antennae (90 to 120 centimetres in most regions). The use of satellite antennae has increased in the last years and we have in 1990 about 30 000 units in Spain, most of them in tourist areas and in hotels.

Nevertheless, the increase in Spanish television channels (to 5 or 7 channels depending on the regions) will make it difficult for foreign broadcasting to enter Spain. But in some municipal areas, where there are small cable systems, there is usually the equipment necessary to distribute channels received by satellite.

### Local radio and television

The law regulating television in Spain does not permit local television. But since 1980 this kind of television has increased in many areas of Spain. Today there are about 150 local television channels and most of them are located in Catalonia. These stations are in general non-profit institutions and in some cases they receive economic support from local administrations. It is expected that by 1991 or 1992 their existence will be legalized, as was the case for cable television.

In the radio field, the law recognizes the existence of local radio stations with low power transmitters. Since 1934 there have been local radio stations, though most of the time they are used as re-broadcasters of regional or national radio programmes, either public or private. As a reaction to the lack of attention given to local radio, *radio municipal* (owned by town councils) began to proliferate after 1981, mainly in Catalonia but also in other areas of Spain. At the end of 1990 Parliament was debating a law allowing this kind of radio. The hottest issue was that of including advertising because it threatens the private radio stations.

### Telematics media

The development of telematic media is very much in its early stages in Spain, although a lot of experiments have been made in the fields of videotex and teletext from 1982 and onwards.

The videotex system (named Ibertex) is managed by Telefónica and it has not been very successful among the professional public or among the domestic public. Nevertheless the interest from some economic sectors, such as banking and general stores, for use in their relationship with the public and the Telefónica advertising campaign can foster future development. At the end of 1990 there were nearly 100 000 customer equipment installations.

The teletext system depends on the television organizations, which are in charge of implementation and production of news and information given through this medium. In 1989 TVE started to offer its public service, while some regional channels (like TV3 in Catalonia) did not start till 1990. However, the lack of advertising campaigns has contributed to the poor situation of teletext in Spain.

## Policies for the press and broadcasting

The dynamics of mass media in Spain are based on the interests of publishing companies and the socialist administration. Press companies want to have a powerful position in radio and in television through the creation of multimedia conglomerates. Socialist policy is based on balancing public and private participation.

Therefore, press groups trying to gain a dominant position in television are opposed by the law passed by the socialist government. This law defines a maximum participation of 25% ownership in the concessionaires and prohibits a company from taking a share in more than one channel. Although the companies protested at first, most of them have finally decided to participate in the competition for private television.

The government has not objected to the entry of press companies in radio (even with a dominant position, as it is the case of Antena 3 Radio or SER) but the telecommunications law of 1987 (LOT) limits the number of radio stations that a company may own in the same geographic area, in order to promote diversity.

At the same time, the regulation of mass media has in recent years tended to allow the participation of foreign companies in the ownership of media. This has been the case with the press since 1986 and television since 1988.

The government has also encouraged the involvement of the public sector in media activities, with the exception of the press. In this way, not only does TVE keep its two channels, but there are also public companies with regional channels. So, instead of giving the third channel to private enterprise, the presence of the public sector has been introduced in regional television. At the same time, central Government and some CCAA Governments have granted an important number of radio station licences to public networks in order to increase their presence, and municipal radio is being allowed to broadcast.

# Statistics

(1 ECU = 130 pesos)

| | |
|---|---|
| Number of inhabitants: | 38.86 m. |
| Number of inhabitants per km$^2$: | 77 |

Broadcasting
Number of national TV channels

| | |
|---|---|
| 2 public | (TVE-1, TVE-2) |
| 3 private | (Antena 3, Tele 5, Canal+) |

Number of regional channels
9 public
(ETB-1, ETB-2, TV3, Canal 33, Canal 9, Canal Sur, Telemadrid, TVG, Telemurcia)

Audience share (total: 26,362 million people)

| Channel | October 1989 | July 1990 |
|---|---|---|
| TVE-1 | 63.7% | 52.4% |
| TVE-2 | 21.3% | 19.3% |
| Regional channels* | 14.7% | 16.4% |
| Private channels** | - | 11.4% |
| Others | 0.3% | 0.5% |

* Regional channels in their respective areas have the following audience share (July 1990): Canal Sur, 26.3%; TV-3 and Canal 33, 19.4%; TVG, 18.2%; Telemadrid, 11.4%; Canal 9, 20.4%, ETB-1 and ETB-2, 14.5%.
** Private channels were only broadcasting in some areas (July 1990).

Radio
Number of national channels
5 public (RNE)
10 private:
2 SER, 2 COPE, 2 Onda Cero, 1 Antena 3, 1 Radio 80, 1 Cadena Ibérica, 1 Radio Minuto

| Frequencies | Audience 1989 |
|---|---|
| All | 16 018 m. |
| AM | 6 172 m. |
| FM | 10 800 m. |

Circulation of the 10 principal newspapers

| Newspaper | 1989 | | 1988 | |
|---|---|---|---|---|
| | Daily | Sunday | Daily | Sunday |
| El País | 377 528 | 862 544 | 376 230 | 819 112 |
| ABC | 280 356 | 546 561 | 267 772 | 486 911 |
| La Vanguardia | 210 624 | 345 348 | 202 741 | 329 033 |
| El Periódico | 164 174 | 285 476 | 157 192 | 246 834 |
| Diario 16 | n.a. | n.a. | 139 956 | 176 570 |
| El Correo Español | | | | |
| El Pueblo Vasco | 127 127 | | 125 555 | |
| La Voz de Galicia | 95 053 | 138 298 | 87 739 | 136 433 |
| Sport newspapers | | | | |
| Marca | 182 632 | | 154,556 | |
| As | 162 881 | 213 810 | 159 915 | 209 744 |

Advertising share in different media (%)

| Year | Newspapers | Magazines | Television | Radio | Cinema | Foreign |
|------|-----------|-----------|------------|-------|--------|---------|
| 1985 | 33.8 | 16.7 | 31.1 | 11.6 | 1.2 | 5.6 |
| 1986 | 33.3 | 16.7 | 31.8 | 12.9 | 0.7 | 4.6 |
| 1987 | 34.6 | 16.4 | 31.5 | 12.0 | 0..6 | 4.9 |
| 1988 | 36.1 | 16.5 | 31.0 | 11.7 | 0.7 | 4.0 |
| 1989 | 36.3 | 16.6 | 30.1 | 11.1 | 0.8 | 5.1 |

## References

Boletín de la Oficina de Justificación de la Difusión. Madrid, monthly.

Bustamante, Enrique and Zallo, Ramon (eds.) (1988) Las industrias culturales en España . Madrid, Akal editores.

Corbella, Joan (1988): Social Communication in Catalonia. General survey in the 1980's. Barcelona, Generalitat de Catalunya.

Fundesco (1989) Comunicación social 1989/Tendencias. Madrid.

Mateo, Rosario de (1990) Els ajust de l'Estat a la premsa a l'Europa Occidental. Barcelona, Generalitat de Catalunya.

Mateo, Rosario de, Corbella, Joan and Vilalta, Jaume (1988) The Press in Catalonia in the eighties. Barcelona, Generalitat de Catalunya.

Situación: "Informe sobre la Información. España 1990". Madrid, Banco Bilbao Vizcaya, 1990/1.

# 15

# Sweden

*Karl Erik Gustafsson*

## National profile

Sweden is sparsely populated. Only in the metropolitan areas does the population density exceed 100 per km$^2$. About 400 000 inhabitants, 5% of the population, are citizens of other countries. About 40% of them come from Finland. Other large groups with foreign citizenship are Yugoslavs, Norwegians, and Danes.

Danish, Norwegian and Swedish are quite similar languages and are understood to a large extent in all three countries. The Finnish language is completely different. There is, however, a large Swedish language minority in Finland – about 6% of the Finnish population. Swedish mass media can be, and are, used in neighbouring countries, and vice versa.

For more than 40 years Sweden was governed by the Labour Party with coalition Governments on two occasions, but all headed by a Labour prime minister. In the 1976 general election the non-socialist parties in Parliament gained the majority. The general election of 1979 showed the same results, although the majority was much smaller this time – one seat in Parliament. In 1982, the Labour Party returned to office and retained it in the 1985 as well as the 1988 general election, when the Greens gained seats in Parliament.

The Swedish political structure consists in practice of two blocks: the Labour Party and the Left Party (formerly the Communist Party) face the Centre Party (formerly the Farmers' Party), the Conservative Party, and the Liberal Party. In media policy questions the basic political pattern is different. The Labour Party and the Centre Party very often make common cause.

Since the 1950s economic life has been characterized by free enterprise and free competition. An Antitrust Ombudsman can intervene against forms of restrictive business practices which are judged to be harmful, and remove these by negotiation. These rules hold for the mass media industry, but the transition period from fair to free competition took longer in this sector of the economy than in other sectors. Restrictions lasted for a longer time in cases like accepting new outlets for single copy selling of newspapers, and the advertising agency remuneration system. There are traditionally two media-related monopolies: broadcasting, and telecommunications.

## Development of the press and broadcasting since 1945

*Birth of radio and television*

As far back as the 1920s the newspaper industry had achieved a superior position in the nation, not only according to press doctrines but by actual readership. When radio was established as a public service in 1925, it was partly on conditions set by the newspaper industry, which also became the major shareholder in the radio corporation.

Television came relatively late to Sweden (1956), which is probably one explanation of the fact that TV-set ownership increased rapidly in Sweden. At the end of 1960 – after four years – the number of television licence holders was one million, equivalent to 138 per 1 000 inhabitants. Another reason for the rapid penetration is that television was introduced in Denmark in 1954 and as a side effect at the same time in the southern part of Sweden.

The newspaper publishers were not able to control television in the same way they controlled radio. However, their firm resistance to advertising on radio and television prevented these media from becoming advertising vehicles. This did not hamper the development of radio and television. The licence fee system has been and still is the only source of financing public service radio and television with one small exception: educational programmes were financed via the state budget until 1985.

The rapid penetration of television did not have any negative effects on the newspaper industry. On the contrary, newspaper benefited from the general interest in what was going on in and around television. The only medium to experience negative effects was the cinema.

*Attacks on the broadcasting monopoly*

The Swedish Broadcasting Corporation has since 1925 had exclusive rights to broadcasting – radio and television. It is a joint stock company, and the shareholders are popular movements (60%), the press (20%) and business (20%). Previously the press and business had larger shares.

Attempts have been made to break the monopoly of the Swedish Broadcasting Corporation. As in other countries, ships off the Swedish coast started pirate radio broadcasting around 1960. These activities changed the contents of radio programmes, but not the system. Light music programmes were introduced (1961), hit lists (1962), and finally a channel for light music (1964).

In the early 1960s the demand for a second channel on television was pushed by industry and advertising interests. With British television as a model – the BBC and ITV duopoly – the industry lobby wanted a second channel, independent of the Swedish Broadcasting Corporation and financed by advertising. Such a system, the advocates said, would create competition to the benefit of the audience. The ruling Labour Party Government did not want to introduce advertising on television, but accepted the argument of competition. A second channel was introduced in 1969. The two channels were to be managed independently – e.g. produce separate news services – but to have the same general management.

The change of Government in 1976 – from socialist to non-socialist – led to some changes in the broadcasting system. As a sign of a new political trend a so-called neighbourhood radio outside the broadcasting monopoly was introduced on a trial basis at the end of the 1970s.

*Home video*

Plans by the electronics industry to market video cassette recorders in the 1970s as a home entertainment aroused anxiety among Swedish politicians. In 1974 a Government commission was appointed to specify measures to ban or restrict advertising on video. The intent was twofold: partly to maintain the ban on advertising on television, partly to protect the advertising interests of the daily press. The Swedish Broadcasting Corporation also regarded the plans for home video as a threat. Its broadcasting monopoly might in practice be undermined.

As in other countries, the development of home video in Sweden took some time. The Government commission had to delay its work and did not publish its report until 1982 suggesting a ban on advertising on video. The proposal was passed on without comment by the Government to a general mass media commission, appointed the same year. In its final report in 1984 it suggested that no measures should be taken against advertising on video. The question was removed from the public policy agenda.

The Swedish Broadcasting Corporation has also changed its view on the competition from home video. The main concern of the Corporation became the question of television programming, because video cassette distributors were able to pre-empt television companies for exclusive programme rights.

The growth of the home video market, and particularly viewing among young people, made brutality and prurience on video tapes the subject of debate. Prepublication censorship of recorded cassettes was demanded. The debate led to a law against video violence in 1982. The question of censorship is still on the agenda.

In 1982 a tax on video cassette recorders and a levy on blank tape (later cassettes) were introduced. In Sweden video cassette recorders are bought, not rented. The motives were both cultural and fiscal. Some of the tax revenues have been used to promote Swedish film culture.

## Cable and satellite

Although modern mass media, from the introduction of radio onwards, have had a considerable impact on Swedish trade and industry, the discussion about new electronic media did not take this type of effect into account initially. Cable and satellites marked a turning point.

In the middle of the 1970s the idea of a Nordic direct broadcasting satellite – Nordsat – was introduced and a Nordic commission was appointed to develop the idea. The project was unique in a number of ways, even internationally. The project was seen as an integral part of the on-going cooperation and collaboration among the five Nordic countries. Nordsat would also be an extension of national cultural policies, since it would make all existing TV-channels accessible to viewers in all Nordic countries. In spite of this the Nordsat project was turned down.

Satellite programming was again discussed when a new project, Tele-X, was presented. The initiative was taken by the Swedish Ministry of Industry, taking over the responsibility for Nordsat from the Ministry of Education and Cultural Affairs, and making Tele-X an industrial policy issue.

Sweden sought collaboration with Finland and Norway in developing Tele-X. Denmark had withdrawn from the negotiations already during the Nordsat discussions. After long negotiations on the distribution of costs and problems pertaining to employment policies between Norway and Sweden, an agreement was finally reached in March 1983. Later Finland joined the project. The Tele-X satellite, scheduled to be launched in 1986, was finally launched in 1989 and again became a wholly Swedish-run project.

Yet another example of industrial policy influence on media development can be found in the discussions regarding cable-TV. The Telecommunications Administration estimated that cable-TV could provide employment for 3 000 workers per year for seven years, which made the project attractive. Another reason to invest in cable-TV was to protect the telephone monopoly, as cable-TV could be used for telephone services. Almost all Swedish households have satisfactory TV-signal reception conditions. There has been no pressure to install cable systems to improve reception of public service television.

In 1982 a Government commission was appointed to analyse cable and satellite techniques from various points of view – maintaining the broadcasting monopoly, the ban on television advertising, the role of the daily press in the Swedish democracy, and violent videos.

The commission on cable and satellites concentrated its work on regulation of cable systems for mass media use. The report of the commission was published in 1984. A cable law was enacted in January 1986.

Initially the Telecommunications Administration was the main actor on the cable and satellites scene. Gradually, this picture has changed. Other actors have shown interest in becoming cable network owners or operators: local authorities, public utility companies as well as private companies. The interest in satellite television increased among the viewers after the introduction of the Swedish-owned commercial channel Scansat TV3 and the pay-TV channel Filmnet in 1987.

## The press

### Policy framework

In 1766 the Swedish Parliament adopted a Freedom of the Press Act as a part of the Constitution. The present Freedom of the Press Act dates from 1949. Public censorship is explicitly forbidden and there are no restrictions on publishing and distribution.

Press freedom is safeguarded in a number of ways. Any periodical appearing at least four times a year must appoint a responsible publisher, alone accountable for any violation of the law. Another measure is that the law explicitly prohibits the investigation or disclosure of sources. This protection is extended even to State and municipal employees. A third measure is the principle of free access to public documents, which gives anyone the right to demand access to any document held in a State or municipal agency. The right of access is guarded by the Parliamentary Ombudsman.

In 1916 Swedish press organizations set up the Swedish Press Council to guard against abuse of the liberties of the Constitution. The first Code of Ethics was adopted in 1923 and the present Code in 1978. The aim of the Code is to uphold high ethical standards, particularly to protect against damaging publicity as invasion of privacy, and defamation. In 1969 a Press Ombudsman was established to supervise the adherence to the Code of Ethics. Serious cases are filed by the Ombudsman with the Press Council. The findings of the Council are published in the newspapers in question and in the trade press, and offending newspapers may be fined.

There are no special laws in Sweden against concentration of media ownership. A proposal was drawn up in 1980 by a Government commission preventing mergers and cross media ownership in the media industry, but the Government did not put any proposals forward in Parliament. The commission appointed by a socialist government delivered its report to a non-socialist government.

## Circulation

In 1989, there were 98 high-periodicity newspapers (4–7 issues per week) in Sweden with a combined circulation of 4 537 800 copies, equivalent to 536 per 1000 inhabitants. Low-periodicity newspapers (1–3 issues per week), of which there were 68, mainly local newspapers or opinion weeklies, added about 10% to the total circulation and per capita consumption. On an average day 72% of the population (9–79 years of age) read a morning newspaper and 34% an evening newspaper.

In Sweden the daily press has always been mainly regional and local. The only exceptions are two Stockholm afternoon tabloids (*Aftonbladet* and *Expressen*) sold on a single copy basis.

As most Swedish newspaper editorials advocate party political programmes, the political structure of the press is also a debated issue. There is a discrepancy between the political line-up of the newspapers and the political preferences of the electorate which puts the socialist parties at a disadvantage. However the newspaper market is governed by economics, not by political power structures. Newspapers derive their revenue from sales to readers and to advertisers.

There are a number of general state subsidies to the daily press: exemption from value-added tax on subscription and single-copy sales, lower tax on advertising than other media, and postal distribution at a special newspaper rate. There are also a number of selective measures, e.g. subsidies to individual newspapers.

## Permanent multi-million subsidies

The number of Swedish newspapers declined sharply during the postwar era, resulting in an increasing number of one-newspaper communities. Since the beginning of the 1960s the structural development of the daily press has been under close official surveillance. In order to prevent newspaper closures and counteract concentration of ownership a series of measures have been introduced since the end of the 1960s.

By the end of the 1980s an elaborate system of subsidies was in place. In 1989, direct subsidies to "low-coverage newspapers", i.e. those with not more than 50% household coverage in their place of issue, totalled approximately 400 million Swedish Kronor, SEK (60 million ECU). These selective subsidies amounted to some 4% of the total costs of the newspaper industry. In addition, subsidies of about 60 million SEK (17 million ECU) were extended to newspapers participating in joint distribution schemes. Papers that cooperate in production are also offered favourable financing.

The objective of the subsidy programme, introduced around 1970, has largely been realized. There are still 18 communities with two competing newspapers. The newspapers receiving the subsidies are, however, economically dependent on the subsidies. Almost any reduction will cause closures.

*Finance and ownership*

Swedish morning newspapers, which are mainly subscriber-based, derive about two thirds of their revenue from the sale of advertising space, and about one third from sales to readers. For afternoon newspapers, single-copy-sold tabloids, the revenue structure is the other way round: one third from sales of advertising space, and two thirds from sales to readers. Subsidies for low-coverage newspapers give the recipient newspapers, only morning newspapers, an average revenue increment of about 15%. The subsidies are financed by tax on all advertising.

In Sweden there are 17 newspaper chains, which include about 80% of all newspapers with at least four issues per week, as well as about 80% of the total circulation of these high-periodicity newspapers. The two largest newspaper groups are the Bonnier Group and A-pressen (the Labour Party newspaper group). The Bonnier group includes the morning newspaper *Dagens Nyheter, the afternoon tabloid Expressen, and the business daily Dagens Industri.* The group holds 23% of the circulation. The share of A-pressen of the total circulation of high-periodicity newspapers is 19%. Measured by turnover the Bonnier Group has increased its share from 22.5 to 25.8 during the 1980s, as shown in Table 1.

Table 1    Major groups of the national and regional daily press by turnover in 1980 and 1989 (%)

| Group: | 1980 | 1989 |
|---|---|---|
| The Bonnier Group | 22.5 | 25.8 |
| A-pressen (The Labour Movement) | 16.5 | 14 8 |
| Göteborgs-Posten | 8.1 | 8.7 |
| Sydsvenska Dagbladet | 5.8 | 6.2 |
| Svenska Dagbladet | 4.6 | 5.5 |

(Source: The Information and Mass Media Research Unit, Gothenburg School of Economics)

The Bonnier Group is the largest media group in Sweden. Besides publishing newspapers it publishes books and weekly/monthly general magazines and trade journals, runs data base information services, produces and distributes film and videos, has interests in the cinema business, as well as in the distribution of television programmes (the pay-TV channel SF Succé).

## Electronic media

### *Legal framework for broadcasting and cable-TV*

General broadcasting policy is laid down by a Radio Act and an Enabling Agreement between the broadcasting companies and the State. Programmes must be impartial, objective, and designed to satisfy a broad range of interests and tastes.

The State exercises no control over programmes prior to broadcasting. However, a Broadcasting Council is empowered to raise objections – or to consider complaints from the general public – to specific programmes after they have been transmitted, if they are found to have violated the Radio Act or the Enabling Agreement. The Radio Council is appointed by the Government.

According to the Cable Law the establishment of cable networks is unrestricted, but licences for distribution channels other than those from direct broadcasting satellites are required in networks connecting more than about 100 flats (originally it was 50). A Cable Board decides on such licences after hearing the communities in question. Some of the rules of operation reflect the broadcasting monopoly: a) a principle of "must carry" will give right of way to the Swedish Broadcasting Corporation, b) a ban on simultaneous distribution of programmes to a number of cable networks preserves the broadcasting monopoly of the Corporation, and c) a ban on advertising in local channels protects the newspaper advertising market as well as defending the ban on television advertising. Operators who regularly offer violent or prurient programmes may lose their concession. In the last case the licences may only be revoked by a court of law. The Cable Board was set up in 1986.

### *Organization of public service broadcasting*

In 1979 a new organization of the Swedish Broadcasting Corporation was implemented: a parent company with four subsidiaries: television, national radio, local radio, and educational broadcasting. This structure has since then been subject to debate. There have been a number of suggestions: to go back to the original, monolithic model; to establish two separate companies, one for radio and one for television; to merge national and local radio; to relinquish educational broadcasting, and so on.

All economic relations between the State and the Swedish Broadcasting Corporation run through the parent company. It is responsible for the allocation of the financial resources, and coordinates the activities. The board of the parent company consists of 14 members besides the Director General. Seven of these – the Chairman included – are appointed by the Government. Five are appointed by the shareholders and two by the employees. The board of the parent company appoints the boards of the subsidiaries, excepting two representatives of the employees.

There are three national radio channels in Sweden. They are mainly of a generic type: Channel One is a talk channel, Channel Two classical music and programmes in immigrant languages, and Channel Three light music. A fourth channel was introduced for local radio stations in 1987. Two years later all 25 local radio stations used the fourth channel. Sweden has two national television channels, independent of each other but with coordinated schedules in order to avoid programme collisions.

The Telecommunications Administration is responsible for broadcasting. The administration also controls the use of the broadcasting frequencies. The Swedish Broadcasting Corporation has for a long time wanted to take over this responsibility. In 1991 a board (telenämnden) will take over.

*Financing of public service broadcasting*

The Swedish Parliament decides upon the annual licence fee as well as the total budget for broadcasting. There were separate licence fees for radio and television until 1969, after that one licence fee for both. From 1970 to 1990 there was an extra fee for colour television. The licence fee is exempted from value added tax.

The Telecommunications Administration collected the licence fees until 1989, when it was taken over by a new subsidiary to the Swedish Broadcasting Corporation.

Advertising or sponsored programmes are not permitted on radio or television. There is one exception. Public information is accepted, but only in separate blocks, and only on television – a so-called notice-board.

In 1989 the Swedish Broadcasting Corporation received 2 700 million SEK out of the total licence fee revenues. The total number of employees was 6 022, about 55% at the Swedish Television Company. About 93% of the financial resources are used by the four programme companies as shown in Table 2.

Table 2     Financial resources of the Swedish Broadcasting Corporation
by programme company 1989

| Programme company | SEK m. | % |
|---|---|---|
| National radio | 513 | 20 |
| Local radio | 298 | 12 |
| Television | 1 560 | 62 |
| Educational | 139 | 6 |
| TOTAL | 2 510 | 100 |

The broadcasting market is mature. The debate on financing public service broadcasting in the future has become intense. Three ways are suggested: a) a substantial increase of the licence fee, b) introducing
advertising as a part financing method, and c) establishing a channel for
pay-TV or pay-per-view.

*Commercial television*

Television channels financed by advertising or subscription were introduced in Sweden in 1987 by satellites and cables. The first two channels
were TV 3 and Filmnet. TV 3 is owned by the investment company Kin-
nevik, with interests in forestry, car imports, and the Astra satellite project.
Filmnet started as a joint venture in the Netherlands with Esselte as one
of the investors. Gradually Esselte, an office and media business, took over
the channel.

Two more channels were introduced in 1989. One was the Nordic
Channel, financed by advertising and owned by the Swedish industrialist
Matts Carlgren (forestry), and the other SF Succé, a pay-TV channel controlled by the Bonnier Group. In 1990 the channel TV 4 was introduced.
It is financed by advertising and owned by a consortium of banks (Wal-
lenberg and the Farmers' Bank), a book publisher, and an insurance company.

Swedes' interest in commercial television has increased but the public
service television has been able to keep its audience ratings as shown in
Table 3.

Table 3     Net reach of television companies 1988 and 1989

| Company | National audience | | Cable areas | |
|---|---|---|---|---|
| | 1988 | 1989 | 1988 | 1989 |
| Public service (SVT) | 76 | 76 | 72 | 74 |
| Private service (All) | 6 | 10 | 38 | 43 |

Note. Foreign channels are included in private channels although some of those are
public service channels (e.g. 3 Sat)

The commercial channels were in 1989 loss-making. The break-even
point is moving as the costs rise due to competition for programme rights.

## Local radio and television

Radio and television were organized as national media. Their regionalization started in the 1970s. In 1975, a subsidiary of the Swedish Broadcasting Corporation was founded, Swedish Local Radio. The services are local in a different sense than the newspapers. The number of local radio stations rose to 25 – about one third of the total number of newspaper regions. The number of television districts stopped at eleven.

Neighbourhood radio was invented as a means of communication within voluntary organizations, of which Sweden has many. Advertising was not permitted, and the broadcasting area was to be very small. This infra-local radio expanded during the non-socialist Government, and continued to grow after 1982 when the Labour Party, at the outset opposed to this medium, regained power. Today, there is political agreement on neighbourhood radio: it will be a permanent, steadily growing, medium in the Swedish mass media landscape.

The Swedish Broadcasting Corporation responded to the neighbourhood radio move. It started Everyman's Radio inside its local radio organization. It was seen as a way of public access. This model was launched on a trial basis in two of the 25 local stations. Lack of money has hampered its development, but also the wider acceptance of the idea of neighbourhood radio as a permanent instrument for infra-local communications.

Local television only exists as cable-TV, and mainly on a trial basis. This is mainly due to the ban on advertising. Also the distribution of the programmes (by cable or by air) is still an open question.

## Telematic media

Teletext has not generated as much interest as other new media. This medium was inaugurated in 1979 by the Swedish Broadcasting Corporation, mainly as an aid to the hard of hearing. Optional sub-titling of programmes and full pages of text were produced in order to enrich the television experience for this group.

Nevertheless – and some say because of that sneaking introduction – teletext has enjoyed a much wider distribution than was originally envisaged. The Swedish Broadcasting Corporation has also gradually expanded the amount and type of material available: general news, financial news, public information, sport, weather and programme schedules. About 150 text pages are broadcast and the medium is being used experimentally in educational broadcasting. The regular transmissions are national but trials of regional transmissions have been made.

Teletext is financed via the broadcasting licence fee. Advertising is not permitted. Teletext will remain a service of the public broadcasting company, at least as long as the present agreement with the State exists.

Teletext is seen as complementing other media. The newspaper publishers do not consider it a threat to their business. The newspaper companies are not directly engaged in teletext. However, an agreement has been reached between the Swedish Broadcasting Corporation and the TT news agency on delivering pages to teletext.

The initiative for videotex in Sweden came from two directions: the Swedish Telecommunications Administration and the Swedish Philips Company. Videotex trials started gradually at the end of the 1970s. Many actors were engaged, among them a number of newspapers. The trials were technical, and did not take place on the open market.

Swedish Philips has reduced its commitment. Its videotex department has finally been taken over by the Postal Administration. The Telecommunications Administration has maintained a position of caution as far as public distribution is concerned. In the autumn of 1982, the Telecommunications Administration launched its videotex system for use in the business sector. Other videotex firms have been established, all of them targeting the business sector.

There is a minimum of regulation of videotex. Free establishment is the rule, and no ban on advertising, but it can only appear in called form, i.e. separate ad pages, indicated ad pages, and so on. As long as the prospects for home videotex were regarded as good, the newspaper industry saw a competitive threat in videotex. A Government commission looked into the question, and by the time it published its report the outlook for home videotex had changed. In 1988 a field experiment started with 100 households. At the beginning of 1991 a sequential introduction of videotex started. The plan is to install the service in 75 000 homes by the end of 1991.

## Policies for the press and broadcasting

### *No coherent policy*

Two main moves have been made towards a coherent mass media policy. In the middle of the 1970s the Swedish Council of Culture suggested that public service broadcasting policy as well as press subsidy policy should be regarded as aspects of a general cultural policy. The cultural policy goals were laid down by Parliament in 1974, and imply: extended freedom of expression, a responsibility for society to further a full comprehensive cultural life, to counteract the negative effects of commercialism, to contribute to artistic and cultural regeneration, to further decentralization, to increase people's opportunities for cultural pursuits of their own, to take into consideration the experiences and needs of neglected groups, to safeguard and bring the culture of bygone days to life, and to further exchange across linguistic and national frontiers. Cultural aspects were integrated in the public service broadcasting policy, but cultural policy did not become the common denominator of mass media policies.

In 1982 a non-socialist Government appointed a commission on mass media with broad terms of reference. Whether this initiative ultimately would have produced a policy for all media – or all new media – will never be known, for after the election the same year a new, socialist Government altered the thrust of the commission's work. The new directives charged the commission to concentrate mainly on the regulation of cable systems. This means that, in effect, all Swedish media commissions so far have been single-medium commissions, although some have had more than one medium in their terms of reference. A coherent mass media policy seems beyond reach. The demand for such a policy might even be seen as an instrument to challenge the medium-by-medium policies, i.e. the prevalent public service broadcasting policy and the existing press subsidy policy.

Initiatives taken by the other actors – the industry, the telecommunications administration, the public service broadcasting corporation, and so on – regarding media development directions have not aimed at a cohe-rent mass media policy.

## Main issues

At the end of the 1980s the issue of advertising on television became the main issue of the political debate on mass media. Suddenly there was a majority in the Parliament for advertising on television, but, should advertising be introduced in one of the channels of the Swedish Broadcasting Corporation, or in a third, independent and privately owned terrestrial channel, or in both? In early 1991 it was decided to introduce advertising only in a third, independent terrestrial channel.

Another issue is the future of the subsidies to the press. The political support for the programme seems to be decreasing, perhaps because the subsidies have made the party press less connected to the party system. Another reason may be the economic recession which has created financial problems for the State (which now wants to use the advertising tax for other purposes) as well as for the newspapers supported.

Besides the issues of advertising on television, and daily press subsidies, video violence has raised an intense debate. This debate has been analysed by the sociologist Keith Roe. He found that the debate, as it was played out in the press, fulfilled very accurately many of the conditions said to be necessary for construction of a moral panic. This Swedish moral panic lasted, according to Roe, from 1981 to 1984. Throughout 1984 it was, he says, clear that the panic was on the wane. There were fewer articles and their tone became increasingly less strident. More and more references were, according to Roe, made to the positive aspect of video technology. Still, in a debate in Parliament in December 1985, demands were put forward for the certification and censorship of all pre-recorded video films. This was turned down. However, from 1986 video films intended for public showing must be previewed by the censorship authorities.

It is hard to tell what issues are interesting to the general public. There have been a number of opinion polls, but they have mainly covered the question of advertising on television, the answers showing that a majority of the population is positive. Judging from letters to newspaper editors, violence on video seems to be an issue of some general interest. Lacking primary information on the subject, one is left with interpretations of the issue – signals such as the buying and renting of, listening to and viewing of new media by the public.

## Statistics

(Conversion rate 1 ECU = 7.50 Swedish kroner, SEK)
All figures from the end of 1989

| | |
|---|---:|
| Population | 8 527 880 |
| Land area in $km^2$ | 449 964 |
| Inhabitants pr $km^2$ | 20 |
| | |
| Public service broadcasting | |
| Number of licence fees | 3 330 000 |
| Licence fee per year | 1 084 SEK |
| | |
| Television 1989 | |
| Number of channels | 2 |
| Hours per week, national | 115 |
| Hours per week, regional | 10 |
| | |
| Radio | |
| Number of channels | 4 |
| Hours per week, national | 44 7 |
| Hours per week, regional | 1 551 |
| | |
| Neighbourhood radio | |
| Number of transmitters | 154 |
| Number of participating organizations | 2 391 |

Commercial television
| | |
|---|---|
| Esselte: | Filmnet (pay-TV) since 1987 |
| Kinnevik: | TV 3 since 1987 and TV 1000 (pay-TV) since 1989 |
| Matts Carlgren: | Nordic Channel since 1989 |
| The Bonnier Group: | SF Succé (pay-TV) since 1989 |
| Wallenberg et al: | TV 4 since 1990 |

| | |
|---|---|
| Video cassette recorders (stock) | 1 800 000 |
| Teletext (stock) | 1 500 000 |
| Home videotex (stock) | 100 |
| Satellite and cable | |
| Tele-X since 1989 | |
| Number of cable households | 1 100 000 |
| Home parabolic antennas (estimated) | 30 000 |

Media use
Use of mass media on an average day by inhabitants of 9–79 years of age

| Medium use | % |
|---|---|
| Radio programmes | 77 |
| TV programmes | 76 |
| Subscribed morning newspapers | 72 |
| Sound cassettes | 35 |
| Single-copy-sold evening newspapers | 34 |
| Periodicals | 24 |
| Records | 20 |
| Weekly magazines | 19 |
| Comic strip magazines | 11 |
| Home video | 9 |

The press

| Circulation of largest dailies | Weekdays | Sundays |
|---|---|---|
| Metropolitan morning papers: | | |
| Dagens Nyheter (independent) | 414 969 | 519 575 |
| Göteborgs-Posten (liberal) | 277 257 | 309 994 |
| Svenska Dagbladet (conservative) | 226 526 | 238 969 |
| Sydsvenska Dagbladet (liberal) | 114 849 | 144 030 |
| Arbetet (labour) | 114 725 | 104 618 |
| Skånska Dagbladet (Centre) | 30 480 | 30 897 |
| Metropolitan afternoon tabloids: | | |
| Expressen (liberal) | 571 197 | 685 226 |
| Aftonbladet (labour) | 397 043 | 493 352 |
| GT (liberal) | 106 175 | 275 137 |
| Kvällsposten (liberal) | 104 341 | 176 273 |

Advertising

| Medium | Million SEK |
|---|---|
| Provincial newspapers | 3 820 |
| Metropolitan morning newspapers | 3 697 |
| Metropolitan afternoon newspapers | 736 |
| Trade and business magazines | 1 048 |
| Consumer magazines | 517 |
| Outdoor advertising | 396 |
| Cinema advertising | 70 |
| Direct mail (estimated) | 4 700 |
| Total | 15 134 |

# References

Bagerstam, K. (1975) "Kabelfernsehen in Kiruna", Media Perspektiven, 1.

Boethius, M. (1980) "Lokalradio in Schweden nach drei Jahren auf sicherer Basis", Media Perspektiven 8.

Gustafsson, K.E. (1981) "Pressepolitik in Schweden", Publizistik 3.

Gustafsson, K.E. (1982) "Die Diskussion über die Einführung von Werbung im Schwedischen Fernsehen", Media Perspektiven, 12.

Gustafsson, K.E. (1984a) "Outlines of a Swedish Mass Media Policy of the 1980s", Masscommunicatie, 4.

Gustafsson, K.E. (1984b) "Forecasting Mass Media Development", EBU Review 4.

Gustafsson, K.E. and Hadenius, S. (1976) "Swedish Press Policy", Stockholm: The Swedish Institute.

Hultén, O. (1980) "Future of Broadcasting - Public Service Broadcasting in the 80s", Masscommunicatie, 3–4.

Hultén, O. (1982) "The Use of Video in Swedish Homes" EBU Review September.

Hultén, O. (1984a) "The Video Trend in Scandinavia and Finland", Nordicom Review, 1. Nordicom, University of Göteborg.

Hultén, O. (1984b) "Mass Media and State Support in Sweden", Stockholm: The Swedish Institute.

Pash, G. (1982) "Nah-Radio in Schweden", Media Perspektiven 12.

Roe, K. (1985) "The Swedish Moral Panic over Video 1980–1984", Nordicom Information 2–3. Nordicom, University of Göteborg.

Wallqvist, Ö. (1982) "The Media Structure in Sweden in Years to Come", EBU Review, 3.

# 16

# Switzerland

## Werner A. Meier and Ulrich Saxer

### National profile

With an area of 41 293 km$^2$ compared to its big neighbouring nations Switzerland is a small state. By the end of 1989 the population was 6 723 000, more than 1 in 7 of them foreigners (1 040 325). This population is, however, unevenly distributed, due to the topography of the country. Half of the population is living in suburban or metropolitan areas, which contrast considerably with thinly populated regions and peripheries. Swiss society is multilingual (German 73.5%, French 20.1%, Italian 4.5%, Romansch 0.9% in 1980). Due to the topography there are many more cultural segmentations. Therefore, the socio-cultural differences between regions are quite evident; furthermore, Swiss society has moved in the last decade even more in the direction of a multicultural society.

The Swiss political system is highly differentiated and therefore especially complex. It functions as a direct democracy on three different levels: the confederation, the regional provinces (26 cantons) and the local communities (3 021). This system is the result of Switzerland's socio-cultural and socio-political diversity and creates not only various opportunities for political articulation but also a variety of tensions among interest groups on these three levels. In spite of linguistic, cultural, and religious differences as well as considerable economic inequalities, Switzerland has managed to develop strategies for solving political disagreement by very elaborate political discourses and to reach a consensus on some basic political values, but by no means on such issues as nuclear energy, disarmament, joining the EC, etc. Consequently, the political decision making process is rather slow, complicated and often inefficient.

At the end of this decade, in general the Swiss economy is still on a relatively healthy footing: its real gross domestic product (GDP) rose by roughly 3%, making 1989 the 7th consecutive year of economic growth enjoyed by the Swiss economy. Sixty percent of the working force earn money in the service sector while 35% have a job in the industrial and trade sector. 24% of the labour force are foreigners. In 1989, the unemployment rate was 0.6 and weekly working hours were 42. The EC countries, especially Germany, France and Italy, are Switzerland's most important trade partners: 57% of exports go to EC countries while 71% of imports come from the EC countries. In the light of these facts it is not surprising that the viability of the Swiss economy in the near future will be even more dependent on the quality of its relations to the EC.

In general the Swiss economy has great political influence on decision making processes. Corporations and banking institutions sometimes influence politics more than the political parties do.

## Development of the press and broadcasting since 1945

The development of the Swiss broadcasting system goes back as far as 1911, when the first licences for radio reception were issued, and to 1921 when the first public radio station began transmissions. Local corporations in the bigger cities ran the first radio stations in the 1920s, different regional interests in the thoroughly segmented confederation determining the broadcasts. Yet there was also an increasing demand for better coordination, for securing access rights for social minorities to the common good of a scarce radio spectrum, for guaranteeing sufficient output of politically nonpartisan and culturally responsible programmes for all segments of the population. Certainly one of the main structural tensions in the Swiss broadcasting system is the struggle between federalist (particularistic) and centralist forces, ever since the Swiss broadcasting corporation (SSR – Sociéte Suisse de Radio Diffusion) was founded in 1931. Mainly it was fear of uncontrolled political influence and the resistance of the influential publishers that delayed the introduction of television till the late 1950s. The SSR did not go on the air before 1958 with its programmes on a regular basis. Radio and television were "public service monopolies" from 1931 to 1983.

This proved to be a type of institutionalization which served the interests not only of the political system but also of the printed press. While advertising was forbidden on radio and permitted on TV in a restricted manner since 1964, the revenues of the press were not jeopardized by the electronic media. The institutionalization of a public monopoly – financed mainly by licence – prevented economic competition between print and electronic media and brought about a financially healthy private and a viable public system.

Pressure from pirate radio stations on the one hand and from the bourgeois parties and the advertising industry on the other, and the general trends towards de-monopolized broadcasting in Western Europe, forced the federal government in 1982 to give provisional licences to 36 private local radio stations in all parts of Switzerland. This "Ordinance on Experimental Local Broadcasting" was in effect as a transitional means of broadcast regulation until the end of 1990. Later on in 1992 the Law on Radio and Television (LRT) will come into force replacing the provisional order. Furthermore, in 1983 a consortium of private entrepreneurs and the SSR procured a government licence in order to find out whether there was a demand for a feature film channel in Switzerland on a pay-TV basis. These decisions opened up the broadcasting system for new private enterprises, and a new era began for the Swiss media system as well as for Swiss media policy.

## The press

### Policy framework

In Switzerland, the press is still referred to in the federal constitution only in a terse sentence, "The freedom of the press is guaranteed" (Art. 55). Additionally, article 55a of the federal constitution, which regulates radio and television, explicitly calls for the protection of the written press. There is, however, no legal obligation on the Swiss press to fulfil a public service. Newspapers are private enterprises and depend on market mechanisms and on the rights of freedom of commerce and trade. Yet, they are expected to be more than just businesses. Swiss media policy thus typifies the democratic paradox of autonomy and obligations which characterize the mass media. The conflicting goals of economy and state apparatus lead to diffuse expectations concerning the public obligations of private enterprises.

In 1985 the parliament voted against a motion calling for the protection of the press, which would have allowed the federal authorities to take measures against any publishing company dominating the market. The reason for such rejection was that the motion implied an encroachment on the freedom of opinion. Nevertheless, the newspapers actually receive annual subsidies from the postal service amounting to more than 100 million ECU through a reduction of transport costs. It seems to be a common belief that the press should be supported without direct state interference.

### Ownership and finance

In Switzerland all daily newspapers with a circulation over 100 000 are owned by multimedia companies. Ringier, the largest publishing company, owns the yellow paper *Blick* (workdays) and *Sonntagsblick* (tabloid), the leading Sunday newspaper (376 473). Ringier also publishes the weekly magazines *SchweizerIllustrierte* (178 221) and *L'Illustré* (102 740). The second largest publishing company – based on turnover – is Tages Anzeiger AG, the owner of the leading regional newspaper *Tages Anzeiger* with a circulation of 261 113 copies. Tages Anzeiger AG also has a minority share (49%) in the publishing company Berner Zeitungs AG, which owns the leading newspaper in Berne (*Berner Zeitung*). Both Ringier and Tages Anzeiger AG are located in Zurich and each is financially controlled by one family. The other two important publishing companies in the German-speaking part of Switzerland are Curti Medien AG (publisher of *Weltwoche*, the leading weekly quality newspaper, *Sport Bilanz* and *ZüriWoche*, a weekly freesheet with a circulation of 358 342 copies) and AG für Neue Zürcher Zeitung (publisher of *Neue Zürcher Zeitung* and *St. Galler Tagblatt*). The leading publishing house in the French-speaking region is Edipresse SA, which owns *24 heures* and *Le Matin*, both regional daily newspapers with the largest and third largest circulation in French-speaking Switzerland.

Advertising provides 60-80% of subscription newspaper revenue. In the last years the indirect financing of newspapers by the advertising industry has grown. Therefore the profitability of newspaper production is more and more dependent on the viability of the advertising industry. In addition the dependence is direct, because most of the newspapers – with the exception of some leading newspapers – have leased their advertisement columns to advertising companies. The biggest leaseholder conglomerate (Publicitas/ofa/assa/mosse) controls more than 65% of all advertisement columns in the Swiss press.

## Structure and organization

Variety of choice cannot be measured by the number of different titles alone, but rather by the independence of the publishers as well as by journalistic performance. The large publishing houses – all of them are multimedia companies, owned and controlled by Swiss capital and management – enjoy an increasing share of the market. The five most important newspapers with a daily circulation over 100 000 are read by almost as many people as the 245 smallest newspapers with a circulation of up to 25 000. More and more small and medium-size newspapers have been forced out of the market or have been taken over by large publishing companies, and simply lend their title to a leading regional newspaper. It is even more difficult to establish new titles on the market; since the Second World War only one new daily newspaper has been launched successfully over an extended period of time in a more and more concentrated market: that is *Blick*, a representative of the yellow press, which has the largest circulation of all daily newspapers in Switzerland with almost 370 000 copies sold.

## Electronic media

### Legal framework

The organization of radio and television is based on Article 55a of the federal constitution, which was passed by the citizens in the plebiscite on 2 December 1984. Legislation on broadcast media became the confederation's task. The act specifies information, education, and entertainment – exactly in this order – as the main functions which radio and television are supposed to fulfil. The independence of the broadcasting institutions is ensured, and also takes other media, especially the press, into consideration. Finally, it mandates an independent board of complaint. Based on this article, a Law on Radio and Television (LRT) has been passed in both chambers of the federal parliament and should presumably become effective in 1992.

After a sufficient majority voted for article 55a of the federal constitution, a legal framework for regulating broadcasting was enacted. Based on this article, a Federal Decree on Satellite Broadcasting was worked out by the government in 1985, submitted to the parliament in 1986 and, after having passed both chambers in 1987, became effective in May 1988. It sets out the conditions for the licensing of radio and TV broadcast by satellite. The applicant for such a licence must be a Swiss citizen and the capitalization of the enterprise must be under Swiss control. Since state subsidies are not provided, advertising, sponsoring and subscription are the main sources of revenue. One of the primary aims of the decree is to promote Switzerland internationally in the political, economic and cultural fields. This implies a certain percentage of domestic programme production, also in order to strengthen the ties with Swiss citizens living in foreign countries (Art. 12). Applications are judged according to their ability to fulfil this requirement.

Pertinent also to broadcasting is the federal government's licence to the SSR, which is obliged to run at least one television and three radio services for each one of the linguistic regions. Programmes have to be produced in the different linguistic regions. In addition the SSR has to produce a radio channel as well as some hours of television programming for the Romansch-speaking population and a short-wave radio service for listeners abroad. Moreover, the SSR is allowed to participate in satellite television programming on the multilateral level (3Sat, TV5, Eurosport) or can supply programmes to satellite channels like Eins Plus, Raisat and CNN. Due to the lack of programmes, however, the SSR has terminated its commitment to the satellite channel Eins Plus at the end of 1990.

The SSR's different programmes as a whole must, according to its licence,

> defend and develop the cultural values of the country, contribute to the intellectual, moral, religious, civic and artistic education of the public, contribute to the free forma-tion of opinions and satisfy their needs for entertainment.

They have to be conceived in such a way that they:

> serve the interests of the country, reinforce national unity and solidarity, and contribute to international understanding (Art. 4.1).

Furthermore the SSR licence demands accurate and balanced news reporting.

The Federal Transportation, Communication, and Energy Depart-ment is in charge of supervising Swiss radio and television broadcasting's performance. Since 1984 the Independent Authority for Programme Complaints, as Article 55a of the federal constitution demands, has evaluated complaints about the programme output. The Authority has developed a set of criteria, according to which it judges the programmes in the light of professional norms and social values. Any Swiss citizen and any foreigner holding at least a temporary residence permit may appeal to this body provided the complaint has been signed by 20 other persons or the plaintiff is able to prove that he/she is closely connected with the content of the programme in question. Public authorities and societies are also entitled to lodge a complaint. The institutionalization of a programme-controlling authority is an interesting as well as a problematic way to evaluate programme performance in general and control programme norms and quality in particular.

## Structure and organization

The SSR is registered as a private company – not as a state institution – and is organized as an association. It is a non-profit organization with a dual structure. The SSR is divided into a parent organization with some 20 000 members, and a professional organization with roughly 3 700 employees and 2 250 regular free-lance contributors (1990). The parent organization comprises the various SSR organs (general assembly, central committee, General Director, auditors), the regional councils and mem-ber societies. Any Swiss citizen aged 20 or older and any foreigner hold-ing a permanent residence permit can join the SSR association of his region and thereby become actively involved in the SSR institution. The aim of the parent organization's structure is to ensure that the organized and unorganized public's interest is represented vis-à-vis the professional organization. It thus should fulfil a social and political function in general and a supervisory and cooperative function in particular.

The SSR structure reflects the fact that Switzerland is multilingual as well as multicultural, and radio and production facilities are distributed over all the language regions. The six radio studios (Zurich, Berne, Basle, Geneva, Lausanne and Lugano) as well as four regional studios (Aarau, Chur, Lucerne and St Gall) produce nine channels, altogether 77 690 hours of radio broadcasting annually (1989). The three television studios in Geneva, Lugano and Zurich produce individual programming for each linguistic region as well as special programming in the Romansch language; their total output is 14 948 hours of broadcasting per year (1989). Swiss Radio International (SRI) produces daily schedules which are broadcast in seven languages (German, French, Italian, English, Spanish, Portuguese and Arabic), and which comprise approximately 15 000 broadcasting hours yearly.

## Ownership and financial/economic aspects

National radio and television, as offered by the SSR, is mainly financed by licence fees and television advertising. On 28 February 1990 there were 2 636 558 radio and 2 395 767 television licence holders in Switzerland. The federal government sets the radio and television licence fees – since 1 October 1987, the rate has been 4.3 ECU per month for radio and 8.5 ECU per month for television. Just recently, in September 1990, the federal government has decided to increase the licence fees "only" 25% for 1991 – to 10.6 ECU for television and 5.42 ECU for radio – although the SSR was asking for a 30% increase. The yearly amount of 192 ECU for radio and television will be one of the highest licence fees in Europe. For its programme services the SSR receives 77% of the licence fees levied by the postal services; PTT keeps 23% for its services which include construction, operation and maintenance of the transmission installations.

The broadcasting of a limited amount of advertising – 29 minutes for pure commercial purposes and one minute for charitable organizations per working day since 1 July 1989 – is allowed on national television. This revenue from television advertising constitutes about 25% of the total SSR income. Advertising is operated by a private company (AG für Werbefernsehen, Berne) in which the SSR holds a 40% share. Ninety-six per cent of the available slots or 7 584 minutes on the German-speaking channel were sold to the advertising industry in 1989. Besides, in 1990 a one-minute TV spot costs 12 912 ECU to be broadcast in all three linguistic regions. On radio advertising is forbidden – except for the private local radio stations.

The analysis of the budget shows on the one hand that television advertising subsidizes the overall radio programme production – overhead expenses included – to an amount of 33 million ECU. On the other hand the revenues from radio licence fees cover almost 75% of the overall radio programme production costs while the revenues from television licence fees defray only 62% of the overall television programme production costs.

There is also a financial compensation by the largest linguistic region for the benefit of the two smaller ones. Although the licence fee revenues from the German-speaking population add up to 73% of the overall licence fee revenues, the programme producers in that region get only 42% of overall licence fee revenues. Without such cross-subsidization it would be nearly impossible to set up and maintain a full line of television programmes in the French-speaking and especially in the Italian-speaking part of Switzerland.

Due to the restricted revenues, the SSR is forced to produce its programmes rather cheaply or to buy on the international market. It spends only 16 538 ECU on an average for an hour of television programming, eight times less than e.g. ZDF. In 1989 the average costs for entertainment programmes added up to 21 978 ECU while those for sports came to 5 934 ECU .

*Programme policies*

Undoubtedly the starting point for the development of programme policies is the SSR's charge and mission. The SSR, however, is confronted – especially in the TV sector – with some structural handicaps which have to be taken into consideration at the very beginning: the small, distinctively segmented Swiss market, steeply rising programme production costs, mighty competitors from different neighbouring countries (ARD, ZDF, RTLplus, Sat1, TF1, and RAI1, among others), limited financial and creative resources. Under such – partly new – circumstances the SSR is developing programme policies which can be described under the headline "helvetization and adaptation". Thus primarily the SSR is fostering the amount of news and information about "Swiss" issues and problems. Secondly the SSR is trying to survive in the different newly emerged transnational broadcasting markets with a more mass-audience-oriented pro- gramme profile in order to be able to compete in the new market environment; and thirdly the SSR is reinforcing the collaboration with major public service broadcasters in Europe.

*Foreign media availability*

Geographically determined factors such as poor television reception in many regions have accelerated the installation of cable systems in Switzerland since the early 1960s. As a result, in the German-speaking part of Switzerland 66% of the households are cabled and 19% are connected to a master antenna at the end of 1990. Only 15% of TV-viewers are entirely reliant on a roof top antenna. Thus, on average a household has access to 12 channels including the three Swiss channels. This figure has been doubled since 1980. As most of the cable systems are privately owned they show a strong interest in gearing the system to the consumers' preference with an array of attractive foreign television and broadcasting channels. As a result, a majority of households in the German-speaking part of Switzerland have access to at least seven channels from Germany (ARD, ZDF, RTLplus, Sat1, Bayern 3, SW 3, 3Sat), to two from Austria (FS1 and FS2) as well as to two from France (TF1 and A2) and one from Italy (RAI1), apart from satellite channels like Eurosport or Superchannel. The high availability of more or less attractive foreign channels – especially in the mother tongue – has a distinct effect concerning the total viewing time and the audience share. In the German-speaking part of Switzerland 56% or 66 minutes daily of the total viewing time – 108 minutes on average per day (1989) – is dedicated to foreign channels. The situation in the two other linguistic regions is even more precarious: 66% of the total viewing time in the French and 68% in the Italian-speaking part of Switzerland is spent on foreign channels. Still the SSR's TV programmes are able to keep their market leader position in every linguistic region, but the market shares were in 1990 only 31% (TV DRS), 30% (TSR) and 27% (TSI). This figure as well as the high availability rate of foreign channels demonstrate the difficulties for the Swiss broadcasting system in holding its position in the new European broadcasting environment.

*Local TV and local radio*

From the early 1970s the federal government allowed short-term experiments with local TV without any advertising. Not surprisingly only a few attempts were made in the cities of Geneva, Fribourg, Lucerne, Solothurn, Wil and Zug, among others. Although these heavily limited experiments were more or less positively received by the local audience, they have been terminated as a result of lack of financial support by the communities.

In 1982, the experimental phase with local television was replaced by a government decree – namely the Ordinance on Experimental Local Broadcasting – that made commercial local radio and television possible. It limited local FM stations to a broadcasting radius of 10 kilometres and allowed advertising for 15 minutes per day. In 1984, this advertising quota was increased to 20 minutes and later even to 30 minutes per day. Theoretically, the main goal of this test phase was to figure out if there was sufficient demand in programming for and using local radio. Moreover it was to evaluate what the effects of local radio were on other media and on society as a whole. In practice, however, the test phase turned out to be an introductory phase for private local radio, fruit of a rather conservative and careful design in order to give all affected actors in the media sector (government, local broadcasters, the SSR, newspaper publishers, etc.) time to adjust to the new situation.

In the first phase in 1983/1984 around 30 of 36 licensed radio broadcasters went on the air, providing programmes and services for their relatively small local audiences in all three linguistic regions. At the end of 1990, 37 private local stations were in operation, in 1989 alone nine more companies were granted a broadcasting licence by the federal government.

## Telematic media

In 1984 – after a test phase – over-the-air teletext was publicly introduced in Switzerland on the basis of a licence given to the SSR and the Swiss Newspapers and Magazines Publishers Association, which each have a share of 50% in the new production company Teletext AG. This service is financed partly by the SSR and partly through advertising, which is not to exceed 20% of the pages offered to the audience. Currently, Teletext AG is providing a news service as well as a radio and television guide in German, French and Italian. Furthermore it airs subtitles for deaf viewers.

In 1987 – after a seven-year test phase – the federal government decided to introduce videotex, which uses a connection to the telephone network as a link to a data bank, as a public service in Switzerland. The national PTT was authorized to market the system to the subscribers and information providers, but the problem of converting a technical system to a useful public service has not yet been solved, despite early optimism. The diffusion of videotex has been rather slow until now. In 1990, PTT had attracted only 50 000 subscribers, roughly 35% of them private households. Although PTT started more than once an expensive marketing campaign to launch videotex and although the charges and expenses for users were massively reduced over the last years, the public service is far from commercially viable. The future of videotex in Switzerland is still uncertain.

## Policies for the press and broadcasting

*Main actors and interests*

At least five interest-groups influence the defining and enforcing of standards, norms, values and regulations in the Swiss media landscape:

— Transnational actors: Among them the Council of Europe is of particular importance for Swiss broadcasting policy, since Switzerland is not (yet) a member of the EC. Swiss government, however, gave its provisional approval – Swiss parliament has yet to confirm it – to the European Convention on Transfrontier Television, whose traditional liberal ideal of free flow of information does not take into consideration the structural handicaps of small, multicultural states.

— National governmental actors: National authorities, mainly the federal government, the department of transportation, communications, and energy, the parliament, administration and jurisdiction – among the last the Independent Authority for Programme Complaints – contribute to the definition, protection and enforcement of norms, standards, values and regulatory activities. Typical for government's strategy in a direct democracy is that it seeks consensus at almost all costs, to avoid plebiscites, whose outcomes are difficult to predict. The result of such a strategy is in any case very often a rather questionable and problematic compromise.

— Political parties: The political parties react – if at all – in the media sector according to their traditional platforms. The liberal and conservative parties in general favour the privatization of the whole media system, the social-democrat party prefers newspapers as independent as possible from commercial pressure and a public broadcasting system.

— Representatives of economic interests: As the economic actors penetrate and control Swiss politics, this makes for an overall policy in favour of the national economy. There is therefore very little chance of establishing media institutions and regulations, if this mighty pressure group opposes them.

— Media organizations: As powerful multipliers, on which the politicians depend to a certain degree, media organizations can challenge or even obstruct government strategies, regulations and values they judge unfavourable to their interests with considerable success. Especially the privately owned media companies usually are only willing to comply with special social, cultural or political obligations as long as the market rewards such activities. The fact that these interests partly differ among the media, however, limits their influence on media policy.

## Main issues

The essential concerns for the survival of most newspapers nowadays are colour printing, an up-to-date marketing system with early morning deliveries and a wide range of special supplements. In order to be able to make the necessary investment in printing, marketing and editorial work, even the largest publishing houses are concentrating their forces through cooperation contracts on the level of printing, publishing, advertising and editorial work. This has e.g. resulted in several publishers' editing joint weekend supplements or in joint advertising sections. The trend towards cooperation is being reinforced by the high marketing costs in competitive environments as well as by the Europeanization of the advertising market. The trend towards economic concentration is being intensified through the doubling of printing capacities in the last years by some large publishing companies which will force some small entrepreneurs out of the market.

The demise of the European Business Channel (EBC) in July 1990 has convinced most of the potential investors that the launching of a new TV channel is a risky business in such a competitive market. Indeed, the combination of different languages, a highly fragmented audience, insufficient advertising money, expensive programme production, exclusivity rights, and marketing costs, the scarcity of creative resources and of technical staff, the lack of a viable audiovisual industry, legal restrictions for some advertising and sponsoring (bartering) activities, and so on may prove to be real stumbling blocks for potential broadcasters.

In Switzerland the effectiveness and efficiency of regulations and controlling institutions is limited. In order to get Article 55a of the federal constitution fulfilled, the federal government set up legal regulations – norms of performance, social, cultural and political obligations – and controlling institutions. Still the question remains, how effectively such measures and activities work and how efficiently these protective systems are executed or controlled in the media field. In general there are a lot of difficulties and limitations for all sorts of regulatory activities in a small multicultural society.

Small states, among them Switzerland, heavily depend on big neighbouring countries and large international centres. They have to comply with many exterior exigencies because the passive balance of trade of their media sector will continue to be rather modest because of international counter-trends and because their legitimation in traditional liberal democracies is precarious.

Under these conditions the attempt, undertaken 1978–1983, to systematize Swiss media policy and structure coherently according to certain general principles largely remained an experiment of thought. Only fragments of it, such as the test phase with local broadcast, were realized.

LRT, the future Law on Radio and Television, is delayed and mainly functions as a framework for present and possible future developments; while its structural potential for Swiss radio and television may be quite remarkable, its steering capacity on the whole is small.

The influence of advertising on decisions in Swiss media enterprises is bound to increase further, as competition for advertising revenues becomes harder and the audience become accustomed to getting media fare cheaper.

The regulation of the Swiss broadcasting system is moving in two directions: cautious opening to private broadcasters and at the same time securing the structures of a productive system of public broadcast, mainly for political reasons. Furthermore there are distinct tendencies to maximize Switzerland's presence in international broadcasting while at the same time strengthening and multiplying the media of local communication.

## Statistics

(1 ECU = 1.74 Swiss francs, Sfr)

| | |
|---|---:|
| Population | |
| Inhabitants in 1989 | 6 723 000 |
| German-speaking Swiss (1980) | 3 986 955 |
| French-speaking Swiss (1980) | 1 088 223 |
| Italian-speaking Swiss (1980) | 241 758 |
| Romansch-speaking Swiss (1980) | 50 238 |
| Foreigners in 1989 | 1 040 325 |
| | |
| Newspapers | |
| Number of newspapers publishing 5–7 days a week (1988) | 110 |
| Number of newspapers publishing 1–4 days a week (1988) | 165 |
| Circulation, 5–7 days a week (1988) | 3 217 629 |
| Blick (1990) | 368 590 |
| Tages-Anzeiger (1990) | 261 113 |
| Neue Zürcher Zeitung (1990) | 149 520 |
| Berner Zeitung (1990) | 122 495 |
| Basler Zeitung (1990) | 115 338 |
| Weltwoche (weekly) (1990) | 103 949 |
| 24 heures (1990) | 96 131 |
| Sport (weekly) (1990) | 79 891 |
| | |
| Number of freesheets (1988) | 178 |

Public broadcasting

| | |
|---|---|
| Radio licences | 2 636 558 |
| Television licences | 2 395 767 |
| Radio licences per 1000 inhabitants | 411 |
| TV licences per 1000 inhabitants | 373 |
| Annual fee (radio) | 65 ECU |
| Annual fee (television) | 127 ECU |

Television

| | |
|---|---|
| Number of channels | 3 |
| Number of hours per year | 14 948 |

Division of TV audience in % (1990)

| German part | | French part | | Italian part | |
|---|---|---|---|---|---|
| Channel | % | Channel | % | Channel | % |
| DRS | 31 | TSR | 30 | TSI | 27 |
| TSR | 2 | DRS | 3 | DRS | 4 |
| TSI | 1 | TSI | 1 | TSR | 3 |
| ARD | 12 | TF1 | 24 | RAI1 | 10 |
| ZDF | 8 | A2 | 14 | RAI2 | 11 |
| FS1/FS2 | 11 | FR3 | 7 | RAI3 | 4 |
| RTL+ | 8 | LA5 | 5 | Can.5 | 10 |
| Sat1 | 7 | M6 | 3 | Ital.1 | 6 |
| Others | 20 | Others | 13 | Others | 25 |
| Total | 100 | Total | 100 | Total | 100 |

Radio

| | | |
|---|---|---|
| Number of channels | 1991 | 11 |
| Number of hours per year | 1989 | 77 690 |

Private broadcasting

| | | |
|---|---|---|
| Number of local radio stations | 1990 | 37 |

New electronic media

| | | |
|---|---|---|
| Videotex subscribers | 1990 | 50 000 |
| Teletext decoders | 1990 | 28% of adult pop. |
| Video recorders | 1990 | 40% of adult pop. |
| Pay-TV subscribers | 1990 | 95 000 |

Advertising expenditures (1989)

| Medium | Amount | % share |
|---|---|---|
| Newspapers | 1 056 m. ECU | 59% |
| Magazines | 2 m. ECU | 18% |
| Outdoor | 202 m. ECU | 11% |
| Television | 113 m. ECU | 6% |
| Local radio | 30 m. ECU | 2% |
| Cinema | 16 m. ECU | 1% |
| Others | 47 m. ECU | 3% |
| Total | 1 776 m. ECU | 100% |

# References

Bollinger, Ernst (1986) La Presse Suisse. Les faits, et les opinions. Lausanne.

Bonfadelli, Heinz and Hättenschwiler, Walter (1989) "Switzerland: A Multilingual Culture Tries to Keep Its Identity", in L. Becker and K. Schönbach (eds) Audience Responses to Media Diversification: Coping with Plenty. Hillsdale, N.J. Lawrence Erlbaum Ass., 133–157.

Fleck, Florian, Saxer, Ulrich and Steinmann, Matthias (eds) (1987) Massenmedien und Kommunikationswissenschaft in der Schweiz, Zurich.

Meier, Werner A. (1990) "Euronews und Eurofiction. Diskurs über kulturelle, nationale und europäische Identität", Medien Journal 14 (2): 66–78.

Meier, Werner A., Schanne, Michael and Bonfadelli, Heinz (1988) "Auswirkungen transnationaler Kommunikationstrukturen auf die Schweizerische Medienkultur: Eine Problemskizze", Schweizerische Zeitschrift für Soziologie, 2, 225–246.

Meier, Werner A., Schanne, Michael and Bonfadelli, Heinz (1990) Auswirkungen internationaler Kommunikationsstrukturen auf die schweizerische Medienkultur. Schlussbericht zum NFP 21 Kulturelle Vielfalt und nationale Identität, Zurich.

Saxer,Ulrich (1989) Lokalradios in der Schweiz. Schlussbericht über die Ergebnisse der nationalen Begleitforschung zu den lokalen Rundfunkversuchen 1983–1988. Arbeitsgruppe RVO-Begleitforschung am Seminar für Publizistikwissenschaft der Universität Zürich.

Saxer, Ulrich (1990a) "Sprachenbabel in Europas Medien", Media Perspektiven 10: 651–660.

Saxer, Ulrich (1990b) "Integrationsrundfunk und multikulturelle Gesellschaft", Media Perspektiven 11: 717–729.

SRG 90 (1990) Jahrbuch der Schweizerischen Radio- und Fernsehgesellschaft, Berne.

Stiftung Werbestatistik Schweiz (1990) Werbeaufwand Schweiz, Zurich.

Verband Schweizerischer Werbegesellschaften (1990) Katalog der Schweizer Presse, Zurich.

# 17

# The United Kingdom

*Jeremy Tunstall*

## National profile

In Britain geography and population distribution as well as language use all favour a highly centralized communications system. In 1990 the UK had a population of just under 57 million living in 22 million households. By European standards there is a negligible labour force engaged in farming. The population is 90% urbanized and concentrated between London and Manchester. Fifty-seven percent of the people live in just four of the 14 commercial television regions – based on London, Manchester, Birmingham and Leeds. At least 97% of the population speak English as a first language. Among other first languages are Urdu and Welsh (spoken by about 150 000 people as a first language.).

The UK has a centralized system of government; but Scotland has a degree of autonomy (including a distinctive legal system) more characteristic of a federal state. In media terms also, Scotland is the UK's most distinctive region. Wales has less autonomy. And a consequence of the continuing conflict in Northern Ireland is that the traditional political dominance of Protestants over Roman Catholics has been superseded by direct rule from London.

Both the national political and economic systems still reflect the "End of Empire" which occurred in the 1960s. Having lost an Empire, the British continue to see themselves as performing some kind of entrepôt role in the world. This perhaps has more reality in both media and telecommunications than in almost any other field.

## Development of the press and broadcasting since 1945

*Characteristics of British media development*

Gradualism – slow change, continuous evolution and policy consensus – has broadly characterized British media in the twentieth century. This

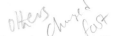 *others charged cost*

slow-change, gradualist, tradition is in sharp contrast to what has occurred in all of the other West European countries in the same century. Germany, Italy and Spain have all seen their media under absolutist control. In 1945, France also attempted to bury the collaborationist past and to effect a re-birth of the national media.

In more recent times there have been remarkable changes of policy. In Italy the policy players managed to drop the broadcasting ball, allowing Silvio Berlusconi to pick up the ball and to shape a multi-channel television empire. Several other countries, not least France and Spain, recently doubled their number of national television channels in one giant policy leap.

Not so in Britain. In media policy Britain is a tortoise. And in British media history there are very few key dates or key events. The modern era offers perhaps just two key dates, one each for newspapers and television. In 1896 the modern mass press was born in Britain. In this year North-cliffe's *Daily Mail* was launched as the first successful half-penny morning daily. The key date for television in Britain was 1955; the launch of a new ITV channel entirely financed by advertising marked the birth of Britain's television duopoly. BBC television had begun a pilot service in 1936, but even the BBC service which started up again in 1946 was still semi-ex-perimental and subordinate to radio.

After gradualism, a second key characteristic of British media is a mix-ture of (or compromise between) "commercialism" and "public service". The element of "commercialism" is a powerful one; Northcliffe established the pattern of the publicly quoted company, complete with shareholders and multi-media properties. The arrival of ITV in 1955 expanded the pat-tern; nearly all British media companies of any significance – including many radio stations and advertising agencies – are public companies. But there has long been a powerful strain of non-commercialism; this is most obviously true of the BBC and the "public service" element legally required of commercial broadcasters. A powerful non-commercial element was also present in Northcliffe's newspaper empire. *The Times* (which North-cliffe bought) had long had a non-profit goal; so also the Manchester *Guardian* and *Daily Telegraph*.

Thirdly the British media have long emphasized the central and nation-al at the expense of the regional. In general the regional element has declined as the twentieth century has advanced. The British regional press saw significant decline between 1918 and 1939 and this has continued after 1945. Both the BBC and ITV emphasized regionalism in their early years; but in both cases the second channels (BBC2 and Channel Four) are pure-ly national channels.

"Eyes West" is another long-running British media tradition. Britain has kept her back turned on Europe; she has long looked toward North

America for new ideas and innovations of all kinds. Northcliffe, himself, was fascinated by the US press. His successor rescuers of *The Times* were the American Astor family, the Canadian Roy Thomson, and Australian-American Rupert Murdoch. Both BBC and ITV history involve an endless series of attempts to adopt American innovations without also accepting their full home-grown commercial logic.

Fifthly, British media policy making has tended to be cautious and consensual. Britain has tried to follow America, but at some distance in time; policy making has been deliberately slow. The arrival of ITV in 1955 was preceded by four years of active debate, lobbying and legislation. Policy making in both broadcasting and the press has relied on Royal Commissions which have taken up to three years to complete their deliberations. Both the Annan Committee on Broadcasting and the McGregor Royal Commission on the Press ran from 1974 to 1977.

In the press the British have followed the Anglo-Saxon tradition of no special body of press law. The general law of the land (such as libel) applies; no further law is believed to be either necessary or desirable. In practice this means that monopoly law is the major part of press law; press policy in fact consists of somewhat half-hearted attempts to limit the size of press companies.

In broadcasting there is a body of law, but this traditionally has been minimalist and vague. The detailed decisions are left to the BBC Governors and the IBA (now ITC) Members. These are amateur regulators with only one individual in each case (the chairman) being a more or less full-time regulator. These amateur regulators are appointed by the government of the day, but for several reasons this indirect system greatly limits the government's power to intervene. Up to 1979 the appointments were not partisan; as amateurs the regulators tend to be "captured" by their professional staffs; and in so far as they are active professional regulators, the chairmen have tended to put their independence and integrity in evidence by resisting the cruder blandishments of government.

Finally, British media policy has tended to be made by the Conservative Party. The Labour Party, when in power, tends to be too split to be able to reach any decision. In the two years 1977–79 the Labour Party failed to legislate on its two massive reports of 1974–77. The Conservatives also tend to be split between market conservatives and cultural conservatives. Typically media (mainly broadcasting) legislation moves slowly and reflects a high degree of consensus, within the Conservative Party, between Labour and Conservatives, and between the politicians and the main media industry lobbies.

*The Thatcher Era (1979–90): radical failure, consensual success*

The eleven years of Thatcher government undoubtedly saw major changes in the British media. But Thatcher government attempts at radical breaks with the past were largely failures.

In this field, as in others, it was not always easy to discern what Thatcher Government policies were. While the Conservative Parliamentary Party often favoured consensus and tradition, Mrs. Thatcher saw communications as exhibiting many of the worst of British sins: consensual complacency, excessive trade union power, corporatism, lack of managerial machismo, inadequate entrepreneurial spirit.

Initially for the electronic media the Thatcher government pursued a twin-track policy. Firstly the Thatcher government – enthusiastic for information technology – placed much faith in expanding video choice via direct broadcasting by satellite and cable; both of these were failures during the 1980s. It was the second track of Thatcher broadcasting policy which had the major impact. This was the decision to go ahead with a fourth conventional television channel.

Channel Four was an "ambiguous innovation". C4 was the spearhead for most of the major innovations in British broadcasting in the 1980s; it was heavily committed to "independent production", which at once turned producers into Thatcherite entrepreneurs and undermined trade union control of production practices. C4 was also largely responsible for an approximate doubling of broadcast hours from 275 per week in 1980 to 550 hours per week in 1990. However, in other respects, Channel Four actually strengthened some of the key aspects of British broadcasting to which Mrs Thatcher was opposed. Channel Four was a "minority channel" – only seeking (and never achieving) 10% of the total UK television viewing. It was a sheltered channel, deliberately protected from the blast of head-on commercial competition. Above all, Channel Four completed the Two-plus-Two design of British broadcasting; it confirmed consensus and duopoly and it enabled both the IBA and its main commercial channel, ITV, to proclaim that they also were in "public service broadcasting".

The difficulty of escaping from consensus and tradition was illustrated by the Peacock Committee (1985–86); Mrs Thatcher asked this Committee to look into the possibilities for the BBC to carry advertising. But the Peacock Committee, despite being packed with free marketeers, reported against advertising on the BBC. The chief casualty of such a scheme would have been ITV (and its advertising monopoly).

The Thatcher government next focused on some of the other conclusions of the Peacock report and produced its deregulatory White Paper, "Broadcasting in the '90's: Competition, Choice and Quality" (1988). This finally led to the Broadcasting Act which became law shortly before Mrs Thatcher was ousted in late 1990. Was this final Act of Thatcher broadcasting policy a radical or a consensual measure? Like much British media policy it was ambiguous (because consensual). We will consider the Act in more detail below. But the Act is certainly not quick. Even the new round of licensing Channel 3 (formerly ITV) companies was not due to take effect until 1993. The Act also favoured a fifth conventional TV channel, but this was unlikely to appear until 1995 at earliest. Since C4 began in 1982, this would be thirteen years between the launch of Channels Four and Five. This in turn is very much in line with Britain's traditional gradualist pattern of television expansion.

Paradoxically it was in the newspaper field, where the Thatcher government had fewer policy thoughts, that it had bigger results. Perhaps the most dramatic press event in the Thatcher years was the move of Robert Murdoch's (then) two daily and two Sunday newspapers in January 1986 to a new electronic printing plant at Wapping in East London. This move had been made possible by the Thatcher Employment Acts of 1980 and 1982, which had greatly strengthened the hand of employers in relation to their trade unions. But the Murdoch move followed union-busting initiatives by Robert Maxwell and Eddie Shah. In this case Thatcher policy had helped to speed up something which would inevitably have happened anyway.

A more genuinely Thatcherite piece of radical press policy had been the Thatcher government's waving through of newspaper mergers on the basis of a get-out clause allowing immediate government approval if the publication subject to the merger bid seemed to be in commercial danger of not surviving. Using this dubious get-out clause, the Thatcher government had allowed News International (Murdoch) to acquire *The Times* and *Sunday Times* from Thomson in 1981. Other such merger wavethroughs were to follow.

On the whole Mrs Thatcher's radical and innovative policies (for example in new technology) did not work. The policies which were successful were ones which followed the patterns of previous decades. Gradual change still amounted to major changes over a decade.

Even if commercialism received the main emphasis, various conceptions of "public service" remained central. Indeed the Thatcher vision of cable and satellite saw commercial entertainment cast in the role of "pulling through" nationally useful high technology.

In the 1980s the British media became more national. Channel Four, unlike ITV, was almost entirely national and was heavily London-oriented. Changes in the national press also led to a downgrading of provincial subcentres; Manchester ceased to play a significant part in the national newspaper industry. The sizable Manchester editorial offices of 1980 had by 1990 been replaced by a handful of provincial reporters in-putting their material direct into the London newspaper's computer system.

In the Thatcher decade the British media kept their eyes focused on the West. With the return of the Thomson clan to Canada, the permanent residence of Rupert Murdoch in New York, the arrival of Conrad Black from Canada to buy the *Telegraph* newspapers, and Robert Maxwell's heavy American involvement, the British press became increasingly integrated with that of the USA.

**The press**

In Britain, as already noted, there is no such thing as a Press Law. There is also no specific subsidy for newspapers; but newspapers still receive favourable treatment in terms of Value Added Tax.

The only important body of law and regulation which specifically concerns the press deals with the issue of monopoly and competition. As previously described there is a major loophole in the relevant law and in recent years a number of substantial mergers and purchases of newspapers have occurred. The Thatcher decade of the 1980s differed from previous decades only in that there were more mergers. The main mergers and purchases between 1979 and 1990 were as follows:

— Murdoch's News International acquired *The Times* and *Sunday Times* in 1981. News International acquired *Today* in 1987 from the Lonrho company which had previously acquired it from its founder, Eddie Shah.

— Robert Maxwell acquired Mirror Group Newspapers (*Daily Mirror*, *Sunday Mirror, The People*) in 1984.

— United Newspapers acquired Fleet (*Daily Express, Sunday Express*) in 1985 from Trafalgar House, which company had itself previously acquired the publications only in 1977.

— The Canadian financier Conrad Black acquired *The Daily Telegraph* and *Sunday Telegraph* in 1986.

— The Lonrho company acquired *The Observer* in 1981.

Of the 1990 survivors five titles had been launched during the Thatcher years:

— *Daily Star*, launched 1979

— *Mail on Sunday*, launched 1982

— *Today*, launched 1985

— *Independent*. launched 1986

— *Independent on Sunday,* launched 1990

There were also several other unsuccessful attempts to launch new national titles. The longest running of these was the *Sunday Correspondent* which lasted just over one year (1989–90).

Of the twenty national daily and Sunday titles in 1990 only five were being published, and by the same company, in 1979. Of the dailies only the *Sun Daily Mail, Financial Times and Guardian* showed no change since 1979. And among the Sundays, only Murdoch's five-million sale *News of the World* was under the same ownership as in 1979. This points to the national Sundays as an especially volatile sector.

Thus three quarters of all the twenty national titles of 1990 had changed ownership and/or been launched since 1979. But this revolution in ownership was only one of two linked revolutions affecting British newspapers. The second revolution has come to be known as the "Wapping Revolution"; but Murdoch's move of four national titles to Wapping in January 1986 was only the single most dramatic event in a comprehensive industrial revolution in the press. In many other countries the switch to electronic printing occurred earlier and more gradually. In Britain, the electronic revolution was also well under way outside London. Previous to Murdoch's move of January 1986, Eddie Shah had launched his *Today* newspaper without traditional trade union labour and with elec-tronic printing.

All of the national newspaper groups by 1985 were making preparations for a switch to new technology. Following January 1986 the floodgates were open and by 1990 a comprehensive revolution had been completed. In the British case the revolution had the following overlapping strands:

— Traditional printing unions were in retreat.

— Massive staff cuts – 50% and more – were negotiated and/or imposed.

— There was a quick move to new printing plants and to new office buildings; Fleet Street ceased to be the newspaper centre. The new locations were mostly scattered along a ten-mile stretch of the Thames river from Docklands in the east to Battersea in the west.

— There was also an uncoupling in some cases of editorial offices from printing plants; and some papers were printed on contract at several centres outside London.

— Distribution practices were radically changed – notably from rail to road. Wholesaling was also radically reformed.

— All national newspapers had acquired the ability to print colour throughout the paper by late 1990.

— There was a strong switch to multi-section newspapers – led by Rupert Murdoch's *Sunday Times* with some ten separate sections.

— The national newspaper groups funded their new plant investments from two major sources – by selling their now valuable shares in Reuters and by exploiting their former sites in the Fleet Street area.

But all of this activity, and the new titles, did not raise total sales. Indeed in the 1980s total sales of British newspapers continued their slow decline from the peaks of the 1950s.

In Britain the dominance of the national (London) newspapers over the regionals was also further strengthened. The major groups of provincial dailies continued to be owned by the same national groups. In the 1980s there were major drops in sales. This was especially marked in big northern cities, but was also true in the West and South, which had grown in prosperity and population in the 1980s. The small band of provincial morning papers in England were in a very weak state indeed by 1990. But the Scottish mornings – further away from London – continued strong. Titles like *The Glasgow Herald, The Scotsman* (Edinburgh) and morning dailies in Aberdeen and Dundee all had sales of over 100 000 – a circulation no longer achieved by any provincial morning title in England.

During the 1980s the local free sheets expanded enormously – from 13.9 million copies a week (1979) to 42.3 million copies per week (1989). British households each receive two free newspapers per week. During the later 1980s the big groups bought large sections of the free newspaper business. By 1990 the large magazine company, Reed, was the largest free sheet owner. Other major owners were Thomson, Pearson (Westminster Press) and EMAP.

There were other indications that the provincial paid-for dailies and weeklies were looking down towards the grass roots and to competition with free sheets and increasingly with local radio coverage. Most of the major provincial groups closed down their once quite large London offices and by 1990 relied increasingly on Press Association and other syndicated national material. A nationally edited magazine section, at one stage carried by 45 regional dailies, was closed down in 1990.

Politically the main provincial daily press (the evening dailies) remained overtly neutral. But the national press continued to lean heavily to the right – this has been the case ever since Rupert Murdoch acquired the *Sun* in 1969. The *Sun's* mixture of sensational journalism with relentless support for Mrs Thatcher has helped to retain its reputation for controversy. During the 1980s the popular papers seem to have become ever more belligerently partisan. The *Daily Mirror* (under Robert Maxwell) has returned to aggressive support for Labour. But of the five largest circulation dailies, four (the *Sun, Express, Mail* and *Telegraph*) are belligerently Conservative.

Among the serious (broadsheet) dailies the political balance has shifted in the 1980s. *The Times* has finally ceased to be the voice of the British Establishment. *The Financial Times* now has Europe's largest newspaper team of foreign correspondents; the *Independent* surged forward after its launch in 1986 and has quickly consolidated its position. It is probably the newspaper most admired, and most read, by British journalists. The *Daily Telegraph* has undergone a commercial transformation, but still has a very elderly readership. The *Guardian* has suffered from the competition, but remains formidably strong in classified advertising.

*The Times* has changed its business plan several times, but contains a lot of good journalism. These five dailies would all claim to be among the best ten newspapers in Europe. Surely no other European city has five such formidable dailies. Paradoxically, of course, no other city has the equivalent of Britain's collection of bare-breasted and bare-fisted tabloids.

## Electronic media

### Legal framework

The Broadcasting Act which finally became law in late 1990 was the culmination of a policy-making sequence which began with the Peacock Committee (on the BBC's finances), established 5 years earlier in 1985. However, the Broadcasting Act 1990 is a complex legal document of 291 pages, which has to be interpreted by the new Independent Television Commission. The ITC (successor to the IBA) retains responsibility for terrestrial television, domestic British satellite television and also cable TV (previously overseen by the Cable Authority). The ITC in turn had its own timetable of events:

— January 1991: ITC came into existence.

— April–May 1991: Deadlines for bids for Channel 3 (formerly ITV) franchises.

— Autumn 1991: Channel Three franchises allocated.

— January 1993: Channel Three franchises commence operation (running for ten years)

— 1993–95: Allocation and launch of Channel 5.

Well before 1995 the UK broadcasting policy focus will have shifted to the BBC. The BBC's legal basis (its Royal Charter) will be re-negotiated for a new period commencing in January 1996. So the gradualistic British policy process will continue on its step-by-step way.

What follows will consider mainly the situation as it is and seems likely to be in the mid-1990s. However, an initial glance back at the 1980s seems essential.

As previously noted, the biggest change of the 1980s was the launch of a fourth TV channel in 1982. By 1990 Channel Four was transmitting 140 hours a week of television. This alone was a 50% increase on the total hours of 1980. But the other three channels also increased hours – breakfast TV arrived, the mornings and afternoons filled up and ITV (Channel 3) began 24-hour transmission. In 1980 there were 275 hours a week and this doubled to 550 hours by 1990.

This large output of hours was one main reason why cable proved unattractive to most potential customers. The 550 programming hours still included a low proportion of repeats by international standards. For example in 1979–80 only 16% of ITV's 103 hours were repeats; and ten years later only 15% of the total 168 hours were repeats. This was possible partly because British television continued to be better financed than in most comparable countries. In 1989–90 the BBC spent £814m. on its television services; the two BBC channels and the two IBA channels had a combined expenditure of about £2 billion, or nearly 3.3 billion ECU.

The British also were eager purchasers of video recorders. According to IBA research, VCRs were in 70% of British households by 1990 (although BBC data indicated about 60%). About two thirds of all video playing back involved time-shifting of programmes (and only one third was the playing of rented or purchased tapes).

The Broadcasting Act 1990 did make some important changes to the previous position. But the change is much more modest than some Conservative government rhetoric of the mid-1980s implied. The BBC, of course, remains in the same legal position until the changes of 1996. The new ITC must now regulate Channels 3 and 4 and it does so in a more "arm's length" manner than before. The old IBA's 1980s responsibility as the "publisher" of ITV programmes has now ceased; from 1993 it is the Channel 3 companies, not the ITC, which are the publishers.

The powers of the ITC are also more limited in other ways. The ITC has to give reasons for its decisions and these can be challenged in court. Consequently British broadcasting regulation in the 1990s takes on a much more legalistic, and court-arbitrated, character.

Even before January 1991 the "Shadow" ITC decided to continue with ITV's map (for Channel 3) divided into 14 regions. The ITC also decided to continue with one weekday and one weekend franchise in London. In addition it continued with a separate breakfast contract and with Independent Television News (ITN) as Channel 3's sole provider of national and international news bulletins. Therefore the pattern of ITC's franchises which commence in January 1993 will have a close family similarity to the new franchises which began in 1955, in 1968 and in 1982.

The ITC quickly made it clear that it also wanted to keep most of the other major aspects of the old ITV system. Under the ITC the Channel 3 companies will again form a network with the bulk of the networked programming being supplied by the five companies based in London (two), Birmingham, Leeds and Manchester.

The ITC insisted that successful bidders for the regional franchises must continue to show as much regional programming as did the IBA's licensees. The core of this regional programming consists of daily news (including 30 minutes of regional news in the 6–7 p.m. hour), plus some regional current affairs, political and sports programming. Some regional licensees are required to supply sub-regional news offerings; this is so for the East Anglian and South and East companies. The Midlands licensee must supply regional news not only from Birmingham, but also separately for the area around Nottingham and again for the area around Oxford.

## *Programming policy*

The programming policy is somewhat ambiguous and is likely to remain controversial throughout the 1990s. The Broadcasting Act (1990) and the ITC's own pronouncement suggest that Channel 3 companies in the decade from 1993 will be expected to retain the previous standards of quality, while facing stronger competition and being more entrepreneurial.

In its allocation of franchises the ITC must firstly inspect programming plans and ensure that applicants meet its "quality" standards. Secondly the ITC must then choose the highest bidder – the franchise process is basically an auction. However, thirdly the ITC can in exceptional circumstances not choose the highest bidder. And fourthly, franchises must post a bond (which can be lost) as a guarantee of meeting their quality programme obligations.

The ITC indicated in its bidding document that all regional companies would be expected to transmit programming in all of the nine following categories: drama, entertainment, sport, news, factual, education, religion, arts and children's. A diet of soap operas and game shows will not suffice.

However, the 1990 Act (and the preceding debates) clearly defined the ITV companies of the 1980s as having been lazy duopolists in programming and lazy monopolists of TV advertising. Certainly the ITV companies in the 1980s were commercial successes only because advertising revenue continued to be buoyant. By 1990 the 15 regional companies still relied heavily on their ITV regional advertising monopoly. Collectively they had tried several sorts of diversification, each of which had been a failure. Firstly their two diversifications into satellite broadcasting (Superchannel and British Satellite Broadcasting) were both costly disasters. Secondly, their attempts to become programme suppliers to Channel Four were largely a failure – Channel Four came to rely almost entirely on small independent producers. Thirdly, some ITV companies diversified into buying United States companies; the major such purchase – by TVS of MTM (a Hollywood production house) – was another disaster. Finally in the late 1980s most ITV companies decided to enter the facilities business – by renting out their studios, editing suites, dubbing theatres and outside broadcast units. This occurred in 1988 as the facilities business was suffering from an over-capacity – yet another diversification disaster.

The 1980s ITV companies would claim that if they were bad at business this was because of three weights around their necks; one was the IBA and its fussy "public service" regulations, another was the trade unions, and a third was Channel Four which the ITV companies were required to shelter from the real commercial world.

In the late 1980s the ITV companies increasingly confronted their trade unions and, especially from 1987 onwards, began to make massive cuts in their personnel. In the years 1986–91 some ITV companies cut their personnel by half; four-person camera crews became two-person camera crews and so on.

Whether the new Channel Three contractors will be able to retain ITV's 40%-plus share of the audience, while offering good quality and staying profitable, remains to be seen. Much will depend upon the trend in advertising revenue and competition from new channels.

Uncertainty in general and uncertainty about programming "quality" in particular surrounds Channel Four. Channel Four's audience settled down at around 8 or 9% of the total UK viewing. It achieved even this level of audience only by backing its "minority" programming with a sizable admixture of Hollywood comedy (from Chaplin to Cosby), and by having its advertising sold by the ITV sales force. In return the ITV companies pocketed the income from selling C4 in their local regions and they paid a "subscription" to the IBA which became C4's income. In addition the ITV gave massive promotion to C4's programming – "now showing over on Channel Four is. . . ".

From 1993 onwards Channel Four will have to swim largely by itself. It will also have to sell its own advertising and to employ its own expensive advertising sales force.

We know that there will be increased competition from commercial radio. By 1991 there were some one hundred commercial local radio stations, and this number will increase (gradually) during the 1990s to several hundred. There will also be three national networks of commercial radio – in addition to the BBC's five national radio networks.

## Satellite television

More significant for television competition will be the development of direct broadcasting by satellite (DBS) and cable. The first Thatcher administration enthusiastically embraced both DBS and cable in a stream of policy pronouncements which began in 1981 and 1982. There were many errors – in particular the government decreed high technology stations but was unwilling to provide finance. The great British public showed little interest in such multi-channel offerings as became available; with take-up rates around 10–15% it simply was not worth cabling additional streets.

However a long string of cable and satellite disasters eventually led to an internationally unique phenomenon – during part of the year 1990 two companies were offering competitive satellite direct-to-home television services. One of these was the official British offering (licensed by the IBA) British Satellite Broadcasting and its high technology (D-MAC), on a high-powered (Marco Polo) satellite with quality programming via a square dish. BSB, owned by a shifting consortium of communications companies, had trouble with its high technology and was disastrously late in offering its service to customers.

British Satellite Broadcasting launched its 5-channel service to cable customers on 25 March 1990 and to square dish owners on 29 April; on 2 November  BSB surrendered. The battle with Murdoch's Sky service lasted just 31 weeks. BSB had taken a disastrous four years from obtaining its licence to getting on the air. Apart from all of the technical delays and commercial mistakes, its service was not very popular with audiences or advertisers; and BSB spent hundreds of millions of pounds on buying Hollywood movies. BSB offered five channels: Now (lifestyle and talk), Galaxy (general entertainment), Power (music videos), Sports and a Movie Channel. BSB's leading consortium members by April 1990 were Granada, the publishing giants Pearson and Reed, the French Chargeurs and the Australian Bond.

Murdoch's winning Sky operation was different in nearly every respect. It began two years later than BSB, but was in operation one year earlier. Sky was licensed, of course, not in Britain, but in Luxembourg – and thus it escaped all of the IBA's requirements for "quality" in programming and technology. Sky used a medium-powered SES satellite (Astra 1); it operated not on MAC, but on old PAL, technology. Its dish was circular. Its four channels of programming were comparatively cheap and aimed at popularity rather than quality. The four Sky channels were Sky One (general entertainment, mainly American re-runs), Sky News (popular with politicians and journalists), Sky Movies and Eurosport. Murdoch's News company exhibited its usual speed, commercial belligerence and political acumen. It resorted to direct selling its own service. Murdoch also ✗ used the free publicity possibilities of his newspapers to an extraordinary degree – full page advertisements, prize offers of hundreds of free Sky television dishes and massive listings of programming alongside the 4 BBC and IBA channels. The *Sun, The Times* and *Today* are seen by almost 30% of UK adults each weekday and the *News of the World* and *Sunday Times* by 35% on Sundays.

By March–April 1990 when BSB at last entered the battle, Sky had already virtually won. Through the summer and autumn of 1990 BSB engaged in a huge media advertising campaign. When the protracted merger talks concluded in the merger announcement of 2 November the rival services compared as follows:

|  | BSB | Sky |
|---|---|---|
| Antennas in use | 117000 | 960000 |
| Cable homes | 630000 | 630000 |
| Total households | 750000 | 1 600 000 |

These figures, however, include many homes in the Irish republic. Irish citizens could receive both services via dish or via cable; much higher household penetration rates were achieved in Ireland.

The Sky–BSB merger involved many legal, commercial and other difficulties. But the merged British Sky Broadcasting (B Sky B) obviously had a much better chance of becoming a commercial success than did either of the two services in competition. By November 1990 Sky and BSB had together lost over £1 billion with the prospect of bigger losses to follow. The future of B Sky B remains one of the key unknowns of the 1990s. But Sky quickly showed that its "cheap and cheerful" programming style could attract audiences. The standard ratings service (BARB) in mid-October 1990 showed that in Astra homes the Astra channels accounted for just over one third of total viewing. The two popular channels were Sky One and Sky Movies.

## Cable

In the 1990s the performance of satellite-to-home will be heavily affected by the performance of cable. In 1991 there are signs that cable – largely quiescent for a decade – may become a success. There are two reasons for this. Firstly the satellite offerings – available on most cable systems – provide a reason for subscribing to cable. Secondly the years 1988–90 saw the Cable Authority appointing cable operators for virtually every urban area; this cable activity was heavily supported with American finance. The American companies include many of the big names in both telecommunications and cable. A major motivation to invest in Britain is the regulatory divide between telecoms and cable in the USA. The biggest of the American investors are the giant regional telephone companies; US West has interests in franchises covering over 2 million UK homes, while Nynex investments are in franchises covering a million UK homes. Until 1989 take up rates for multi-channel cable in Britain were around 15%. But during 1990 some cable operators were claiming more promising rates of 25–30%.

The likelihood, then, is of a gradual expansion of cable in the 1990s – with cable and satellite together posing a major challenge towards the end of the 1990s.

In the 1990s both satellite and cable in Britain will clearly be heavily dependent on United States companies. This obviously further increases the salience of anxieties about the quantities of US programming. In the late 1980s two quite clear – and contradictory – trends were evident.

### The US influence

There was a gradual tendency for more American programming to appear on British screens. Extra early morning hours were often filled with American imports; and Channel Four showed the most American programming, much of it comedies. Britain is an especially good market for US comedies because British audiences can probably understand at least half of the jokes (although even in Britain many US jokes are not widely comprehensible).

But there is also a counter-trend. US programming was undoubtedly losing some of its audience appeal in Britain. There were no US series as popular as Dallas was around 1980. Lists of the top 50 programmes each week, month and year are increasingly dominated by British programmes. For example, in the middle four months of 1990, of the 50 most popular series, the highest placed import was the Australian soap, Neighbours, at number 16. There were only three US entries, the highest placed being Murder, She Wrote (at number 20), which starred a British born actress. A second Australian soap (Home and Away) was number 46. No less than 45 of the top 50 series were British-made.

Only two categories of American programming have been amongst the most popular in recent years. One is feature films – and these were among the leading offerings of both BSB and Sky. But among the most popular (audience of 15 million plus) offerings of 1982–89, only about 3% were American films. Much the most popular films on UK television were the

James Bond films, which are classified as British and have a British star actor.

The second category are the American format shows – such as This is Your Life and Blind Date. But such shows in Britain, as elsewhere in Europe, are peopled with local personalities, local accents, and local/national culture generally.

## Policies for the press and broadcasting

Probably more important for the overall shape of British broadcasting in the 1990s will be the evolution of the "independent" production companies. These companies have since 1982 been the main suppliers of programming to Channel Four. Most of these are still small, but in 1989–90 C4 bought over £1 million worth of commissioned programming from 28 separate independent suppliers. In the late 1980s both the ITV companies and the BBC started to commission from independents on a sizable scale; by 1992 both BBC and ITV will be placing 25% of most categories of programme production with independents. A quarter of three channels (BBC1, BBC2 and Channel 3) and all of Channel Four's programming being made on an independent production basis constitutes a massive change.

But like many changes in the British media, it remains somewhat ambiguous. At first sight this looks like a successful attempt to break up the industrial pattern of vertical integration which has characterized British television to date. The trade unions certainly believe that independent production has been used to introduce a casual employment system.

But there is already evidence of some independents becoming quite large. Such companies are seeking "output deals" – contracts to produce large chunks of programming over a period of several years. They also are seeking to own the programming, so as to exploit rights to additional showings.

The other great unknown is what will happen to Channel Five. The ITC is empowered to license a fifth conventional channel; but this seems to be slipping further into the future. We know that this channel will only be receivable by about 70% of UK households via conventional means. We do not know what Channel Five will look like; it might be a completely national channel, but it could be a channel focusing on city-level television. However, given the British (and ITC) preference for "quality" (meaning expensive) television, the city option has obvious problems.

The second half of the 1990s is especially hard to predict because around 1996 three things will be happening simultaneously: the BBC will be operating under a new Charter; cable and satellite may be reaching big audiences; Channel Five may be launched.

## Statistics

(1 ECU = £0.65)

|  |  |
|---|---|
| Population | 57 million |
| Number of households | 22 million |

Broadcasting

|  |  |
|---|---|
| Number of TV channels | 4 (BBC1 and 2, ITV/Ch3 and Ch4) |
| Number of national radio networks: | 5 BBC and 1 commercial |
| Number of local radio systems: | 2 |

Number of local radio stations in late 1990

|  |  |
|---|---|
| BBC | 46 |
| ILR | 100 |
| By 1996 | "several hundred" |

Division of audience between channels

|  |  |
|---|---|
| BBC 1 | 39.2% |
| BBC 2 | 9.9% |
| ITV | 42.5% |
| Channel 4 | 8.4% |

Advertising expenditure (total expenditure £8.313 million)

|  |  |
|---|---|
| Press display | 33.3% |
| Press classified | 24.5% |
| TV | 27.5% |
| Direct mail | 9.1% |
| Other | 5.6% |

The press
National newspapers

|  |  |
|---|---|
| Daily | 11 |
| Sunday | 9 |

Political allegiance, circulation and readership (April–June 1990)

| Newspaper (political affiliation) | Circulation ('000) | Readers support in % Conservative | Labour | Lib/Dem | Green |
|---|---|---|---|---|---|
| The Sun (Cons) | 3817 | 33 | 54 | 6 | 4 |
| The Star (?) | 895 | 16 | 67 | 9 | 4 |
| Daily Mirror (Labour) | 3821 | 13 | 77 | 7 | 3 |
| Daily Express (Cons) | 1574 | 58 | 29 | 8 | 4 |
| Daily Mail (Cons) | 1727 | 60 | 27 | 8 | 4 |
| Today (?) | 525 | 43 | 37 | 12 | 7 |
| The Times (Cons) | 423 | 53 | 29 | 10 | 5 |
| The Guardian (Labour) | 442 | 12 | 70 | 8 | 8 |
| Fin. Times (Cons) | 295 | 56 | 27 | 11 | 3 |
| Independent (?) | 366 | 28 | 46 | 13 | 8 |
| Daily Telegraph (Cons) | 1075 | 70 | 15 | 9 | 3 |

(Source: MORI)

| Paid for regional newspapers | Number | Circulation in 1988 |
|---|---|---|
| Morning | 15 | 1 234 272 |
| Evening | 72 | 5 149 112 |
| Sundays | 9 | 386 171 |
| Paid for weeklies | 570 | 7 567 627 |
| Free weeklies | 961 | 38 020 546 |

# References

Annan, Lord (1977) Report of the Committee on the Future of Broadcasting, HMSO Cmnd 6753.
BBC, Annual Report and Handbook. London.
Barwise, P. and Ehrenberg, A. (1988) Television and Its Audience. London: Sage.
Briggs, A. (1985) The BBC: the first 50 years, Oxford.
Collins, R., Garnham, N. and Locksley, G. (1988) The Economics of television: the UK Case. London: Sage.
Curran, J. and Seaton, J. (1988) Power Without Responsibility. London: Methuen.
Independent Broadcasting Authority. The IBA Annual Report and Accounts. London.
Lambert, S. (1982) Channel 4 - television with a difference?, London: BFI.
Madge, T. (1989) Beyond the BBC: broadcasters, broadcasting and the public in the 1980s. London: Macmillan.
Negrine, R. (ed)(1988) Satellite Broadcasting. London: Routledge.
Negrine, R. (1989) Politics and the Mass Media in Britain. London: Routledge.
Palmer, M. and Tunstall, J. (1990) Liberating Communications: Policy Making in France and Britain. Oxford: Blackwell.
Potter, J. (1990) Independent Television in Britain Volumes 3 and 4. London: Macmillan.
Sendall, B. (1982 and 1983) Independent television in Britain. Volumes 1 and 2. London: Macmillan.
Tunstall, J. (1983) The Media in Britain. London: Constable.
Tunstall, J. and Palmer, M. (1991) European Media Moguls. London: Routledge.

## Selected Official Documents of the Thatcher Government

Broadcasting Act 1990, HMSO.
Report of a Home Office Study (1981) Direct Broadcasting by Satellite, HMSO, May.
Cabinet Office, Information Technology Advisory Panel (1982) Report on Cable Systems, HMSO, February 1982.
Lord Hunt (chairman), Home Office (1982) Report of the Inquiry into Cable Expansion and Broadcasting Policy, HMSO, October.
Sir Antony Part (chairman), Home Office and Department of Industry (1982) Direct Broadcasting by Satellite. Report of the Advisory Panel on Technical Transmission Standards, HMSO, November.
Home Office and Department of Industry (1983) The development of Cable Systems and services, HMSO, April.
Peacock, A. (chairman) (1986) Report of the Committee on Financing the BBC, HMSO.

# Index